SUEZ
THE DOUBLE WAR

Other Works by the Authors

By GEOFFREY POWELL

The Green Howards

The Kandyan Wars

*Men at Arnhem**
(Originally under the pseudonym of Tom Angus)

*Plumer: The Soldiers' General**

*The Devil's Birthday: The Bridges to Arnhem**

Buller: A Scapegoat?

The Book of Campden

*The History of the Green Howards: 300 Years of Service**
(with Brigadier John Powell)

By ROY FULLICK

*Shan Hackett: The Pursuit of Excellence**

Titles marked* are currently available through Pen and Sword Books Ltd
(February 2006)

Biographical Notes

Roy Fullick commanded a company of the Parachute Regiment in the Suez operation and left the Army, after sixteen years' service, about a year later. He retired as chief executive of a London-based printing group and is living in Highgate, London.

Geoffrey Powell, who died in 2005, was a Regular officer of the Green Howards, but was seconded to the Parachute Regiment in 1942 and served throughout the battle of Arnhem where he won the Military Cross. He began to write seriously after he retired from the Army in 1964 with the rank of Colonel. He was a Fellow of the Royal Historical Society.

SUEZ
THE DOUBLE WAR

By Roy Fullick and Geoffrey Powell

Pen & Sword
MILITARY

First published in Great Britain in 1979 by Hamish Hamilton Ltd.
Reissued 1990 by Leo Cooper.

Published in this format in 2006 by
Pen & Sword Military
An imprint of
Pen & Sword Books Ltd
47 Church Street
Barnsley
South Yorkshire
S70 2AS

ISBN 1 84415 340 1

Printed and bound in England
By CPI UK

Pen & Sword Books Ltd incorporates the Imprints of Pen & Sword Aviation,
Pen & Sword Maritime, Pen & Sword Military, Wharncliffe Local History,
Pen & Sword Select, Pen & Sword Military Classics and Leo Cooper.

For a complete list of Pen & Sword titles please contact
PEN & SWORD BOOKS LIMITED
47 Church Street, Barnsley, South Yorkshire, S70 2AS, England
E-mail: enquiries@pen-and-sword.co.uk
Website: www.pen-and-sword.co.uk

CONTENTS

What the Critics said about
Suez: The Double War

...this is a book with an angle all of its own...the best concise account of the affair...candid and fair-minded.

OBSERVER

I doubt if any clearer, fairer, more objective account of that extraordinary – episode? adventure? aberration? – will ever appear: certainly none more readable ever will.

BERNARD FERGUSSON, LATER LORD BALLANTRAE

...should be compulsory reading for all who aspire to authority over Her Majesty's armed forces.

SPECTATOR

...conspicuously well written.

THE ECONOMIST

...their writing is so lively that the non-specialist can enter into the arguments and the operations...the book should be compulsory reading for everyone of ministerial rank in the Ministry of Defence.

DAILY TELEGRAPH

FOREWORD

WITH THE archives closed until 1986, we have relied for our primary sources on the memories of participants, both published and recounted to us in letters and interviews and upon our own personal knowledge of the events of the summer and autumn of 1956. After twenty years or more, nearly everyone's recollections clash on the facts, on the motives and on the consequences of the affair. In the future quite a different book or books will probably be written when the Public Record Office does reveal its secrets but even then it is highly unlikely that the complete truth about Suez will be revealed. Some of those whom we approached did not want to talk to us, while others expressed a wish that their names should not be revealed. Respecting as we did their motives, we have decided that it might be invidious to mention the names of those, both in this country and abroad, who have been so generous with their time and their confidences.

The staffs of the British Film Institute, the Fleet Air Arm Museum, The Imperial War Museum, the London Library, the Royal Air Force Museum, the Tank Museum and the Royal United Services Institute for Defence Studies all gave us the generous help which is characteristic of librarians, archivists and curators but special mention must be made of the R.U.S.I. librarians who seemed to have the happy knack of anticipating one's wants.

Literary collaboration is far from easy but we managed to put this book to press without exchanging a single harsh word, so confounding the predictions of our friends and surprising even ourselves.

Foreword to the 2006 Edition
A few misprints were corrected in the 1990 edition and an Afterword written by both authors. Geoffrey Powell died in 2005 and this edition includes a revised Afterword by Roy Fullick that reflects the views of them both.

INTRODUCTION

WHEN THE news of the nationalisation of the Suez Canal burst in July 1956, the British people were broadly united by a strong sense of personal and public morality. They had borne well the exhaustion of fighting throughout the whole of Hitler's war, although this exhaustion had perhaps cut deeper than was generally realised and had never been relieved by the necessity of rebuilding a society from its foundations as the defeated had experienced. They seemed also to be bearing with patience and no little common decency the difficult task of dismantling their Empire. Eleven years after the end of the war the British Army, with the support of the other two services, was still engaged in operations (euphemistically termed "in aid of the Civil Power") in Malaya, Cyprus, Kenya and elsewhere; operations which had as their purpose the controlling or slowing down of the pace of separatist and independence movements either to allow a more orderly transition to full sovereignty or to frustrate those externally-supported insurrections which threatened British interests.

At home the people respected the traditional structure of the state and the means by which it exercised its powers and responsibilities. The elected legislative and the executive were regarded as the essential elements in a society which was based on consent: the rise of non-elected groups to positions of overwhelming power was seen, if at all, as a phenomenon likely to occur in certain foreign countries but not in the United Kingdom. The more powerful trades-union leaders, whose opinions and actions were reported with an infrequency that would surprise the reader of today's newspapers, were expected to be yeoman figures with their hearts in the right place—cast in the mould of J. H. Thomas who could talk with kings without the slightest intention of losing the common touch, or in that of Ernie Bevin, the bluff, forthright and able figure whose policy as Foreign Secretary in the Attlee administration he himself enshrined in the memorable phrase "to be able to go to Victoria Station and buy a railway ticket to anywhere he bloody-well chose". There was still a belief in the essential rightness of Britain, a belief, however insubstantial the under-lying evidence, that somehow British achievements would always match those of other countries, that whatever might be lacking in quantity would be more than made up in quality. The feeling of God-given national superiority which was the foundation of such beliefs was by no means limited to those who by reason of income or position exercised a superior freedom of choice; it pervaded all social classes and automatically mani-fested itself in the presence of or even in the contemplation of foreigners and their funny ways.

With such an underlying philosophy, it was not surprising that the British were reluctant to see changes in their national institutions, and that they took rather too much account of what they thought had worked well in the past when they planned their actions for the future. When national disasters occurred, their causes tended to be concealed behind individual or collective acts of heroism and self-sacrifice; the ability to conduct searching post-mortems on failures had never been a conspicuous trait, nor had the IBM philosophy that "there must always be a better way" figured large in national decision-making. The consequence was that in their response to the Egyptian seizure of control of the Suez Canal, both politicians and military turned to precedent and prejudice as proper bases for action.

So it was that the British people entered the Suez crisis with their self-confidence still substantially intact and with a belief, founded on a measure of historical evidence, in the ability of doggedness to carry the day. When the extent of the failure of the Anglo-French efforts came home, the shock to the nation was all the greater because it was clear how easily the allied aims had been thwarted, how small were the military resources which could be put together for the reoccupation of the canal, how isolated the two allies had been from the rest of the world, and how vulnerable the United Kingdom was when its major ally manifested its disapproval.

Anthony Nutting chose the title *No End of a Lesson* for his personal account of the events of the Suez crisis. Two of the definitions of "lesson" provided by the *Shorter Oxford Dictionary* are "an instructive occurrence or example" and "a rebuke or punishment designed to prevent the repetition of an offence". Whichever, if either, of these two definitions more nearly fits the course of history since Suez has been, and will continue to be, the subject of debate. What is certain is that the door through which the British people passed in 1956 slammed behind them.

The authors and publishers are extremely grateful to the following for granting permission to quote: Faber and Faber Ltd. and Editions Bernard Grasset for extracts from *The Suez Expedition, 1956* by André Beaufre; H.M.S.O. for extracts from *Hansard*; Cassell Ltd. for extracts from *Full Circle* by Anthony Eden; MacGibbon and Kee Ltd./Granada Publishing Ltd. for extracts from *The Rise and Fall of Sir Anthony Eden* by Randolph Churchill; William Kimber and Co. Ltd. for extracts from *Airborne to Suez* by Sandy Cavenagh; the *Daily Telegraph* for extracts from General Sir Hugh Stockwell's article "Suez from the Inside" which appeared in the *Sunday Telegraph* on 30 October, 6 and 13 November 1966; Weidenfeld (Publishers) Ltd. for extracts from *Diary of the Sinai Campaign* by Moshe Dayan; Punch Publications Ltd. for extracts from *Punch* during 1956; Mr. John Reed for allowing the authors to make use of his manuscript *History of the British Army in Egypt (1950–1956)*; and Lieutenant Colonel J. M. Barstow for the sketch map published in the *Infantryman*, No. 67, February 1957.

CHAPTER ONE

NATIONALISATION

EGYPT'S LEADERS had hoped for too much from Hitler's defeat. Although the British Government had removed its troops from Cairo and Alexandria during 1947 and 1948, to abandon control of the Suez Canal was a risk hardly to be contemplated. The experience of two world wars had confirmed the importance of the waterway to British trade and security, while the vast base which had grown along its west bank was seen as the fulcrum of the country's military strength in the Middle East and North Africa. Thus even though Egypt was now a member of the United Nations and the leading state of the Arab League, she still suffered the indignity of having a large and important area of the country occupied by foreign troops.

The 1948 war against Israel, in which the Egyptian armed forces were humiliated, provided further impetus to the Society of Free Officers, the revolutionary movement led by Gamal Abdul Nasser and dedicated to liberating the country from what were seen as the three enemies: imperialism, the monarchy and the feudalism imposed by the wealthy. Since Britain had first become embroiled in Egypt in 1882, the aims of successive governments had been to create a stable country, economically sound, which would secure the protection of the Empire's communications. One of the tools used to try to achieve this stability had been the Egyptian Army, modelled on British lines. Despite its limitations, so quickly revealed by the Israelis, this army had developed into a comparatively efficient force, western in professional outlook, and one which reflected the military characteristics of cohesion and dedication, qualities rare in Egyptian public life.[1] Britain had, in fact, created the instrument which was to be responsible for her departure from the Middle East and which was to establish Egypt as the least unstable power in the Arab world.

During 1951 relations between Egypt and Britain were to worsen. Food supplies to the British Canal Base were cut off, Egyptian civilian labour was withdrawn, and guerilla attacks were carried out by a variety of different groups, including both the Moslem Brotherhood, which preached a fanatical creed of Islamic revivalism, and the communists. Some of these guerilla groups were trained by the Free Officers. The British were forced to increase their garrison, and in the January of the following year, needled by these terrorist attacks, they were manœuvred into attacking the police headquarters at Ismailia. In the subsequent fighting, British officers were astounded by the stubborn defence of the Egyptian auxiliary policemen, fifty of whom died with double the number wounded. The next day the centre of Cairo was in flames. Foreign-owned property was gutted and a number of innocent Europeans met unpleasant deaths at the hands of the mob. Order was restored only by the firm action of regular units of the Egyptian Army which were rushed into the city.

The time had come for the Society of Free Officers to act. On 23 July 1952 in a well planned operation Nasser seized power but used as his figurehead a Major-General Neguib. Both men had distinguished themselves in the 1948 fighting and both had been wounded in battle, Neguib seriously, to the benefit of their standing and influence with their fellow-officers. It was the prototype of the new-style African and Arab army coup. Four days later Egyptian troops surrounded the Ras-el-Tin Palace in Alexandria, and the same evening the dissolute King Farouk, the last member of the Mohammed Ali dynasty which had ruled Egypt in name if not in fact for the past century and a half, sailed for the pleasure resorts of Europe, his possessions packed into a couple of hundred trunks.

Nasser was now Prime Minister with Neguib as President. The former took just two years to tighten his grip upon his country. Land reform, combined with the abolition of political parties and the confiscation of their funds broke the oligarchical power of the upper classes. The vast possessions of the Royal Family were impounded and the leading members of the old régime dealt with by a revolutionary court, but in a manner surprisingly mild. The activities of the Moslem Brotherhood, which had seen in the revolution its own opportunity to gain power, were held within bounds, while the communist threat on the left was eliminated. Unreliable officers in the police and armed forces were retired, and all the senior command positions, together with the key ministries of government, were filled by young officers who had helped to create the revolution.

British public opinion gave grudging and on the whole patronising approval to this national resurgence, but the man in the street did not find it easy to take Egyptians seriously. Since 1914, hundreds of thousands of British civilians in uniform had endured often long periods of boredom and discomfort there. Sound judgement tended to be smothered by prejudice. To many of these men, and to their friends and relations at home, the Egyptians were a people which in contrast to most of the other races of the Empire, and in particular the Indians, had done little to help win the Kaiser's war and had proved to be more of a liability than anything else in the next one. Egyptians were remembered as street-hawkers or pimps, as thieves of unparalleled ingenuity, as wealthy idlers flaunting their possessions in the Cairo cafés, or sometimes as street-louts hurling bricks and abuse. Closer acquaintance with an individual, probably a house or mess servant, could reveal a pleasant human being, but such contacts were rare. The common cliché was that the Egyptian was in no way an Arab and that it was presumptuous of him to claim the title. Subjects like the Egyptians were for mockery and few British thought it in any way bad taste when Churchill made a habit of deliberately mispronouncing Neguib's name as "Neegwib". Such attitudes did not escape the Egyptians, whose own Moslem and xenophobic prejudices were all too often inflamed by inebriated soldiers bawling insulting songs on their way back to camp or barracks. Beyond living memory, the British in company with the French and other foreigners had run their country and it was only too easy to blame them for every ill.

Nasser's other major task was to rid the Canal Zone of British troops and in this he was helped by the fact that the British Government had at last come to understand that there was little point in incarcerating 70,000 servicemen in a base which could be used only with Egyptian co-operation. Negotiations for the withdrawal had started in May 1953, but it took eighteen months for agreement to be reached between the two countries, and at one stage Nasser loosed guerillas once again against the base installations as if to demonstrate that they were worthless in the face of Egyptian hostility. This intransigence fostered a growing dislike and distrust of Nasser in Britain, particularly in the ruling Conservative Party, but in October 1954 Anthony Nutting, then the young Minister of State at the Foreign Office, signed with Nasser an Anglo-Egyptian Treaty which provided for British forces evacuating Egypt within twenty months, with the proviso that for a further seven years a body of civilian technicians was to be allowed to maintain the base for use in the eventuality of any Middle Eastern country, including Turkey, being attacked. Even before this treaty was signed, British troops were being shipped to Cyprus. At the same time Sir Norman Kipping, the Director-General of the Federation of British Industries, was organising the new body which was to maintain the base. Backed by such famous industrial names as Vickers, I.C.I., Rootes and Wimpeys, Suez Contractors Ltd. was to employ 1,200 civilian technicians, 800 of them British. Middle East Command Headquarters also moved from Egypt to Cyprus, which was still a peaceful island. Unfortunately it lacked the airfields, harbours and other installations needed for a military base.

The Treaty was far from popular in both Britain and Egypt. It was condemned by the so-called Suez Group on the right of the Conservative Party, while Clement Attlee, the leader of the Opposition, mocked Churchill for sponsoring an evacuation which hitherto he had so resolutely opposed. The Moslem Brotherhood, which was still a power in Egypt, saw the Treaty as a further act of treachery by the new rulers against their country's real interests. When a member of the organisation emptied his pistol at Nasser as the latter was addressing a public meeting at Alexandria on 24 October, the Prime Minister had the excuse he sought, both to crush the Brotherhood and to remove Neguib, who not only had links with the conspiratorial organisation, but whose popularity and standing in the country had grown to the extent that he was on the brink of becoming the *de facto* rather than the titular ruler of Egypt. As a consequence Neguib retired to his villa, and Nasser added the office of President to that of Prime Minister.

Britain had hoped that the signing of the Anglo-Egyptian Treaty would be followed by the setting up of a Middle East Defence Organisation. With the Arab countries the source of much of the world's oil reserves and with the shortest sea and air routes to Asia and East Africa lying either through or across them, the danger to the West of leaving a vacuum in the area for the Soviet Union to fill was only too clear. Nasser and the rest of the young Arab revolutionaries saw it otherwise. France had already been expelled from the Middle East at the end of the war against the Axis powers, and now the British were starting to leave as well. An organisation such as Britain was canvassing was seen as an instrument to prolong Western influence in the Middle East, and one which would help to sustain the despotic monarchies of Saudi Arabia, Jordan and Iraq, all of which were friendly towards the West. The Soviet Union, on the other hand, was quietly making friends, but was also taking care to avoid any overt interference in Arab affairs. Nasser was more than an Egyptian nationalist; he was a Pan-Arabist who wished to eliminate foreign influence and corrupt misrule, not just in Egypt but throughout the Middle East. It was ironic that his critics always saw him as a protagonist of either the right or the left, even though he had little knowledge of political theory or interest in the subject. As a young man, however, he had immersed himself in history, and he understood well the roots of his country's misfortunes.

Nasser, therefore, became the focus for resistance to the Baghdad Pact, with such success that Iraq was to be the only Arab country numbered among its members. His main weapon in the struggle was Cairo's radio station, "The Voice of the Arabs", which fed neighbouring countries with virulent propaganda, directed against both their own rulers and Western influence. With the proliferation of cheap radios, the announcer's voice could reach the illiterate peasant or herdsman in the most remote villages and encampments. To many in the West, this seemingly unjustified interference in the affairs of others increased their distaste for Nasser and all he represented.

Although no Arab leader could dare to be known as less than a bitter enemy of Israel, Nasser's attitude towards his neighbour was more restrained than most, and in private he even seemed to welcome the possibility of an eventual settlement. In any case his struggle to eliminate his rivals and to rid his country of the British, combined with the antique equipment of his armed forces, at first put any idea of war out of the question. Then on 27 February 1955 the Israelis, exasperated by murderous raids into their country by Palestinian border-guards, attacked an Egyptian post near Gaza and slaughtered a lorry-load of reinforcements.

From that date Nasser was compelled to consider the likelihood of war, but his need was for weapons. A number of unsuccessful approaches had already been made to the Americans, and to a further request made after the Gaza raid, Eisenhower's Administration equivocated, insisting on payment by cash. In June, the British provided a small quantity of material, but a little later they refused to release ammunition from their Suez stocks for the Centurion tanks which had been included in the consignment, a decision afterwards described by a future C.I.G.S., Field-Marshal Sir Richard Hull, as driving Nasser "straight into the arms of Moscow".[2] It was the chance for which the Russians had patiently been waiting and working. In September 1955, Nasser announced to the world that Czechoslovakia was to provide Egypt with arms. At the time the details of the deal were kept secret, but it was subsequently revealed that Egypt received 300 Soviet medium and heavy tanks of the latest types, 200 MIG-15 fighters, 50 Ilyushin bombers, 100 armoured SP guns, 2 destroyers, 4 minesweepers, together with large quantities of every type of military equipment, including guns, small arms, radar and spares.[3]

Israel also needed arms, and France supplied them. Despite France's traditional concern with all things Arab, since 1945 she had discovered that she had much in common with Israel. The people of both countries had similar memories of Hitler's persecutions, and French revulsion for what was seen as British treachery in Syria and Lebanon in 1945 stimulated sympathy for the Israelis in their fight to eject the British from Palestine and to smuggle further immigrants into their country. A decade later, as a consequence of *fedayeen*[4] raids into Israel and Egyptian support for Algerian independence, Egypt had become the focus of both their enmity in the Middle East.

Guy Mollet, the twenty-second post-war premier of what seemed to be an ungovernable France, was a socialist in sympathy with Israeli socialism. Ten years after the end of the war, the French had little with which to console themselves. Liberated by Americans and British, and with only the exploits of the Resistance and the Free French to remind them of past military glories, they had since 1945 watched the progressive liquidation of their Empire. Manœuvred out of Syria and the Lebanon, they had been embroiled in an eight-year long conflict in Indo-China, which in 1954 had ended with the disastrous defeat at Dien Bien Phu and independence for Vietnam. By 1956 both Morocco and Tunisia were on the verge of gaining their freedom after bitter years of violence, and since 1949 there had been sporadic trouble in Algeria itself, an integral Department (or rather three Departments) of Metropolitan France, a country in which ten per cent of its 9,500,000 people were *colons* of French or other European origin. With Egypt providing a refuge for the revolutionary Algerian leaders and lending covert support to their cause, a guerilla war proper had been launched in November 1954. At the time France had 50,000 troops in the country; eighteen months later the number had swollen to a quarter of a million. It was a struggle marked by the usual type of massacre and subsequent bloody retribution, with Egypt providing weapons and political support, and using "The Voice of the Arabs" to exult over the slaughter of European women and children and of Arabs and Berbers who co-operated with the French. It was hardly surprising that Mollet, who like most of his colleagues had fought with the Resistance, should have equated Nasser with Hitler, and his book, *The Philosophy of the Revolution*, with *Mein Kampf*. To Mollet Nasser became an obsession.

In contrast to France, Britain's withdrawal from Empire had not been too untidy. Ceylon had left in an atmosphere of goodwill, and India, despite everything, had departed without too much bitterness. In Malaya a communist uprising had been defeated with the help of indigenous support, at the time a unique feat. The Mau-Mau in Kenya (who were also crushed) and EOKA in Cyprus were to prove troublesome, but the scale of the insurrections was in no way comparable to the wars which the French had to fight.

Britain was still a great power. Despite inflation and adverse trade balances, she was the most prosperous country in Western

Europe. Although dwarfed materially by both the Soviet Union and the United States, her influence was great; even her enemies respected her standards and values. Although troubled by the problems at home, a reader of *The Times* would still look outwards towards the world overseas: after scanning the centre page, where the main news still faced the leading articles, he was more likely to turn next to the foreign rather than the home pages, unless his interest lay in the sporting columns, which continued to ignore any mention of horse-racing odds.

Churchill's last major speech in office dealt with Britain's decision to join Russia and America in the manufacture of H-Bombs. His continued and inspiring leadership had contributed much towards his country's self-confidence, misplaced though it may have been, and when he handed over as Prime Minister to Anthony Eden in April 1955, it was to a man whom both the Conservative Party and the country at large held in high respect. In the May general election the new Premier was returned with an enhanced majority. As Foreign Secretary during the previous three and a half years, Eden had consolidated the international reputation which he had acquired before and during the war. At the height of the Cold War he seemed to have the knack of solving any problem, however troublesome it might be; whatever the crisis, he was at the centre of the negotiations. He had helped to end the Korean War, and to persuade the major powers to reach agreement over Indo-China. When Mossadeq nationalised Iranian oil, he negotiated a settlement and the oil ran once again. With his assistance, a clash between Italy and Yugoslavia was settled without bloodshed. He helped to bring West Germany into NATO and to persuade the Russians to allow Austria her independence.

In dealing with problems at home, Eden failed to display the same dexterity. To curb inflation and reduce the drain on the gold and dollar reserves, a number of unpopular fiscal measures had to be introduced in October 1955 which had not been forecast during the election campaign. Government and private spending were cut; taxation was increased. Strikes were rife. The Cabinet seemed to lack a firm guiding hand, and public opinion started to turn against the new Prime Minister, who was compared unfavourably with Churchill. As might have been expected, the *Daily Herald*, the *Daily Mirror* and *Punch* lampooned him, but even the *Daily Telegraph* mocked his lack of firmness. Eden was seen as a master of conciliation, but not the strong man the country sought. The brilliant and successful statesman, who had waited so long for his inheritance, was unused to this sort of criticism. Nutting, who was then Eden's close friend, saw him writhing under the insults and describes the consequent harm to his self-confidence.[5] Even worse, the nervous strain started to produce physical effects, and his bile-duct, which had been damaged during an operation in 1953, began to trouble him once again.

An Arabic speaker, Eden had read Oriental Studies at Oxford, and his subsequent work in the Middle East as a young man had made him sympathetic towards the Arabs. Later he had been shocked by the plight of the Palestinian refugees, and unlike Churchill he had never supported Zionism. So it was unfortunate that he took a particular dislike to Nasser, even though he welcomed the expulsion of King Farouk. On the one occasion Eden met Nasser, when he was passing through Cairo in February 1955, he handled the Egyptian President more than a little tactlessly, summoning him to the British Embassy and condescending to him.[6]

For all that, Eden accepted the Czech arms' deal philosophically and he showed no more than resentment at the excesses of Radio Cairo.[7] Even the violent protests of Jordanian nationalists, demonstrating against Britain's attempt to induce King Hussein to join the Baghdad Pact, and which Eden with some justification believed to be the product of Nasser's intrigues, did not affect his early support with Eisenhower for Egypt's High Dam project.

The turning-point in the Prime Minister's attitude towards Nasser was King Hussein's dismissal at twenty-four hours notice of General Glubb from his post as commander of the Arab Legion. In 1956 it was not customary for British advisers to be dismissed in this summary fashion, and the blow to prestige was unpleasant. Eden immediately blamed Nasser, ignoring the evidence which indicated that the dismissal was primarily an attempt by a young king to assert himself against an altogether too experienced counsellor. To make matters worse,

Selwyn Lloyd, the Foreign Secretary, who was in Cairo at the time of the dismissal, was congratulated by Nasser, who suggested that the British Government had itself removed an out-dated symbol of colonialism. It is possible that Nasser did not mean the remark as an insult, but Selwyn Lloyd took it as such. In London, when Nutting tried to defend Nasser's conduct, Eden retorted "I say he is our enemy, and he shall be treated as such".[8] On another occasion he shouted at Nutting over the telephone "I want him destroyed, can't you understand? I want him removed . . ." To Nutting's reply that Nasser's removal might produce anarchy and chaos in Egypt, Eden retorted "I don't give a damn if there's anarchy and chaos in Egypt."[9]

The progress of the negotiations for the construction of the High Dam at Aswan further embittered Eden. In this project lay Egypt's hopes for economic betterment. The original Aswan Dam, built by British engineers in 1898 and later enlarged, had served the country well, but it was too small to store the excess of water which flooded down from the Ethiopian Highlands and ran to waste in the sea. This new High Dam, to be built four miles upstream of the other, was to hold twenty-six times more water and increase by one sixth the patch of green earth which fed Egypt's proliferating millions. It would serve new industries by making Egypt self-sufficient in electrical power, and it would also remove the ever-present threat that an enemy in control of Uganda's Lake Victoria could cut off Egypt's water.

In October 1955, a month after the Czech arms' deal had been signed, Russia offered to help build the High Dam, but Nasser was reluctant to pledge his economy as well as his armed forces to a single power. Not too enthusiastically the American and British Governments agreed to pay the foreign exchange costs, with the World Bank adding dollar for dollar. However, as the detailed bargaining proceeded, the Egyptains became alarmed that the budgetary conditions of the loan would put the Egyptian economy once again under Western control. At the same time Eisenhower's Administration was being pressed to drop the scheme. The Zionist lobby was outraged by Nasser's ban on Israeli shipping using the Canal and the Nationalist China lobby by his recognition of Red China. There was annoyance in government circles that Nasser seemed to be playing off the West against Russia, apparently to obtain a better offer. Above all, however, Congress had recently cut the foreign aid appropriation, and with Eisenhower seeking a second term in November 1956 it was hardly advisable for him to ask for a vast loan to aid a country which looked as if it was veering rather too close to the Eastern bloc. So when on 19 July 1956 the Egyptian ambassador to Washington suggested to John Foster Dulles, Eisenhower's Secretary-of-State, that if the West did not help, Egypt would accept Russian backing for the High Dam, the opening for which Dulles had been waiting presented itself. American support was withdrawn and the following day Eden followed suit.

This should have dealt a crushing blow to Nasser's prestige. In fact, few Arabs thought that he could survive. With the Western press laying bare his discomfiture, it was essential for him to hit back hard and this is what he did. Speaking on 26 July from the same balcony in Alexandria from which he had escaped death two years before, he announced to an exultant crowd that the Suez Canal was to be nationalised and that its £35,000,000 annual revenue would be devoted to building the High Dam. It was a speech in which Nasser revealed new and more powerful skills in demagogic oratory than he had before displayed, and in which he spelt out once again every wrong which the West had committed over the years.[10] Even his enemies in Egypt greeted the speech with rapture.

Before he had finished speaking, armed men had quietly taken over the offices and installations of the Suez Canal Company. Nasser had anticipated by thirteen years the end of the hundred-year concession granted to de Lesseps to build the Canal.

CHAPTER TWO

THE IMPERIAL VISION

NASSER'S SPEECH on 26 July announcing the nationalisation of the Suez Canal cemented his leadership of the Egyptian people. In some ways it had a similar unifying effect in Britain. Despite Mossadeq's nationalisation of Iran's oil in 1951, the expropriation of the property of international firms was still something of an innovation. The bewildered rage with which the British heard the news that the Canal was to be nationalised revived a unanimity a little reminiscent of the war years, a unanimity which was all too short-lived. The French also reacted in a similar fashion, remembering as they did with perhaps rather too much emotion the consequences of Hitler's occupation of the Rhineland twenty years before.

The British people were persuaded that they had good reason for their rage. They sensed that they had for years been trying to mollify the Egyptians, only to suffer yet more abuse and to see more of their soldiers murdered in the Canal Zone. Although these troops had now been withdrawn, new weapons provided for the Egyptian Army and blocked sterling balances released, Egypt had given no signs of reciprocating these gestures of goodwill. Radio Cairo's propaganda, directed at Britain as much as her allies in Iraq and Jordan, continued to flood the bazaars and market places of the Arab world; not only had Egypt done everything possible to destroy the Baghdad Pact but she appeared prepared to allow Russia to obtain a foothold in the Middle East.

By a coincidence the news of Nasser's speech arrived in London as Eden was holding a dinner party at 10 Downing Street for King Feisal of Iraq and his Anglophile Prime Minister, Nuri es-Said, who had been a personal friend of Eden for the previous thirty years. So it happened that the two main architects of the Baghdad Pact heard about the nationalisation in each other's company. Nuri's reaction was to encourage the British Prime Minister to respond with resolution, but at the same time he issued a warning about the danger of Britain allying herself with France and Israel to destroy Nasser, since to do so would have a serious effect upon Anglo-Arab relations.[1] Within two years both the King and Nuri were to be brutally murdered with their families and their mutilated bodies exposed to the derision of the Baghdad mob.

At the end of the dinner party, which included Hugh Gaitskell, the Labour Leader of the Opposition, those Cabinet Ministers who had been present remained for an impromptu meeting in the Cabinet Room. Full evening dress (knee-breeches in the case of the Prime Minister and Lord Salisbury, who were wearing the Garter) increased the dignity of the occasion. Also present at the meeting were the Chiefs-of-Staff, the French Ambassador and Andrew Foster, the United States Chargé d'Affaires, who reported that night to President Eisenhower that the British Cabinet had agreed that the Western governments must consider possible economic, political and military measures against the Egyptians, regardless of what the legal aspects might be, so as to ensure that the Canal remained in operation. He also informed the President that the British Cabinet had asked him to find out how far the United States would go in supporting any necessary economic sanctions or military action. Foster learned also that the British commanders in the Mediterranean had been alerted, and that the Chiefs-of-Staff had been ordered to produce immediately a study of the forces needed to seize the Canal. Before he left the meeting, he reported that Selwyn Lloyd, the Foreign Secretary, took him to one side to say that he was moving towards the conclusion that the only solution lay in a Western consortium taking over and operating the Canal, establishing itself by force if need be.[2] It was a measure of the "special relationship" existing between Britain and the United States at the time that a representative of the latter country should have been so quickly and completely taken into the confidence of the British Government.

The next day in the House of Commons, speakers from all three parties were united in their support for the Government and in their execration of Nasser. Gaitskell protested that "on this side of the House, we deeply deplore this high-handed and totally unjustifiable step by the Egyptian Government",[3] and the Opposition supported the Government in freezing Egypt's sterling balances. A few days later he likened Nasser's action to that of Hitler and Mussolini,[4] and Herbert Morrison, the former Labour Foreign Secretary, expressed the mood of the country with the words "If the United States will not stand with us, then we may have to stand without them . . . but I ask the Government not to be too nervous."[5]

Other than the *Manchester Guardian,* the *Observer,* and the *New Statesman,* all of which in varying degrees cautioned a measure of restraint, the press was united in its abuse of Nasser and a demand for firm action. *The Times,* the *Daily Sketch* and the *Daily Mirror* all produced similar sentiments using different vocabularies, although the last-named was soon to perform a *volte-face* and attack the Government. A *Daily Telegraph* leader demanded that if there was a lurking desire to appease Colonel Nasser, it should be brought out into the open.[6] In *Punch* a demonic and bandoleered Nasser proclaimed from a minaret that "Nasser is great and Suez is his profit",[7] a cartoon which reflected a disdain for the religious susceptibilities of others not unusual at the time. In the same magazine a couple of weeks later, Nasser had become a monstrous bull-frog, inflating himself to explosion point.[8]

Within a week most Labour politicians were expressing reservations about the jingoistic euphoria which had swept the country, and many on the left were savaging the Government hard. Gaitskell was among those who were now expressing their doubts, which provided the subsequent criticism from his colleague "Manny" Shinwell that he had exploited the crisis to further his own position as Labour Leader, and that in seeking public support in this way for Party and personal reasons he had managed to misjudge the mood of the country.[9]

From the start there was no question of the British having to act on their own. On 29 July Christian Pineau, the Foreign Minister of France and like his Prime Minister a veteran of the Resistance, had flown to London with a team of military advisers to discuss the military resources which might be made available for joint action. On both sides the outcome was disappointing. The best units of the French Army were tied down in Algeria, and a high proportion of their warships were out of commission. The British Army was either in Germany or spread around the world in bits and pieces, with some of its best commando and parachute troops chasing EOKA over the Cyprus hills. Even though Pineau made it clear to Eden that his Government was unanimous in its desire for urgent and decisive action, there were no troops either French or British immediately ready to go into action.[10]

Alerted by Andrew Foster's report, President Eisenhower had despatched Robert Murphy, a senior State Department official, to London, briefed to find out just what was happening. Murphy describes how he gathered from Eden and Selwyn Lloyd that Britain had decided to use force if necessary, and that the Chiefs-of-Staff had been instructed to prepare a military plan, something which he well knew was no more than routine staff procedure. Dining with Harold Macmillan, then Chancellor of the Exchequer and an old friend with whom he had worked in war-time Algiers, he recounted that he learned from his host and from Field-Marshal Lord Alexander that the invasion could take place in early August and that France would participate. The danger of Britain becoming "another Netherlands" if Nasser's challenge was not accepted was emphasised.[11] Murphy himself was sympathetic towards the British and French stand, and according to Macmillan this conversation was a deliberate attempt to alarm him,[12] on the grounds that if the Americans were under no illusion that the British meant business, they would help their allies to get what they wanted without force being used.

Murphy had discovered a confident assumption that the United States would go along with her allies, and despite the anti-British feeling prevalent in the oil industry and openly displayed by some elements of the State Department, there was at the time a lot of sympathy for the stand which the British and the French seemed to be making. Eisenhower himself recorded in his diary on 8 August that Nasser was wholly arrogant and that the United States would have to support any reasonable counter-measures, including the use of force which might conceivably be necessary under extreme circumstances.[13]

CHAPTER THREE

EARLY PLANS

WHEN THE first members of the British planning teams started to assemble in London that August Bank Holiday week-end (it then fell at the beginning of the month) there were few doubts about the action contemplated by their Government. For most service officers, the issue was straightforward: with Nasser deposed, Britain's decline as a world power would be checked.

Major-General André Beaufre did not learn until 7 August that he had been selected to take charge of the French troops earmarked for the invasion. To him the idea of war with Egypt was something of a chimera, and he was reluctant to relinquish his operational command in Algeria to take up a nebulous job which could, as he put it, result in his being remembered as "ex-Commander Designate, Expeditionary Force".[1] Two days later, in Paris, he learned more about his task. Integrated Anglo-French Task Forces were to be assembled, with the staffs integrated too. This was the NATO system, one which had been evolved in the war years and which had stood the test of time. At each level, British officers were to be in charge with French deputies under them who could also command their own national contingents. At the top of the pyramid was General Sir Charles Keightley, the Commander-in-Chief of the Middle East Land Forces, with the French Vice-Admiral P. Barjot as his Deputy. Beaufre himself was to be Deputy to Lieutenant-General Sir Hugh Stockwell, the Land Forces Commander. The British Vice-Admiral M. Richmond (who was to be succeeded by Vice-Admiral Robin Durnford-Slater on 14 October) and the French Rear-Admiral P. Lancelot were in charge of the naval forces, while Brigadier-General R. Brohon was to be the French Deputy to Air-Marshal Denis Barnett, the New Zealander Commander of the Air Task Force. Beaufre noticed

CHAIN OF COMMAND:OPERATION MUSKETEER

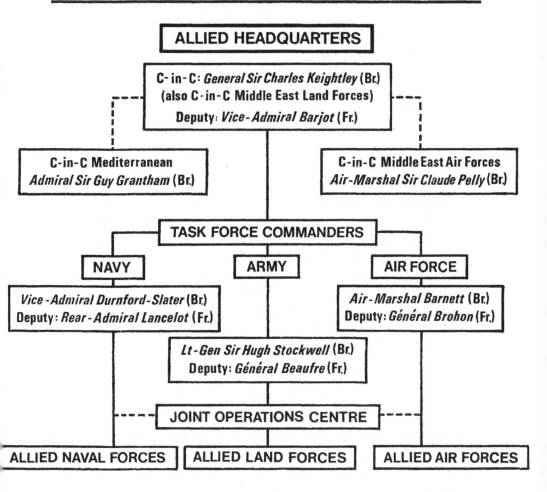

ALLIED HEADQUARTERS

C-in-C: *General Sir Charles Keightley* (Br.)
(also C-in-C Middle East Land Forces)
Deputy: *Vice-Admiral Barjot* (Fr.)

C-in-C Mediterranean
Admiral Sir Guy Grantham (Br.)

C-in-C Middle East Air Forces
Air-Marshal Sir Claude Pelly (Br.)

TASK FORCE COMMANDERS

NAVY

Vice-Admiral Durnford-Slater (Br.)
Deputy: *Rear-Admiral Lancelot* (Fr.)

ARMY

Lt-Gen Sir Hugh Stockwell (Br.)
Deputy: *Général Beaufre* (Fr.)

AIR FORCE

Air-Marshal Barnett (Br.)
Deputy: *Général Brohon* (Fr.)

JOINT OPERATIONS CENTRE

ALLIED NAVAL FORCES **ALLIED LAND FORCES** **ALLIED AIR FORCES**

how the French officers had been chosen with an eye to smooth co-operation with the British.[2]

In invading Egypt, the choice of landing-place lay between either Alexandria or Port Said. From both the strategic and the tactical standpoints, the former was by far the more suitable. If the purpose of the invasion was to threaten or occupy Cairo, unseat Nasser, and beat the Egyptian Army in battle if the need to do so arose, Alexandria should be the objective, for the Desert Road started there, the traditional invasion route to the capital 125 miles away. If, on the other hand, the strategic aim was merely to occupy and control the Canal Zone as a preliminary to establishing some form of international body to run the waterway, Port Said was the choice, particularly if it was important to avoid the invasion forces becoming involved elsewhere in Egypt. From the tactical standpoint, however, there could be few places worse than Port Said for landing troops. The beaches were shallow and shelving, and the port facilities limited. Once ashore, the army would have to deploy down a causeway twenty-five miles long and less than 300 yards wide in places; two roads, the railway and the Sweet Water Canal all used this causeway, which was connected to Port Said by two bridges, only one of which could carry Centurion tanks. In Stockwell's descriptive phrase, Port Said was like a cork in a bottle with a very long neck and "we would have to extract the cork and squeeze the neck before enjoying the rich juices of the bottle."[3] If the Egyptians put up anything of a fight at all, or if they planned their demolitions with care and carried them out thoroughly, progress would be very slow indeed. Moreover, fifty miles would have to be covered before an adequate airfield was captured. As against this, Alexandria possessed everything which Port Said lacked—an excellent airfield, good assault beaches to the west of the town, and first-class port installations.

With their new weapons from Eastern Europe the Egyptians could not be dismissed too lightly as opponents, or so the British and French planners were to be persuaded. No one knew much about the quality of their pilots and tank crews, but there was a distinct danger that their equipment might be manned by Russian or other Eastern European "volunteers", of whom large numbers were known to be advising the Egyptians. Even the four Egyptian infantry divisions and the growing National Guard could not be ignored. Dug in behind an obstacle, these men might fight tenaciously, despite the fact that they were untrained for mobile operations. Many officers, including Beaufre, remembered that Egyptians could behave resolutely on occasion: the defence of the Ismailia police station was still fresh in everyone's memory. The historically minded also may have recollected that Mohammed Ali's Egyptian Army all but conquered the Ottoman Empire in the first half of the nineteenth century and how gallantly the *fellahin* soldiers had fought for Arabi at Tel-el-Kebir and later for the British in the Sudan.

As a consequence the two allies decided that some 80,000 men would be needed to invade Egypt. The British, given time, could produce two-thirds of this massive force, which was to include 16 Parachute Brigade, 3 Royal Marine Commando Brigade, 3 Infantry Division from the United Kingdom and 10 Armoured Division from Libya. The latter, however, was a division in name only, consisting as it did of merely two armoured and one gunner regiments together with a single battalion of infantry. The French share of the combined force was to be the tough and experienced 10e Division Parachutiste and the 7e Division Mécanique Rapide (or 7 DMR), both from Algeria. Some sixty squadrons of aircraft could be made available by the two countries, together with the naval forces necessary to escort the convoys and support the landings.

The problems of mobilising, assembling and transporting a force of this size were such that there could be no question of launching it until mid-September. This delay of six weeks was unacceptable to many and a strong lobby pressed for the immediate use of airborne troops, to drop either at Cairo or to seize and hold the Canal Base installations. Such a *coup de main*, it was argued, might well result in Nasser either fleeing or being toppled by a counter-revolution. But neither the British nor the French parachutists had had much recent opportunity of practising their specialist skills, while the British lacked the anti-tank weapons needed to cope with the Soviet-built Egyptian tanks. Furthermore no link with even an improvised assault force could take place in under ten days and so far as the British Army was concerned, the disastrous defeat at Arnhem was still remembered. A member of the Government later told Hugh Thomas, the historian, that the Chiefs-of-Staff had hinted that they might resign if the Government were to insist on such a dangerous venture,[4] an admission which Anthony Head, as Minister of Defence, all but corroborated in Parliament.[5]

Within the Ministry of Defence devilled an organisation of picked staff officers known as the Joint Planning Staff, whose task it was to have ready to hand plans for dealing with any military eventuality which might arise, however esoteric its nature. When Nasser announced the nationalisation of the Canal, no plans for a return to Egypt appear to have been prepared, probably because the last British troops had withdrawn only six weeks earlier and the prospect of returning had not yet occurred to anyone. If this is true, and the tale may be a *canard*, the deficiency was quickly remedied. When Stockwell arrived in London from Germany on 3 August, where he had been commanding 1 British Corps, he found awaiting him a Joint Planners' paper in which he was directed "to be prepared to mount operations against Egypt to restore the Suez Canal to International Control"[6] with the troops landing at Port Said after the Egyptian Air Force had been neutralised. Stockwell did not favour the idea of a Port Said landing and he relates how he and his colleagues managed to reject this concept. By 6 August they and their staffs had an alternative ready—outline plans for an assault on Alexandria. The codeword *Hamilcar* was chosen to describe this operation, but the British and French had not standardised their vocabularies. When later the British troops started to paint the letter H upon the bonnets of their vehicles to enable their own aircraft easily to recognise them, they learned too late that their allies spelt the Carthaginian's name without the initial letter. As a result *Musketeer* was substituted.

Two days later, on 8 August, these plans were presented to the Chiefs-of-Staff, with Lord Mountbatten, then First Sea Lord, in the chair. The main conference room of the War Office building in Whitehall, finely panelled and well-proportioned, was an appropriate setting. On the fifth day of the invasion, the Chiefs-of-Staff were informed, the Egyptian Army, which was likely to be concentrated around Cairo, should have been beaten in battle just north-west of the city, where Napoleon had broken the Mamelukes. Then, turning east, the allied forces should, by the eighth day, control the Canal. Much to the relief of the Task Force Commanders, among whom no inter-service disagreements have been reported, their proposal that the landing should take place at Alexandria and their outline plans for so doing were accepted. On 10 August, the Prime Minister listened to their proposals and added his agreement.[7]

Beaufre first met Stockwell and his colleagues that same afternoon in their Whitehall headquarters. Only a short time before, on August Bank Holiday Saturday, when the Chief-of-Staff had entered these subterranean offices the only person he encountered was an official of the Post Office, hastily and reluctantly summoned to connect the telephone. His seniority could be judged from his bowler hat, and that only he could be made available was perhaps an augury of the lack of readiness of the Government for war.

Beaufre relates that the two commanders were equally repelled by the conditions. The French were to feel a lowering of morale and the onset of *cafard* every time they entered these cellars, where "much work was done but much time wasted", as Beaufre put it.[8] Among the tiny rooms, connected by a warren of passages, the staff had no idea whether it was light or dark, sunny or raining outside, until a military policeman was directed to provide the information on a blackboard. It was perhaps a pity that someone should have chosen the codeword *Terrapin* for the activities of the hundred or so staff-officers who eventually gathered in these uninviting surroundings.

At this point accounts of what then happened become a little confused. A cool and lucid officer, but reserved and more than a little touchy, Beaufre was in many ways more of the Anglo-Saxon than the lively, extrovert Stockwell, whom Beaufre described as being "as volatile as a continental", a comment with which his British colleagues would have agreed. Beaufre had immediate and justifiable cause for concern when Stockwell told him that the plan for the invasion had already been prepared but that the British Prime Minister had rejected it because an approach through Alexandria was too indirect, the Canal being the political objective. It was as the Frenchman feared might happen: he and his countrymen had neither been asked to approve the plan nor been a party to rejecting it. If Beaufre's account is accurate, it is difficult to understand what Stockwell's motives were in telling him that Eden had rejected the Alexandria plan. Stockwell mentions in his account of planning that things were in confusion; this may well have been so but a senior staff officer who was present at the meeting remembers the astonishment with which he and his British colleagues received this revelation of a complete change of plan, but later understood the purpose as an attempt to conceal the intentions of HMG from the French.[9]

If the two allies had agreed a clear political aim and communicated it to their service chiefs, much time would have been saved in planning and confusion of this sort might not have arisen. Both the British and French Governments were equally guilty, although it should be said that Beaufre was certain that the aim was to topple Nasser,[10] as were many of the British officers concerned with the operation. The choice of landing-place to a large extent depended on what the politicians were trying to achieve. A landing at Port Said was enough if the aim were no more than to return the Canal to international control, but to remove Nasser would probably require the occupation of Cairo with a consequent assault through Alexandria. A British commander told Thomas that some officers spent fruitless hours trying to get the aim of the operation clarified.[11]

Beaufre, who knew the British and spoke their language fluently, had formed doubts about the integrated command structure when he was first told about it.[12] General de Gaulle too, living in retirement and waiting for the expected call, advised against the command going to the British, but it is difficult to see how such a decision could have been avoided. Someone had to be in charge and they were providing the higher proportion of troops, the whole of the long-range bomber force and most of the cargo ships; Malta and Cyprus, the two invasion bases, were both British, and they alone had recent experience of Egypt. The consequence was, however, that the omens for successful and harmonious co-operation between the British and the French were worse than usual. Some allies tend to be instinctive friends; others not so. At working level, British and Americans rarely clash, nor do members of the Old Commonwealth. But with the British and French the suspicion and disdain which so many individuals feel for the characteristics and habits of those living across the Channel make goodwill difficult to achieve without a deliberate effort from both sides.

At home the French were united to such an unusual degree that even the communists were making no more than formal noises of protest at the idea of military intervention in Egypt. The nationalisation of the Canal was just the excuse needed to obliterate Nasser. Convinced of the connection between the Egyptian leader and the extension of the revolt in Algeria, they were sure that with him out of the way the Algerian liberation movement would collapse and the country revert to being a peaceful Department of France.

Some members of the British Government, including the Prime Minister, were as single-minded as the French in planning to remove a dictator who was both a danger to British interests and a general nuisance, but in the Cabinet opinion on the subject was far from unanimous and as the days slipped by, the Government could see opposition building up both at home and overseas. Opposition from the members of the Soviet alliance was as expected: for them the crisis was an opportunity to be exploited in the struggle against the West. Nor was support anticipated from the leaders of the Third World countries. But the British Government had hoped that the United States would at least display a benevolent neutrality, even if armed help was not to be forthcoming. It was, after all, only six years since the British had unhesitatingly joined their old ally in the United Nations action to halt communist aggression in Korea.

The reasons for the American opposition to the French and British plans were complex indeed and have still to be properly unravelled. Rab Butler, then Lord Privy Seal, was one of the many who understood that both Russia and the United States were primarily concerned throughout the crisis with winning or retaining the goodwill of the Third World countries—a vital aspect of the Cold War.[13] Reinforcing this pragmatic

approach were the remnants of Franklin D. Roosevelt's dogma
that Britain and France, together with the rest of the colonial
powers, should divest themselves of their remaining colonial
possessions without further delay, an attitude irritating indeed
to many Western Europeans who detected in the United
States itself many of the characteristics of an imperial power.

Nor did it help that Eisenhower was standing for re-election
as President in the coming November. Alarmed by Murphy's
reports on the belligerent attitudes of the British and the
French leaders, on 31 July he had despatched John Foster
Dulles, his Secretary of State, to join the talks in London. At
the same time the President wrote a personal letter to Eden in
which he urged caution and pointed out that unless the
occupying power was ready to employ the brutalities of
dictatorship, guerilla resistance in Egypt would grow and
might develop into wide-scale conflict.[14] This was an issue
which the British and French were reluctant to face.

Eden and Dulles did not find it easy to understand one
another. Their minds worked in different ways, and when they
met either around a conference table or in private discussion,
their opinions differed and their attitudes clashed. Dulles was a
man of strange duplicity. Although he had decided that
British dominance in the Middle East was near its end and
despite his determination that his country would be on good
terms with those on whom power was about to devolve, he left
Eden with quite the wrong impression of the support Britain
and France might expect, encouraging him with the statement:

> A way had to be found to make Nasser disgorge what he had
> attempted to swallow . . . We must make a genuine effort to
> bring world opinion to favour the international control of
> the canal . . . It should be possible to create a world opinion
> so adverse to Nasser that he would be isolated. Then if a
> military operation had to be undertaken it would be more
> apt to succeed and have less grave repercussions than if it
> had been undertaken precipitately.[15]

Dulles was a dying man and Murphy well understood that
statements of this type from his superior needed to be taken with
a "warehouse of salt",[16] but it was not surprising that Eden
was misled. One consequence was that Dulles obtained Eden's

agreement to a conference of the major maritime powers involved with the Canal. In any case, Eden had little to lose by talking as he had already accepted the advice of his Chiefs-of-Staff that no invasion was possible until mid-September.

Egypt was represented only by an observer at this conference of twenty-two nations which met in London on 16 August, but Nasser's refusal of the invitation had been both polite and conciliatory. Although the Egyptian stand had the full support of Russia and the independent Asian nations throughout the conference, the smaller countries represented were ready to follow any lead which the United States might give and which held out the promise of a peaceful solution. The consequence was that eighteen nations supported proposals prepared by Dulles, Mollet and Eden which included international control of the Canal, the guarantee of freedom of navigation, compensation for the Canal Company, and an equitable financial return for Egypt. Russia, India, Ceylon and Indonesia backed an alternative plan conceived by Pandit Nehru, which left Egypt's sovereignty undisturbed. But despite the stand that Shepilov, the Russian delegate, had made in public, he indicated privately to Dulles that his country was ready to impose international control on Egypt, provided that the plan did not alienate the Arab countries from the Soviet Union. This the Americans saw as a too obvious attempt to try to split the Western allies.[17]

The decision was then taken to send the Australian Prime Minister, Sir Robert Menzies, that staunch friend of Britain, with a small team to discuss the terms in Cairo, a proposal which appealed to France and Britain who knew well that Nasser could never accept such a solution and survive. It was a mission with small prospect of success. Not only did Menzies lack any real powers to negotiate with Nasser but he was hindered by his slightly old-fashioned approach to the Egyptian leaders. Nor was he helped by a press statement by Eisenhower that the United States would go to any length to secure a peaceful settlement, an accurate but untimely remark. As had been anticipated, Nasser finally rejected the plan on 9 September and Menzies is said to have protested vigorously to Eisenhower when he stopped off in Washington on the way home that the rug had been pulled from under his feet.[18]

During these political discussions, the military plans had
been gathering momentum. Back in Paris from London on
11 August, Beaufre contemplated the many tasks awaiting his
attention. The French part of the joint force had to be withdrawn from the fighting in Algeria and trained for its new role.
Detailed plans for its use had to be made. At the same time
Beaufre had to share with the British in the higher planning
which was taking place in London, where he had left his
Chief-of-Staff and a small team. Other than these individuals,
he possessed no staff of any type, so it was with some astonishment that he discovered that nothing had been done in Paris to
provide him with a proper headquarters. The British were at
least a couple of weeks ahead of their allies in their preparations.

After a series of discussions, including one with shipping
experts who depressed him with an estimate of fifty-five days to
collect the necessary merchant vessels, load them, sail, land and
build up the forces, Beaufre returned to London on 15 August
to be further irked by finding the French part of the inter-
service team crammed into a single small and remote cell in the
underground labyrinth. However, the French were now fully
integrated into what Beaufre described as

> . . . the tedious process which the British call "planning".
> The method is as follows: instead of the commander doing
> his work and making the overall decision, after which the
> staff does the drafting, the staff gets to work first; it produces
> a draft, which is then submitted to the "committee" formed
> by the three commanders, Land, Naval and Air. One
> therefore arrives knowing nothing of what will be proposed
> and one hums and haws over each paragraph, the general
> idea still remaining obscure.[19]

There was some justification in Beaufre's criticism. The system
had evolved in the previous war to eliminate friction between
different services and different allies, and to ensure that the
action of the three arms was fully co-ordinated. It had proved
its value but it could be ponderous, particularly when a quick-
thinking commander was a couple of jumps ahead of his colleagues and staff. In general, however, Beaufre was impressed
by what he saw of the British at work, and his tedium was
relieved by what he describes as a number of interesting meals

arranged for him by the French military attaché between the interminable sessions, a compliment indeed to London restaurants.

The plans for *Musketeer* which evolved from this toil were based upon the Egyptian Air Force being destroyed by bombing, after which the troops were to land on 15 September, two days after the initial air strike. Royal Marine Commandos would capture the port itself at Alexandria, supported by a naval bombardment, and the French were to assault over the beaches to secure the west and south-west exits from the city. These assault landings were to be combined with drops by British and French parachutists. In the next phase tanks and infantry were to break out towards Cairo, where the "Second Battle of the Pyramids" was to be fought some time between $D+6$ and $D+14$, and not on $D+5$ as forecast in the draft plans which had been presented to the Chiefs-of-Staff. If it were found necessary to force a passage over the Nile, French *paras* were to be launched at the Nile Delta Barrage.

Although Stockwell later claimed that the troops were not to enter Cairo,[20] there seems to be small doubt that the plan did envisage the city being occupied. As Field-Marshal Lord Montgomery propounded to an audience of Egyptian officers eleven years later, "To dominate Egypt, you must dominate Cairo."[21] It is all too easy to imagine what the consequences might have been if Cairo had been bypassed and left to xenophobic rioting and as a base for guerilla action against the extended allied lines of communication.

A limiting factor in planning *Musketeer* was the prohibition against taking risks, the first of the eight principles established by the Task Force Commanders.[22] In a campaign such as this when the fighting qualities of the enemy were uncertain and when political success could well depend on military speed, it was possibly an unfortunate stipulation. The British were also inhibited, and rightly so, by a desire to avoid casualties both among their own men and among the Egyptians, but the French after their bitter experiences in Indo-China, and faced with another ruthless struggle in Algeria, were rather less squeamish.

Such attitudes of mind, combined with the complexities of collecting troops, ships, stores and aircraft from a number of diverse locations and a shortage of the landing-ships and craft required to put vehicles ashore quickly, was starting to impose delays upon the timetable. In some ways also, the situation seemed a little unreal. The absence of a clear political directive was worrying some of the British staff officers. What is more they were accustomed to working hand-in-glove with the Americans in such an enterprise, with the consequence that it seemed inconceivable that military action could take place without this ally's wholehearted co-operation. With the massive Sixth Fleet in the Mediterranean and their air bases in Libya, they were the only power with the resources to intervene quickly in such a dispute. For all that, most of the officers concerned understood how remote was the possibility of American intervention, and useful though the planning was as an exercise for their military skills, it hardly seemed possible that it could all end in bloodshed.

Beaufre was now concerned that the slow rate of the proposed build-up in the Alexandria bridgehead would allow world opinion to be mobilised in support of Nasser. Nevertheless, when he touched down in Paris *en route* from Algiers to London for the fourth time to attend the presentation of the *Musketeer* operation orders to the Commander-in-Chief,[23] he was dumbfounded to hear Barjot assert that the landing should take place at Port Said, and not at Alexandria. Only a small force would be needed to capture Port Said, Barjot declared, and the place could then be held as a hostage while the British, if they so wished, could carry on at Alexandria with all their paraphernalia.[24] After thirteen days of detailed planning for a very complex operation, and only twelve days before the planned sailing date, the Deputy Supreme Commander was casually postulating an entirely new concept, one which in Beaufre's view was as irresponsible as it was pointless.

Beaufre had already expressed doubts about Barjot's appointment but had been told that there were good political reasons for it.[25] On paper he seemed to be a sound choice. The most brilliant and most decorated French naval officer of his day, he was a restless individual of panache and enthusiasm, well accustomed to working with the Royal Navy. But in Beaufre's view, his imaginative mind had become muddled with age.

The following day when Barjot put his proposal to Keightley, Stockwell and the rest in London, they found it difficult to follow his barely comprehensible English and were a little slow to understand that a complete change of plan was being suggested. The pained surprise which Beaufre noticed on their faces was understandable when the purpose of the meeting was to approve plans so complex that the naval disembarkation orders alone were as thick as the London Telephone Directory. Embarrassed though Beaufre was by his senior's performance, he could hardly openly disagree with him. So, to Keightley's clear relief, he suggested that plans should be prepared for an attack on Port Said, to be available for use should the need arise.

At the end of the meeting a new timetable was approved. The landing date had been delayed to 17 September, a mere forty-eight hours, but later dates were chosen on which further delays or modifications to the programme could be inserted if such proved necessary. This, Beaufre was told, had been done at the request of the British Prime Minister. The Frenchman sensed a lack of determination.[26]

CHAPTER FOUR

THE CONDITION OF THE WEAPON

IN RETROSPECT it is hard to understand why a country such as Britain, which was then spending ten per cent of its gross national product on defence and had 750,000 men and women under arms, should have lacked the capacity to seize the Canal as soon as Nasser nationalised it, even without help from an ally. It may be facile to compare Wolseley's expedition to Egypt in 1882 with Stockwell's invasion force, equipped as the latter was with weapons rather more complicated than those which sufficed to smash Arabi's infantry, but the Victorian general did manage to mobilise, embark and land a force similar in size within five weeks of receiving his instructions, and this despite rudimentary communications and staff machinery. But then the Victorians could get things done quickly: it took them only eighteen months to design, build and open the Great Exhibition of 1851.

The contents of the 1956 White Paper on Defence, which emphasised the need to be prepared for limited wars makes this lack of readiness even more surprising. Published at the beginning of the year, the White Paper started by declaring that there had been no change in Soviet long-term policy which fundamentally aimed at world domination and that the objectives of the Western powers were defensive and that they would never be aggressors. It then went on to say that the United Kingdom had to be ready for the outbreak of localised conflicts on a scale short of global warfare, with the Army "primarily organised so that it can bring force to bear quickly in cold or limited war".[1] In addition the armed forces were required to make a contribution to the Allied nuclear deterrent and to fight effectively in a global war should one occur; strategic reserves were to be maintained for the cold and limited-war tasks and emphasis was to be placed on forces which were "flexible, mobile, well-trained and versatile".[2] This, like so many of these Defence White

Papers was more of an optimistic soporific for Parliamentary critics than a calculated statement of military potential, but the emphasis was on fighting limited wars and for this the British Army was singularly unprepared.

At the time Britain's armed forces were still encumbered by equipment and organisations which dated from the war and by many of the accompanying attitudes of mind. When Germany collapsed in May 1945, 5,000,000 men and women were in uniform, over 3,000,000 of them in the Army. The Women's services alone numbered 215,000, all but the size of Britain's pre-war Army; 4,000,000 civilians had been labouring to produce the supplies and equipment to keep this vast force in being. The subsequent pace of demobilisation was slow and deliberate, much more so than in 1919, and fresh drafts continued to join the colours to replace those who had returned to civilian life. With plenty of jobs available, low rates of pay in the armed forces and a natural post-war reaction to service life, there was little to persuade men to enlist on regular engagements. But the military commitments of an imperial power remained and if enough soldiers were to be available to meet them, there could be no question of abolishing National Service (that very British euphemism for conscription).

The result was that by 1956 one soldier in three was a conscript in an Army just under 300,000 strong. The induction, training and administration of these national servicemen swallowed up a high proportion of the regular *cadre* with the consequence that the number of conscripts in units increased dramatically as one approached the sharper end. Those who needed to acquire specialist skills often arrived in their combatant units so late in their two-year period of service that they could contribute no more than a few months of effective work.

Most gunner and infantry units were, in fact, manned almost completely by national servicemen, with no more than a handful of regular private soldiers and junior N.C.O.s, many of the latter unfit for further promotion and settled into the agreeable niches to be found in stores and messes. Nearly all the infantry section leaders and even the occasional sergeant would be conscripts, inexperienced but intelligent and keen. Of the subalterns, all but a few would be eighteen or nineteen year-old national servicemen, usually talented youngsters destined to

make their mark in later life but whose qualities at the time were
often not fully appreciated by their seniors. The regular captains and majors could be old for their rank, far too many regular
commissions having been granted at the end of the war with
consequent promotion blockages and redundancies. The result
was that many of the company commanders, able though they
usually were, could be disappointed and disillusioned men, some
of whom had held the rank of major for a dozen years at a stretch
and were a generation older than the boys they commanded.

For all that, these largely conscript units were usually very
efficient indeed, even though they were filled with men who
knew their date of discharge to the day and who talked of little
else. To a large measure this competence was due to the officers
and senior N.C.O.s who manned the training depots and
moulded the never-ending drafts of fresh-faced and naïve
youths into effective soldiers, but their task was made easier by
the inherent goodwill which was manifest in these young men
faced with a situation over which they had no control and which
they knew they had to accept.

But it was with a politician's license that Mr. Head, Secretary
of State for War in 1953, boasted that the United Kingdom had
the best equipped, the best trained and the best prepared Army
ever in peacetime,[3] a remark which begged the question of the
standards of comparison being used. Certainly the quality of the
equipment was lamentable. During the post-war decade of
national austerity and reconstruction, the British armed forces
had been saddled with an enormous stockpile of military stores
painfully and expensively assembled during the war, the very
existence of which was a deterrent to any programme of re-
equipment. Not that the equipment had been particularly good
when it was first produced to fight the Germans and the
Japanese. In fact, with few and rare exceptions and these
usually in the gunner arm, the weapons and other tools handled
by the British soldier were inferior in design and performance
to those of both his allies and his enemies. Perhaps it was a
symptom of the industrial decay, the first signs of which were
apparent towards the end of the nineteenth century, that no one
seemed capable of properly defining the task to be carried out
or of providing an effective tool to do the job if by chance it had
been accurately defined. Unorthodox or eccentric solutions

might be found for specific problems: in new fields such as radar and nuclear energy Britain was still able to demonstrate great powers of innovation and invention. But so far as the traditional technologies were concerned, in the long chain which linked battlefield experience or conjecture with the production engineer—somewhere in ministry, research establishment or factory—purpose and fitness for purpose often became irretrievably separated and the soldier had to make do with the outranged anti-tank gun, the dangerous or unpredictable sub-machine gun, the lorry for which there were no spares or the spares for which there was no lorry.

In this field of motor transport, the Americans had excelled. Faced before Pearl Harbour with the need to build a national army upon a regular *cadre* which was in 1939 half the size of the British pre-war Army, the Americans decided on the range of vehicles with which they would fight the coming war: the Willys-Overland 5 cwt. jeep, the General Motors 15 cwt. weapons carrier, the Studebaker 2½ ton general-purpose truck, and so on. Whether built in new or existing factories, the jeep from one would be identical to the jeep from another. In contrast, the multiplicity of vehicle types in the supply column of a British armoured division could resemble an old-timers' rally. Then, in the early post-war years, the British managed to find cash to produce a standardised range of vehicles. All-purpose, they could be used anywhere from the Arctic to the Tropics: with the aid of a schnorkel they could ford rivers and were driven by Rolls Royce engines of the appropriate power, in which nearly everything except the blocks and the head were interchangeable. It sounded too good to be true, but specialist vehicles which are not based upon commercial production runs have snags; the new models were not only bigger and heavier than anything which had gone before, but were so expensive that the Champ cost four times as much as the American jeep which it was intended to replace. Moreover, the Champ was far from reliable, and seemed to have been designed by men isolated from military reality. The front and rear ends of the early model had the curved and flowing contours of the old Morris Minor, surfaces which were quite unsuitable for those essential military tasks of spreading maps, carrying additional loads, or even for balancing a hot mug of tea.

The result was that in 1956 the British Army was equipped mainly with the left-overs from the last war, a state of affairs which according to the Grigg Committee, meant units sent two cars on a journey in order to ensure that at least one of them arrived, and in equipment being borrowed from other armies stationed in Germany so that a passable show could be made on combined manœuvres.[4]

As this Committee also noticed, the Royal Navy and the Royal Air Force were, on the whole, reasonably equipped and the same could be said about the French Navy and Air Force in 1956. As a result the two countries between them disposed of enough warships for convoy protection and bombardment support for the assault landings but, on the other hand, none of their carrier-borne aircraft was capable of tackling Egypt's MIGs. So far as land-based aircraft were concerned, the British medium-bomber force was mostly in England, while neither country had long-range fighter squadrons stationed nearer to Suez than northern Europe.

But the shortages of ships and aircraft needed to carry the troops into battle were serious. This was not really surprising. When money is short, and often when it is not, sailors and airmen quite naturally become more absorbed in the urgent problems of convoy protection or the submarine offensive, in fighter defence or strategic bombing; what to them are the more mundane tasks of dropping parachutists or landing soldiers from small craft tend to take a lower place in their lists of priorities. It might have been different if the Ministry of Defence had been strong enough to enforce its will on the three very independent fighting services but in 1956 this was beyond its capacity. Even though Churchill had assumed the title of Minister of Defence in 1940, the creation of a ministry proper did not come until 1946. But although the task of this new ministry was to allocate resources and co-ordinate the defence effort, it lacked teeth, consisting as it did of little more than the secretariat of officers and civil servants required to service the various defence committees and planning staffs, the individual members of which owed primary loyalty to their own service. Not until 1963 were the three independent empires reduced in status to mere departments of the Ministry of Defence.

Despite the demand for a quick parachute *coup de main*

against Egypt, the sad fact was that the R.A.F. possessed a mere five squadrons of Hastings and Vickers Valetta troop-carrying planes, enough to lift a single parachute battalion and its supporting arms. The four-engined Hastings was the product of a 1939 design study for a civil aircraft which came to nothing because its range and its payload of thirty passengers were surpassed by the aircraft which the Americans were developing so successfully at the time. The smaller Valetta was the British reply to the American D.C.3 or Dakota, swarms of which had made Slim's victory in Burma possible and lifted the allied airborne divisions into Europe during 1944 and 1945, a sturdy and reliable plane which is still flown by "bush" airlines in odd corners of the globe. So the British parachute troops were left to gaze with envy at the American Fairchild Packet and its French equivalent, the Noratlas, both twin-boomed aircraft which could load and parachute heavy cargoes through the tail, a simpler and quicker operation than slinging the loads beneath the undercarriage, as was necessary with the British aircraft.

But as well as the shortage of aircraft, two other problems inhibited quick use being made of 16 Parachute Brigade. Two of the battalions which were operating against the EOKA in Cyprus had done no parachute training for more than a year. The pilots of the aircraft needed practice too, the dropping of parachutists being an exact science, errors in which could lead to costly consequences as had been shown in 1943 and 1944. Secondly, there was the equipment. It was discovered rather late that the new Champ when lashed upon its platform and prepared for parachuting was too bulky; slung beneath a Hastings, the load would prevent the landing wheels from touching the ground. The alternative was the jeep but the British Army had by now disposed of the lot. The consequence was that officers with briefcases stuffed with money had to be despatched to accost local farmers around the Middle East Command, who were astonished and gratified to discover that their battered second world-war runabouts were worth a fortune. The vehicles so acquired were rushed to workshops where a crash programme rendered them fit for an airborne operation.

The next casualty was the BAT, or recoilless anti-tank gun, the only air-portable weapon which could deal with Egypt's

new and modern tanks. Unfortunately the BAT ammunition
could not be passed for active service as it had not been properly
tested under tropical conditions. The alternative was to remove
a number of the United States 106 mm R.C.L.s, the jeep-
mounted equivalent of the towed BAT, from NATO stocks in
Europe, and this was done. Despite the American opposition
to what the British and French were planning, co-operation at
working level in some spheres remained good. As an example,
Robert Amory, the then evaluation chief of the C.I.A. has
stated that his service went out of its way to collaborate with
their old allies by flying U2 photographic missions over Egypt.[5]
The "special-relationship" was strong in the military field. A
British officer who was attending a course in the United States
in early 1957 remembers a visiting British civilian lecturer
criticising his country's actions at Suez; when the officer concerned rose to protest at question time, his American fellow
students applauded him with unrestrained enthusiasm.

Yet a further blow was the withdrawal of the new F.L.N.
self-loading rifle from the parachute battalions because of the
fear that Egyptian sand might jam the re-loading mechanism.
So back came the recently discarded No. 4 Rifle, a hand-
reloading weapon, the machine-tolerances of which were all but
proof against sand, as had been demonstrated in the fighting
against Rommel. With Head's words on the condition of the
British Army still remembered, the members of a force which
prided itself on being an *élite* spearhead found it all rather
frustrating.

Because there was to be no question of airborne troops
invading Egypt unsupported, an assault landing from the sea
had to be mounted. This required specialist landing-ships
(L.S.T.s in the British nomenclature), assault landing-craft to
carry the infantry ashore (either L.C.A.s or the lightly
armoured amphibious Buffalos) and tank landing-craft to
perform the same function for the armour and the vehicles.
All such vessels were as difficult to come by as transport aircraft.
With the continued existence even of the Royal Marines in
doubt at the end of the war, it was hardly surprising that by
1956 the Royal Navy had in commission only two L.S.T.s at
Malta, each of which carried eight L.C.A.s and two L.C.T.s,
hardly enough to land a single infantry battalion and a troop of

tanks at the same time. Other craft and ships were held by the Royal Navy in "mothballs", and some had been sold to ply as ferries or pleasure steamers, from which peaceful pursuits they were commandeered and repainted in more sombre and war-like colours.

The techniques at least of amphibious warfare had been kept alive in the inter-service school of Combined Operations at Fremington and in the attenuated Combined Operations Head-quarters, which had just managed to survive the post-war cuts. Some thought it a pity that even this amount of effort should have been spent on studying combined operations, particularly when the tools of the trade were so conspicuously lacking. How-ever, during the last three years of the previous war amphibious operations had brought major victories to the Western powers, not only in the Mediterranean and Normandy but also in the Pacific and the Indian Oceans. Forces vast by comparison with any other than those of the Russian front had been landed across beaches against bitter and determined opposition. For the British it had been a continuation of their traditional strategy of using the mobility conferred by sea-power to strike at the enemy at his weakest point (a strategy which had, in fact, been marked by far more disasters than successes). Many of the senior commanders at Suez had established their reputations in amphibious operations, with the result that they and their staffs, skilled as they were in the preparation of the complex plans necessary to embark and land under fire thousands of men and vehicles, settled into a familiar routine. However, their task was complicated further by shortages of nearly everything they needed and the frustrations of mobilising forces in a country which had not been placed upon a war footing. There could be no question of taking short cuts: Gallipoli and Norway were awful warnings of the consequences of hurried improvisation. Everything was carried out in a most thorough manner, but the pace was not always of the fastest. Montgomery's maxim for efficient staff-officers had been the catch-phrase "Foresight, accuracy and speed". Some of his successors forgot the last, hard though they worked.

A further difficulty for the planners was the lack of suitable invasion bases within striking distance of Egypt. Two hundred and fifty miles to the north lay Cyprus, the new site of the

British Middle East Command Headquarters and planned as the main British Mediterranean base now that the Canal had been evacuated. Unfortunately Cyprus lacked nearly everything needed in a base for a combined air-and-sea-borne invasion. Workshops and depots barely existed but equally serious was the absence of an adequate harbour. Only at Famagusta could ships berth alongside but numbers were limited to five and these to no more than 5,000 tons. At Limassol, the only other port, there were no wharfs at all and loading of both men and cargoes was from lighters. It was all a reflection on how little Britain had done for the island during eighty years of occupation. Cyprus was no better served by airfields. That August, only the international civilian airport at Nicosia was operational. Akrotiri, planned as the R.A.F. base near Limassol, was still being built, while the only other one at Tymbou, just outside Nicosia, was a neglected field used for emergency landings. Not until the end of October were these two last-named fields fully operational. A further complication, to put it no stronger, was that the campaign against the EOKA guerillas was then at its height.

The next nearest base was Malta with its magnificent harbours and fine airfield. But the island was nearly 1,000 miles from Port Said, six days in a slow convoy, while its chequer-board of minute fields provided little room for troops either to camp or to train. Libya was rather nearer and the home of 10 Armoured Division, the imposing designation for a force less than a brigade in strength, but the Libyan ambassador had already made it clear to Selwyn Lloyd that no Libyan government could dare to allow their country to be used as an invasion base, even though Nasser would not have been mourned once he had disappeared.[6] For all that, the early plans for a landing at Alexandria included a land thrust by the units stationed in Libya, which suggests a lack of proper liaison somewhere in the ministries. However the chance of many of the armoured vehicles ever reaching Egypt from Libya was remote as there were no tank transporters to carry them.

It was easy for the servicemen to blame the politician for the lack of a small and mobile strategic reserve, equipped and trained and backed by the necessary transportation and bases.

Why was it not possible to bring force quickly to bear against an opponent such as Egypt, despite the exhortations of the Defence White Paper? With such numbers of men and women in uniform in 1956 and with so high a proportion of the citizens' taxes being spent upon their maintenance, were the armed forces providing proper value for the money they were spending?

Certainly it is arguable that when the war was over and the time came to demobilise the vast field army, too much of its complicated top-hamper of research establishments, training schools and the machinery for administration and command was retained, often protected by vested interests. To such an extent did training establishments proliferate in the post-war years that it was often difficult to fill the vacancies on the courses and units were dragooned to find students, having already lost too high a proportion of their better leaders as instructors for these schools. Research establishments, operational research groups and the like lingered on, often looking for work or performing functions which could have been better carried out at the universities. An example was the Royal Military College of Science at Shrivenham.[7] Such places devoured men and cash at the expense of fighting units and perhaps may do so still. Unwieldy and bureaucratic headquarters, blowing and yawning like somnambulant hippos, performed few functions other than to provide occupation for their commanders and staffs in accordance with Parkinson's immutable principles. In the decade following Suez four ponderous Army Commands in the United Kingdom alone were replaced by a single entity without any obvious loss to efficiency. In fact their departure speeded-up decision-making. Each had been commanded by a general or lieutenant-general, with a lesser general to assist him, together with cohorts of brigadiers, colonels, majors, military clerks and civilians. The other two services were much the same with the ratio of admirals to ships and air-marshals to planes ever rising.

Nor did the taxpayer necessarily receive full value from the money spent on the fighting units. An example was the infantry whose varied tasks required many differing skills, a battalion moving from field force duties in Germany to anti-guerilla patrolling in the Malayan jungles, and then to join an armoured

division in the Libyan desert, or possibly to ceremonial duties
in London, needing training in a fresh set of both individual and
collective skills each time it moved. The economic answer to the
problem would have been to have kept the battalion per-
manently in one station, posting officers and men to it for a
limited tour of duty, two or three years in the case of regulars
and eighteen months or so in the case of the conscripts. This
was the usual procedure in most arms other than the infantry
and the armoured corps—the latter moved less because most of
their tank units were stationed in Germany. The consequence of
rotating units in this way, rather than the men who manned the
units, was that a number of battalions were always out of action,
either packing or unpacking, training for a new role, handing in
or drawing stores, enjoying either embarkation or disembarkation leave or being shunted in slow-moving troopships from one
end of the world to another. At any one time about one quarter ·
of the infantry was not available for use, but with the single-
battalion regiment which, except for a limited period, was the
post-war norm, it was quite impossible to leave that battalion's
officers and men to stagnate for most of their service in some
backwater such as Gibraltar or Suez. This game of musical
chairs was, in fact, one of the consequences of the regimental
system, but for some unaccountable reason the expense it
entailed was rarely mentioned in the passionate controversy
which raged for nearly a quarter of a century on the merits or
demerits of a corps of infantry.

At the time few officers seemed to be conscious of the basic
ills which had beset the armed forces since the end of the war.
The self-confidence engendered by the victories of 1944 and
1945 blinkered them to deficiencies, and at the same time
encouraged them to condescend towards their allies. The
successes in Korea, which once again demonstrated the dogged
fighting qualities of the British Commonwealth units, did much
to reinforce these attitudes, for Canadians, Australians, New
Zealanders and Indians were still thought of as British rather
than mere allies. Most officers understood full well that the
multiplicity and size of the headquarters caused delay and
resulted in compromises, but such bureaucracies were a fact of
life, as was the shortage of equipment. If parachutists and
commandos complained about the lack of opportunity to

exercise their skills, this was nothing new. Thought for the future there was in plenty but much of this was devoted to the use of the new nuclear weapon, both strategically and tactically on the battlefield. Sometimes ideas could be esoteric and naïve at the same time. At a major conference just before Suez, a presentation was made to the senior commanders of both Britain and the Commonwealth showing how a single (or possibly two) atomic bombs could be used to repulse a Vietnam-type army in an imaginary Far Eastern jungle.[8] Above all, it was perhaps sad that an army which prided itself on flexibility so often relapsed into stereotyped action. This was illustrated by the counter-measures which always seemed to be adopted at the start of a colonial insurrection. Repeatedly, massive sweeps of the jungle or mountains, often supported by area bombing, failed to catch small and mobile guerilla bands. Only when the soldiers learned to operate in the same way as their opponents did they gain the upper hand, but in each campaign the lesson had to be learned anew.

Rather insulated by their own experiences, there were surprises awaiting those British officers who had anything to do with the French during the autumn of 1956. From time to time staff-officers and others met their allies on courses and at international headquarters but it was comparatively rare for anyone to have seen the fighting end of the Army of the Fourth Republic. Therefore when units of the French parachute division began arriving in Cyprus, their tough, professional and battle-hardened look came as an unexpected shock. This impression was brought into sharp focus at a dinner party given for them by the officers of a British parachute battalion. The French officers did not share the custom of their British counterparts to change out of uniform and into civilian clothes whenever possible. Among the guests were some exquisites from the Household Brigade, clad in white dinner-jackets and exuding the unmistakable whiff of Mr. Trumper's products from their beautifully-cut hair. Alongside them the French in clean and pressed camouflage battle uniform with sleeves rolled up to the elbow and with their hair cut to a stiff bristle, caused more than one of their hosts to ponder on the military and sociological implications.

Since 1947 the French had been fighting colonial wars on a

scale and intensity outside recent British experience. By the end of the seven-year-long disaster in Indo-China, 175,000 regular troops of the French Army, not to mention sailors, airmen and local forces, were toiling among the swamps and jungles. One third of the French officer corps and half of the regular N.C.O.s were there. Of the six classes of young officers which had graduated during this war from St. Cyr,[9] 2,000 had died in Indo-China.

But this army, which Général de Gaulle is said to have described as "La plus belle armée que la France ait jamais connue depuis Napoléon" was embittered and divided. Despite the successes of the Free French and the Resistance, the final allied victory of 1945 was a hollow triumph for an army which took its grandeur seriously and which was unused to feeling inferior to Anglo-Saxons. The memories of 1940 were still close. Now the tragic losses in Indo-China had proved purposeless and the concept of Empire had been still further shaken by the grant of independence to Morocco and Tunisia. For the past seventeen years the French Army had been at war, its regular *cadres* separated from their families and isolated from the changes which were occurring in their native land. They felt that they were at a distance from all sections of the population; without sympathy from anyone—politicians, the left-wing workers, the commercial community or even the *petite bourgeoisie*. The officers saw the colonial battles which they were fighting as part of the war against international communism and there was more than an element of truth in this concept of *la guerre révolutionnaire*, its battlefields stretching from Korea and Indo-China, through Egypt and the rest of North Africa to the "red belt" around the *environs* of Paris. To many a French officer, linked by ties of comradeship and mutual respect with his Tonkinese or Moroccan soldiers, both spiritually and physically their army was all that stood between France and the communist conspiracy.

The regular colonial troops and *les paras*, the Foreign Legion and the marines, the men who were so to impress their British allies, were far from typical of the mass of the French conscript army. Because of the political reluctance to commit *le contingent* outside France, the war in Indo-China had been fought by these regulars. Algeria, a constitutional part of France, was another matter and when, in early 1956, the Government found itself obliged to recall several classes of conscripts for service there, disorders erupted in Paris and Rouen and in the boat-trains to Marseilles, but the outcome was not as serious as many members of the General Staff feared. Although this initial dis-obedience did not develop into anything worse, in the following years the mass of the French Army soldiered on in Algeria, apathetic in its attitude towards the struggle, despite the indoctrination carried out by the highly organised psycho-logical warfare teams of the *Cinquième Bureau*. Their duties limited to the drudgery of routine guards and patrols in the *Bled*, with the regular units of the *Réserve Générale* summoned whenever a tough or interesting job arose, the less glamorous line units relapsed into the role of second class troops. The dif-ference was emphasised even in equipment—French in the case of the élite divisions, but outdated American for the rest.

Not only the panache of the French parachutists (whose units did, in fact, now include quite a high proportion of conscripts) but also their equipment made a deep impression on their British allies. One of the reasons their officers wore camouflaged battle-dress to dinner was that they spurned the miscellaneous "lend-lease" garments worn by the rest of the Army. The air-craft which carried them into battle were French, as were the parachutes which each soldier packed himself. As yet unseen by most British soldiers, if not undreamed of, were their SS10 wire-guided ground-to-ground missiles, the revolutionary anti-tank weapon which the French took to Suez. Even their medical packs were pre-sterilised and standardised for single treatments, the envy of the British medical officers. For those who knew their history, there must have been a sense of *déjà-vu* among the Cyprus olive groves. Just a hundred years earlier, the British had reason to envy the training and the equipment of their French allies in the Crimea: then the British lacked everything; the French, straight from years of campaigning in Algeria, were tough and experienced and they were equipped with all the British lacked and needed most—tents, ambulances and proper medical supplies.

There is perhaps an analogy here. France had been building new industrial plant and technologies to replace those destroyed in the war. Britain, far less damaged, still managed to maintain the highest standard of living outside North America and

Scandinavia, oblivious to the occasional economic Cassandra. The French, left at the end of the war with motley and disillusioned armed forces, had developed an efficient regular force suited to the limited colonial and quasi-colonial wars which were to be a feature of the post-war years. The British armed forces, rather like British industry, were saddled not only with the equipment but also with the ideas of previous decades.

CHAPTER FIVE

THE COLOSSUS MOVES

BEFORE THE forces earmarked for the invasion could be made ready to fight, reinforcements in the form of reservists had to be called to the Colours, some as individuals to bring their units up to war-establishment and others to man specialist units which did not have an existence in peacetime. On the whole, the British mobilisation machine ran smoothly, with only the minimum of the ordered chaos inseparable from such occasions as the reservists reported to their depots or units, suffered their inoculations and medical inspections and drew their clothing and equipment. At Arundel, where she was staying for Goodwood, the Queen on 2 August signed the Royal Proclamation recalling them. A few days later many were already on their way to the Mediterranean.

The main difficulty was to move them. The old troopship *Dilwara* was at hand to ship a couple of infantry battalions to Malta on 9 August, but it was necessary to requisition a variety of other ships, including the *New Australia* which had been about to sail for the Antipodes with 1,200 emigrants, all of whom had to suffer postponement of their fresh start in life. It was also announced on 2 August that a number of squadrons of Canberra bombers were flying from the United Kingdom to Malta and that all R.A.F. Transport Command scheduled services had been cancelled so that the aircraft could be used to ship ground staff and stores for these squadrons. It was the start of the "great airlift", as the press christened it, although a mere 5,000 troops were moved, and Transport Command was helped by the independent airlines, which were far from reluctant to being pressed into service. The prospect of a continuing demand for air-trooping in the future was appealing, but the total of aircraft they could find was no more than 200, only half of which were four-engined. It was strange that a major trading nation should have found it so difficult to move a few troops and stores.

The Royal Navy also helped to move the troops. The sole aircraft-carrier in the Mediterranean at the time was H.M.S. *Eagle*, whose fighter and ground-attack planes were somewhat out-of-date. In UK waters were two light fleet carriers, H.M.S. *Ocean* and H.M.S. *Theseus*, both in use as floating training establishments, together with the Fleet Air Arm training ship H.M.S. *Bulwark*. Between 5 and 7 August *Ocean* and *Theseus* sailed south crammed with parachutists and gunners, with about 2,000 men in each ship.

Theseus carried the parachutists. Some were drafts for the three battalions (the third having arrived there only the week before the Canal was nationalised); the rest consisted of the gunner, sapper and other supporting units together with the headquarters of 16 Parachute Brigade. As these men embarked at Portsmouth, the red-bereted soldiers saluted the spectators with the V sign. A truck painted in the light desert-sand colour, which was becoming a conspicuous novelty on British roads, bore the words "Look out, Nasser. Here we come." It was familiar stuff, reminiscent of the newsreels which the younger soldiers had watched as schoolboys, but a newly commissioned R.A.M.C. doctor in the party was impressed by the remarkable philosophy with which the reservists had cast off their civilian clothes and their jobs.[1] However, their wives saw it all in a different light. Some of their men had been in Korea; a few of the older women had even experienced the relief of VJ Day. Now it was hard that their husbands should once again be snatched away, leaving behind growing children and the hire-purchase debts accumulated in setting-up their proper homes. On 15 August, *Punch* published a *Troop Deck Ballad*. The lines provide an ironic insight into the cheerful fortitude with which the average reservist faced the call-up; they also serve as a reminder of contemporary attitudes:

I could talk like one o' Kipling's ruddy 'eroes if I tried
(Ballads in the barrack-rooms and royalties galore!)
But I'm just a paratrooper, and I've not much time for side,
And dialect is really such a bore.
Oh, I'm just a paratrooper and I'm sailing to the East
To bolster up the shares in the Canal;
And what it's got to do with me I don't know in the least,

And in spite of all the papers, I dare say I never shall.

But it's: Call out the Reserve!
Call out the Reserve once more!
There's a lot of chits that say
Class A! Class A!
Fall in the Reserve for the war!

I did five years with the Colours and I got discharged last
  May
(Wallop in the sitting-room and all the neighbours round!)
And I got a job as fitter in a works up Luton way
That brought me in a steady fifteen pound.
But when they called the old Reserve I gladly packed it in—
I wouldn't see Old England up the creek.
But we'll Hang Out the Washing on the palace of Abdin
And knock this dastard Nasser to the middle of next week!
For it's etc.

There's another whole division coming out to fight the Wogs
(And a squadron's-worth of Canberras no further off than
  Malta)
And three small aircraft-carriers to show the dirty dogs
Who owns the Med from Jaffa to Gibraltar.
For the serried ranks of Gyppos (Backed by Jordan and Iraq)
Are Egyptians we'll be very glad to spoil,
When the voice that breathes from Eden says we've got to
  have a crack
So the motorists of England shall never lack for oil.[2]

The "Class A" of the Ballad was the recently discharged
regular soldiers who, for a fixed term of years, were liable to
recall. Many had so recently left the Service that they could be
absorbed into their old units quickly and painlessly; most of
the men rejoining the parachute and commando brigades were
in this category. The other reservists belonged to the Army
Emergency Reserve. A proportion of these A.E.R. were
volunteers, liable for a fortnight's training each year; others
were national servicemen, all of whom served for a spell in the
reserve after their discharge from full-time duty, either with the
Territorial Army or with an A.E.R. unit.[3] Morale often started
to drop when the time came to weld these part-time soldiers

into their units. The call-up had in some cases been selective and it was difficult to persuade anyone why he in particular should have been chosen. Many were specialists such as electricians, plumbers, Post Office engineers or clerks, who could not be properly occupied in their trade. Even worse, some did not even seem to be needed; enough men were recalled for the armoured regiments to provide five-man tank crews when the Centurion required a complement of only four. Nor did it help when politicians and the press voiced their criticisms of British policy and intentions towards Egypt. It had been a long time since the country had mobilised civilian soldiers to fight in a war about which an influential and voluble section of their nation were both so ready and so free to express their moral misgivings.

The movement of units and individuals was not all one way. Two of the Royal Marine commandos which had been operating against the EOKA, were withdrawn from Cyprus to Malta for amphibious training, where they were joined by 42 Commando, which had been hurriedly extracted from its training role in the U.K. and brought up to strength. The 1st and 3rd Battalions of the Parachute Regiment, which had also been trying to flush Grivas' men out of Cyprus hills, were transported back to the Parachute Training School at Abingdon; they had not jumped for more than a year and like the pilots of the aircraft they were badly in need of practice. With these two battalions flew home some of their reservists who had arrived in Cyprus in H.M.S. *Theseus* only four days earlier. 3 Infantry Division, the major British component of Stockwell's force, for the time being stayed put in the United Kingdom.

There were other problems as well as those of moving the troops. When it came to assembling the units and preparing them for their role, many of those concerned felt as if they were sinking into a bureaucratic morass which at times could verge on the malevolent. The number of staffs with which the regimental officers had to deal and through which orders had to percolate, could be surprising. Brigade and divisional headquarters were superimposed on the complicated territorial hierarchy which ran from the War Office down through commands, districts and sometimes even garrisons. As a result one unit discovered that it was receiving orders from six

different sources; even worse, these orders were often con-
tradictory.

The two Centurion tank regiments earmarked for the
operation, 1 and 6 Royal Tanks, suffered rather more than
most. For a start, they were based at Tidworth in Southern
Command with their brigade headquarters in Eastern Command. At the end of July the officers and men of both regiments
were scattered around the United Kingdom, helping the Territorial Army at its summer camps, demonstrating at the
School of Infantry and busy on other similar duties. 1 R.T.R.
had returned from the Suez Canal just a year before and
6 R.T.R. during the spring from Germany. Neither had a
strategic role nor mobilisation plans and both were short of
tanks and soft-skinned vehicles. Virtually every type of store
was lacking and their training was rusty, particularly in range
work. Some reservist officers had not been in uniform for ten
years.

In the words of one of their commanding officers, the next
four weeks were a confused nightmare. When the units started
to collect their vehicles and stores from depots which were
spread around the country and manned mostly by civilians
who took the week-end off, it was found that mobilisation
scales were out-of-date, that numerous items were out-of-stock
and that many of the vehicles were, to say the least decrepit.
To move the tanks from Tidworth to Portland and Southampton, where they were to be loaded into L.S.T.s, help had to be
sought from Pickfords to supplement the few tank-trans-
porters still left to the Army. Pickford's men were subject to
trade-union rules and civilian regulations, and their massive
transporters took a week for a journey which an army convoy
could complete in three days; behind each bunch of their
vehicles trailed a number of empty spares, as was required by
the Regulations of British Road Services. It was hardly
surprising that it took four weeks to move and load ninety-
three tanks, but this was not all, for their brigade commander
had decided that 1 R.T.R. should support the initial landing.
As a result this regiment had priority in everything, and its
tanks were the first to be loaded into the L.S.T.s. Then the
brigade headquarters was disbanded and the regiments
placed under direct command of 3 Infantry Division. Plans

were changed: 6 R.T.R. were allocated 1 R.T.R.'s role in the
initial assault and they sailed first, two weeks ahead of their
sister regiment. When they arrived in Malta, no one was
expecting them.

The Royal Navy also had its problems. Only two L.S.T.s
were in commission, with thirty-two in reserve; when the latter
were taken out of mothballs, many were found to be unsea-
worthy and in the end only half could be used. Wooden-hulled
minesweepers were found to have rotted. The loading, a
joint-service responsibility, often went awry: convoys of
vehicles could find themselves redirected from one port to
another, seeking a vessel in which they could roost. Nor did it
help that the Port authorities and the civil servants concerned
interpreted peacetime rules with unrelenting severity.

The French also were gathering their strength. On 2 August
the press in London and Paris spelled out the details of the
ships of the French Mediterranean Fleet assembling at Toulon:
the 35,000-ton battleship *Jean Bart*; the two aircraft-carriers,
Arromanches and *Bois-Belleau*; the three cruisers, the four heavy
and fifteen light destroyers; the seven frigates and six submarines. No details were lacking, except the state of readiness
of the ships. According to an informant of Professor Thomas,[4]
Jean Bart possessed only a single gun-turret, *Arromanches* was
under repair and much else was needed to make the ships
battleworthy. Three weeks later came the further startling
press announcement that French troops were in Cyprus to
protect French nationals in the eastern Mediterranean, their
stores having arrived a week earlier.

Well equipped and trained though the French troops
appeared to their allies, Beaufre faced problems not very
different from the trials which were aggravating the British.
Les paras, too, had been fighting guerillas and had not jumped
with their heavy equipment for a long time. Their 106 mm SR
anti-tank gun was new to them and they also were short of
transport. It was the same with 7 DMR, the mechanised
division, which for the past six months had been dismounted
and operating in Algeria on a reduced establishment: drivers
required training, armoured vehicles had to be drawn from
depots and motorised tactics had to be practised. The French
staff, their signals, air-support system, services and bases had

all been thrown together in a hurry and now needed to be run in and trained. As he complained

> . . . provision of personnel and equipment constituted the most serious difficulty. Units, and even more the staffs, were below strength; everyone had to be kitted out in tropical clothing, water tanks fitted, sand tracks provided. The painting of the vehicles, for instance, required a greater tonnage of yellow paint than the French market could provide at short notice. As for 7 DMR's tanks, disturbing shortages came to light; complete consignments of tank spares, including all the gun sights, had been misrouted by Marseilles base.[5]

Amphibious craft were a major problem. Some were still on their way from Indo-China, where they had been worked to the point of collapse; the floating dock *Foudre* was creeping around the Cape at a speed of 11 knots. The few amphibious tanks needed a complete overhaul, while the Amphibious Centre at Arzew had only recently been disbanded to form the Marine Brigade. There was, in fact, very little to choose between the state of readiness of the two allies.

There is small doubt that the extensive publicity given to the movement of ships, aircraft and men was designed deliberately to build up the tension which Eden and Mollet hoped might scare the Egyptians into submission, an entirely laudable and economic purpose.[6] At the same time, the two Prime Ministers were careful to avoid allowing anyone, except their closest colleagues, to know exactly what they were planning; one consequence of this was that Gaitskell suffered the indignity of learning the scale of the proposed operations from Mr. Mintoff, the Prime Minister of Malta,[7] to whose country so many troops and aircraft were being moved. Yet this sabre-rattling produced little in the way of a reaction from Nasser, who did no more than call up some reservists, move half his 60,000 troops in Sinai to the other side of the Canal and promote the *fedayeen* into an "Army of National Liberation". Confident of the strength of his position, it was to his advantage to appear conciliatory and moderate abroad; in any case, he was determined to avoid providing the pretext which Britain and France needed to launch their invasion, faced as they now were by opposition not only from the Soviet bloc and the Third World but also from some of their NATO allies.

If ships had ceased passing through the Canal, this might have furnished the two allies with the necessary pretext. Of the 205 highly paid men who piloted the ships through the waterway, only 40 were Egyptian; 115 were British or French, and the rest mainly Dutch, Norwegian or Greek. It had become accepted dogma that these pilots needed at least two years' practice to learn their esoteric craft and that Egyptians were, in any case, incapable of running the installations and navigational systems without outside help. When the time came for the Canal Company to order their expatriate staff to resign and leave Egypt by 15 September, the Egyptians took no steps to hinder their departure. The day after they left a greater number of ships than the daily average was passed through and to nearly everyone's surprise, shipping continued to move smoothly during the subsequent weeks, piloted at first by Egyptians and a few Greeks who had stayed on as a measure of protest over Cyprus. To justify their generous salaries, the old pilots had, of course, been engaged in a quiet game of bluff. Not only were the Egyptians quite capable of running the Canal effectively without outside help but new pilots could be trained in a mere four months. Eisenhower had been sceptical about the whole matter and he had warned Eden that he doubted the validity of the argument that no one could run the Canal except the European technicians then engaged on the task. Thirty years earlier, the American President had gained personal knowledge of the Panama Canal, a much more complex mechanism, and he could not accept the proposition that a high level of technical competence was needed to run the one at Suez.[8]

Interference with the work of the British employees of Suez Contractors Ltd., who still continued to operate the British base, would have also provided a reason for the invasion but the Egyptians had gone out of their way to ensure that the staff at Moascar, Tel-el-Kebir and Fayid were not molested.[9] In early August, 894 women and children had been evacuated, mostly by Solent flying boats, probably the last big job done by these planes, leaving behind their menfolk, a few women staff, and some thirty stubborn wives of the old school who refused to leave their husbands. Early in September, these remaining women and children were forced to follow the others but the 500 male employees quietly carried on maintaining the British war equipment or at least that part of it which had not been lifted by local entrepreneurs over the perimeter fence.

CHAPTER SIX

FRESH PLANS

As the military preparations ground on, politicians continued to argue. Nasser's final rejection on 9 September of Dulles' plan for an international board to run the Canal had done nothing to help Britain and France. Indication of support from among their allies and friends had, if anything, diminished. An exception was that old friend of Britain, Monsieur Spaak, the Prime Minister of Belgium; an enemy of anything which might be likened to Hitlerism, Spaak was convinced that the West must stand firm to avoid the start of a long series of defeats in Africa and the Middle East. The Congo was not far from his thoughts. The Netherlands still held to a strongish line, suggesting that shipping dues should be withheld and the matter taken to the Security Council,[1] but other countries were hostile or wary.

In particular, the attitude of the United States had hardened. On 3 September, Eden had received a personal letter from Eisenhower, warning him that American public opinion flatly rejected the use of force, an admonition which the Prime Minister found both disquieting and disturbing.[2] He answered Eisenhower on 6 September in a long and closely argued letter, in which he reminded the President of the success of the West's reaction to the Berlin blockade and likened Nasser's machinations to those of Hitler, suggesting that the seizure of the Canal was the opening gambit in a planned campaign to expel all Western influence and interests from Arab countries.[3] His letter ended "We have many times led Europe in the fight for freedom. It would be an ignoble end to our long history if we accepted to perish by degrees".[4]

Eden's letter was written eleven days before the fleets were due to sail for Alexandria but Britain and France still lacked an excuse for invading Egypt. As a consequence they had decided to take the dispute to the Security Council. It was an astute move. With the near-certainty that the Soviet Union would veto their resolution, such action would go a long way towards satisfying public opinion both in Britain and overseas. But the United States questioned the legal basis for the Franco-British stand against nationalisation, (even though Dulles had never expressed such doubts at the London conference), at the same time opposing their plans to refer the dispute to the Security Council. A lack of common ground with the United States was something to which the French had become accustomed in the post-war years but to the British such open hostility was new. The "special relationship" was losing even more of its meaning.

With the United States taking such a stand, there was little purpose in referring the dispute to the Security Council. This led Eden and Mollet to agree to a fresh proposal from Dulles for a Suez Canal Users' Association, abbreviated to SCUA or the Users' Club. It amounted to a watered-down method of international control by a body whose functions were ill-defined but which included the organisation of navigation, the hiring of pilots and the possible stationing of ships at either end of the Canal to collect the dues in the event of the Egyptians refusing to do so. Why anyone should have thought that Egypt would be ready to co-operate in such a scheme is hard to understand, as SCUA was based on the premise that the Egyptians were incapable of running the Canal themselves.

As Robert Murphy all but admitted, SCUA was Dulles's delaying device to allow Western European opinion to harden against the military adventure[5] and in this it succeeded. Nevertheless, by now Eden himself was not averse to the delay. Not only had he been beguiled into hoping that the United States might back SCUA with force if the Egyptians proved difficult, but he was becoming very worried about the state of public opinion at home. The Opposition and a large section of the press were by now vociferous in their dislike of the idea of war and opinion in his own Cabinet was divided. The French, more united on matters of foreign policy and far less concerned about the disapprobation of foreigners, were more resolute. Exasperated by the procrastination of Dulles and by what they correctly determined as a lack of resolution in the British, they were ready for action but were reluctantly persuaded by Eden to accept

SCUA. As Pineau is reported to have said at the meeting between the French and British leaders in London on 10 September, "Trying to unravel this latest scheme will get us all so involved that by the time we find the whole affair is impracticable, everyone will be bored to death by our threats."[6]

One aspect of the planned invasion had already become very clear. A landing at Alexandria was no longer feasible. Even if France and Britain did manage to find some excuse to land their forces in Egypt, a major battle in a large port, followed by the occupation of Cairo, was certainly in no way acceptable to world opinion. Any landing would now have to take place at Port Said with the Canal Zone as the initial objective, just as the British Joint Planning Staff had originally envisaged; a subsequent advance on Egypt's capital might then be both necessary and possible but the decision would have to await the political turn of events.

This change of plan, announced only a few days before the invasion fleet was due to sail for Alexandria astounded everyone who was concerned with launching the operation.[7] For Beaufre in particular it was galling indeed, as he heard the news almost by chance in the course of an unplanned visit to Paris. He was already exasperated enough without this failure of communication. During the previous week he had been in Algeria and Malta with Stockwell and had been put out by the last-minute cancellation of a reception—due to the latter's late arrival—at which the British general was to have met the notables of Algiers. But when the next day Beaufre put his *paras* through their paces for Stockwell's benefit a better mood was encouraged: the visitor found the beribboned veterans a tonic to meet and gave him cause for satisfaction that they would not be fighting on the opposite side. Two days later, when Beaufre arrived in Malta to observe a British amphibious exercise he suffered the slight of being met only by an A.D.C. Then he discovered that one minute office in the command ship H.M.S. *Tyne*, measuring two metres square, had been allocated for the use of his entire staff, together with only a single radio channel over which to issue his orders. The consequence was that he decided to install his command-post in the French ship *Gustave-Zédé* even though this would separate him physically from Stockwell.

That evening the British exercise force sailed. Beaufre
described it in the following words: "From the fortress two
trumpeters answered our buglers and Admiral Guy Grantham,
the Commander-in-Chief Mediterranean, standing on the
balcony, replied to our salute. We might have been Hamilcar
leaving Tyre or Carthage; it was all in the style of the great
British naval tradition of the past."[8] It was disappointing that
this fine naval exercise should have culminated in the landing
of a mere battalion, minus its equipment, on one of the island's
few beaches. Beaufre described his visit to Malta as a foretaste
of what British attitudes were to be during the operation—
extreme formal politeness balanced by a complete disregard
for the extent of the French resources.

After this subsequent visit to Paris on 10 September, where
he learned of the change of objective, Beaufre went straight to
London where he met Stockwell once again, downcast and edgy
(in Beaufre's view) and fulminating against the politicians.
Again the planning staffs set to work in a mood of cold, disillusioned fury and within a week they had ground out yet
another set of complicated plans, this time for the capture of
Port Said, with the first ships sailing from England on 21
September and the troops landing on 1 October.

The planned assault on Port Said was to be much on the lines
of what had been prepared for Alexandria, "a second-rate copy
of the Normandy landings, applied in a nineteenth-century-
type colonial context",[9] to quote Beaufre again. *Musketeer
Revise*, as it was at first christened, was divided into three
separate phases, which were:

1. The neutralisation of the Egyptian Air Force.
2. Combined with a psychological warfare programme, a
   continual [sic] air offensive to disrupt the Egyptian
   economy, morale and armed forces.
3. The domination of the Canal Zone and its occupation by
   land, sea and air forces as might be necessary.[10]

However, this new plan did possess one fundamentally different
twist. In some ways it was a reversion to the old concept of
victory by air-bombing, but this bombing was to be very
selective indeed so as to avoid heavy civilian casualties and
material damage. The "aero-psychological" phase, as it became

known, was a well-meaning effort to find a cheap and politically acceptable way of bringing the Egyptians to heel without too many people dying—either Egyptian civilians or British and French servicemen. No thought seems to have been given to the likely death from starvation and disease of large numbers of Egyptians as a consequence of the disruption of their economy.

The senior soldiers responsible for the new plan appear to have had every sort of reservation about its efficacy. Stockwell well understood that an air offensive tends to stiffen resistance and he lacked faith in psychological warfare. To Beaufre, the whole thing seemed to be both fanciful and dangerous. He could hardly believe his eyes when he read that a landing would take place "only when there is no opposition or when the opposition is negligible and can be ignored."[11] How, he asked, could one paralyse the life of the country and so demonstrate the incapacity of the government and the armed forces when there was no question of bombing towns and when one's attacking force amounted to a mere 300 planes? Thousands had failed to do the same thing over Germany. In any case, how would one know when the resistance had reached the stage of being negligible? Dangerous too he considered the tempo of the operation. Eight to fourteen days had been set aside for the bombing of these economic and strategic targets, more than enough time for world opinion to be mobilised against what would seem to be brutal and old-fashioned aggression.

The psychological side was possibly even more fanciful. In late August, the then Brigadier Bernard Fergusson was pulled off the night train to Perth to learn that he had been appointed Director of Psychological Warfare. He tells the story in his amusing book, *The Trumpet in the Hall*. To date, the career of this very able officer had encompassed about every type of military activity other than psychological warfare. When he told his fellow author, Peter Fleming, about the job, he was consoled with the words "I cannot think of a more certain way of bringing a promising career to an abrupt end!"[12] But then the British Army was not in the habit of subjecting officers of his calibre to such uncongenial chores except in dire emergency.

With a couple of Foreign Office officials and his late adjutant to assist him, Fergusson set to work with his usual enthusiasm. His resources included the Sharq al-Adna broadcasting station in Cyprus, and a printing press to produce the leaflets which the R.A.F. was to drop. Otherwise he had a unit of some two dozen men mounted in trucks and equipped with loud-hailers and a "voice-aircraft" which had been summoned from Kenya where it had been busy exhorting the Mau-Mau to behave themselves. Nothing went right for him. The reservists who were to man the press were unfamiliar with the machinery, which broke down, and the scattering device for the leaflets was found to explode not at 1,000 feet but at Egyptian head-height. When at last the "voice-aircraft" was extracted from a protesting Kenyan Government, someone pinched all the loud-hailing equipment during a refuelling stop at Aden, while the only Arabs who could be cajoled into broadcasting anti-Nasser sentiments from Sharq al-Adna were a miscellaneous bunch of Palestinians whose accents were such that Egyptians unhappily mistook them for Jews.

This rather amateur approach was not too untypical of the British attitudes to esoteric subjects of this type. The French arrangements for psychological warfare were in sharp contrast. In Algeria, the year before, *bureaux psychologiques* had been set up at each operational command level—regions, divisions and sub-divisions—with the twin objects of protecting their own troops from F.L.N. propaganda and of helping the civil authorities to retain the loyalty of the mass of Muslim peasants and townspeople. A *Centre d'Instruction de la Guerre Psychologique* had been opened in Paris and chairs on the subject established in all the major service schools; officers of the *Cinquième Bureau* were posted to all commands and in each unit one officer was made responsible.[13]

When Beaufre protested to his allies that the "aero-psychological" plan was inept, they agreed but pleaded that orders were orders, an argument which made little impression on the Frenchman. The planning progressed, however, on the assumption that the third phase of the operation—the domination of the Canal Zone and its occupation by land forces—would certainly be necessary. The capture of Port Said by a combined air and sea assault was allocated to the British, with the French landing east of the town with Port Fuad as their objective. The two contingents were then to push southwards on either side of the Canal, with the British turning west at Qantara to seize Abu

Sueir airfield and the stores in the nearby bases, and their allies crossing the Canal at that point to capture Ismailia and Suez. With the whole of the Canal in allied hands, the two forces could then turn towards Cairo, if this proved to be necessary. There is, in fact, no ambiguity at all in Beaufre's statement that the capture of Cairo was intended.[14]

There were a number of snags to the *Musketeer Revise* plan. Because of the poor facilities at Port Said, the rate of build-up of the forces would, at the best, be no more than half of what had been envisaged at Alexandria. It would take about a couple of weeks to land all the fighting troops and their vehicles, and only the 100 tanks which were to come ashore in the assault would be available for the break-out to Qantara. Here, at the end of the fifty kilometre causeway running between the Canal and the salt marshes, the Egyptian armour and artillery would probably be waiting to give battle. For speed further parachute drops would have been necessary and, although these were discussed, nothing appears to have been arranged. The burnt fingers of Arnhem were taking a long time to heal and in 1956 the scars were still painful. This psychological blockage was reinforced by an intelligence picture which was a further discouragement to bold action. The causeway to Qantara was, it was reported, defended every few hundred yards by prepared positions which could be occupied by the formidable Russian SU 100s, devastating adversaries for British Centurions advancing on a ten-yard front.

For this full-scale operation, with forces sailing from England, Malta and Algiers, eight or nine days' notice was required, a period which equated with the length of the "aero-psychological" phase. However, to cater for the eventuality of Egyptian resistance collapsing after a couple of days of bombing, a variant of the plan was prepared. Part of the amphibious fleet carrying tanks and equipment would be based on Cyprus, the numbers being limited by the absence of harbours and the submarine threat. Then at the start of the bombing, the French parachute troops and others needed for the operation would be moved in one quick lift from Algiers in the battleship *Jean Bart* so that an immediate airborne and seaborne assault could be mounted if resistance appeared to be collapsing. Meanwhile the main invasion fleets would be making their slow and steady way from Malta and Algiers. It was an operation much on the lines of that proposed by Barjot over a month before.

Beaufre claims to have made a startling discovery when he arrived back in Algiers on 19 September to start work on the detailed staff studies for his own divisions. He was handed air photographs which showed that there was no longer a road running south from Port Fuad along the east side of the Canal. It had been destroyed years before when the Canal had been widened. Port Fuad was, in fact, an island, without even a bridge connecting it to the Port Said bank of the Canal. After the initial assault, there would be no alternative other than to ferry the French troops across the Canal and for them then to follow the British down the causeway roads.

If Beaufre was aware at such an early date of the unfeasibility of the two-prong plan, he kept the news to himself. General Massu, commander of the French *10ᵉ Division Parachutiste*, claims in his book *The Truth about Suez 1956* that it was not until late October that he received an updated map of the Canal south of Port Fuad that indicated clearly a gap of two kilometres between the quarantine station and firm ground beyond. An explanatory note told him that recent aerial surveys showed the planned axis of advance to be impassable to wheeled vehicles.

It was startling that plans based on such a failure of intelligence could have been made by officers of an army that had so recently quit the Canal zone. It was all one with the tale of the imaginary city of Talata. In the early 1950s, while the British Army still stood upon the land in question, a military intelligence review published an article on the problems of the Middle East, illustrated by a map of the Suez Canal. The signal stations which regulated the flow of water-borne traffic along the waterway were numbered from one onwards from north to south beginning at Port Said, the third station standing in the desert on the east bank opposite the teeming city of Ismailia. On the survey map these small but essential installations were designated by British transliterations of the Arabic numerals (*wahad, etnein, talata*, etc.) but on the map in the military intelligence review the city of Ismailia was faced across the Canal by the equally large township of Talata. It can only be supposed that the task of reading and passing the article had been given to an officer who, unusually, had never served in Egypt.

These alleged errors could well have been symptomatic of the rather niggardly attitude of the British Army towards providing proper resources for operational intelligence. In most major armies, including that of the United States, staffs were organised with the senior intelligence officer of a unit or formation ranking as equal with his colleagues in charge of operations, supply and personnel. In the British Army, however, the intelligence officer was subordinate to the senior operations officer and he would rank one or two steps below him. Nor was intelligence work, except in its more unusual forms, fashionable. The Intelligence Corps itself, a *parvenu* of the previous war, lacked status, and its officers, whose cap-badge was said to represent a pansy resting on his laurels, received the humdrum jobs, while the senior and the more active intelligence appointments were filled by staff officers from other arms, who had rarely undergone proper specialist training. Altogether it was an amateur approach for a country which prided itself on the high standards of its more recondite intelligence agencies. The results were apparent in the Suez planning, as they had so often been in the past particularly in the many British amphibious failures.

Active though life was for the staff, the politicians and many civil servants, to the troops and the general public nothing much seemed to be happening. *Punch* summed it up with a cartoon of a uniformed Prime Minister marching a column of soldiers up a hill to the refrains of

> The grand old Anthony Eden,
> Recalled thirty thousand men.
> He marched them up to the top of the hill
> And he'll march them down again.[15]

Despite a press leak about the choice of Alexandria as the invasion point, information about the operational plans of the allies was confined to a very close circle; at battalion and company level little was known of what was happening. It was, therefore, a shock to one of the authors, who was paying a social visit to old French *para* friends just after their arrival in Cyprus, to be taken into a tent patrolled by armed sentries and marked as being strictly out-of-bounds. There he was shown a map which displayed the entire operational plan for the Alexandria operation, including the use which was to be made of his own battalion.

As Pineau had so accurately predicted, for most people the Suez crisis was already becoming something of a bore. For example, when SCUA did at last meet, it quietly talked itself asleep, having been emasculated in advance by Dulles. Three days after Britain and France had consented to co-operate with the proposed organisation, and on the day of a particularly acrimonious debate in the Commons, the American Secretary of State chose to announce that his country had no intention of shooting its way through the Canal. It was, as Eden complained with justification, a statement likely to cause the maximum disunity and disarray among the allies.[16] Nasser, reassured by the remark, two days later denounced SCUA as "an association for waging war" in a speech which was scattered with references to thuggery and imperialism.

During this time pressure had been mounting on Eden, from both within and outside his party and from British friends overseas, to take the dispute to the United Nations. The result was that despite continuing opposition from America, France and Britain referred Suez to the Security Council on 23 September. In anticipation of this political action, the sailing dates for the convoys were again postponed, this time to 29 September and the landing date was put forward to 8 October. War, so imminent in early August, became very much less credible as September slipped by. The crisis started to disappear from the main news pages; in the six consecutive numbers of *Punch* between 5 September and 10 October, there were only five references to it. When the military staffs emerged from their troglodyte existence into daylight London, they found their friends more concerned with the end of the cricket season than the possibility of war.

It was not surprising that this unreality affected the morale of the reservists, both those who had been moved to Cyprus, Malta or Germany and those who were kicking their heels in the United Kingdom. The difficulty of occupying the soldiers' time was in many units aggravated by the lack of operational equipment and vehicles, most of which was packed or loaded into ships. Nor did it help that life for those regulars who had their wives with them in places such as Malta gave the impression of it being just one long party, a problem which the authorities recognised but found difficult to control. In Cyprus, 16 Parachute Brigade was more fortunate than most: busy chasing EOKA, boredom was not a problem.

Tedium, combined with worry about the money problems of their families, made for unrest. In early October it came out into the open. After a noisy demonstration on a hotel roof in Cyprus, twenty-one junior N.C.O.s of the G.H.Q. Field Records Office were arrested. In Crookham medical N.C.O.s and orderlies of the R.A.M.C. complained to their chaplain that their time was being wasted. In Malta about 150 guardsmen vociferously objected to a kit inspection, following which a number of gunners took part in a similar demonstration, the consequence, in the opinion of *The Times* Military Correspondent,[17] of no disciplinary action having been taken against the guardsmen. It was especially difficult for those reservists who had been sent to Germany to understand why they were there and the indiscipline of some R.A.S.C. drivers at Minden took an ugly turn.

Although some of this dissatisfaction stemmed from minor military aggravations like chlorine in the tea and a shortage of wash-basins, the feeling underlying the trouble was well expressed by one of the R.A.S.C. demonstrators who complained that they had "come to fight Nasser, and as they were not going to do so, they wanted to go home."[18] On B.B.C. TV on 9 October, the Secretary of State for War remarked that he would be a very complacent man if he were not worried about the incidents but—badly briefed—he declared that only two of the 363 units which had received reservists had been involved. However, the following day, a week's special leave for reservists was announced but only for those who were stationed in Germany and the United Kingdom. Five days later, a troopship landed 1,500 exuberant reservists from Germany to the delight of the press, whose members were provided with an unrivalled opportunity to bombard the men with loaded questions. A few weeks later a handful of the mutineers received short sentences of detention.

The sailors, isolated in their ships, had less opportunity for introspection and even less knowledge of what was happening in the world than the soldiers. A pilot of the Fleet Air Arm in H.M.S. *Albion* recalls that he and his fellow officers never discussed the likelihood of taking part in a war against Egypt and assumed that the assembly of landing craft and bombers in Malta was part of a large amphibious exercise. Army and R.A.F. officers tended to be rather more aware of the implications of what they could see around them. With civilians reinforcing so many units, in many messes debate on the desirability and ethics of invading Egypt could be lively. Even the great Monty's reservations about the practical sense of the operations percolated back to Cyprus by way of an officer who had been his A.D.C. and who had seen him while on leave in England.

Meanwhile the staffs continued to regurgitate modifications to the plans. The next was to be known as the *Winter Plan*. Its need arose from the length of time everything had taken and the consequent requirement to unload some of the ships: not only men but vehicles as well were rusting with inactivity. In many cases the ships into which they were unloaded had been swinging at anchor or tied up at the quayside for months. Batteries were running down and much maintenance was overdue: in some ships there was a danger of accumulated petrol fumes exploding. With changes in the order-of-battle, cargoes required adjusting and loads also needed checking because so many dockers had exercised their traditional tribute, regardless of the consequence to their fellow-countrymen who might need the equipment to fight for their lives.

Because of the danger of ships being caught half-loaded while all this checking and adjusting was taking place, the state of readiness had to be relaxed with the consequence that the *Winter Plan* was based upon ten days' notice having to be given to the force. Due to come into effect on 19 October, it was ready a week before, following six days' intense work by staff officers whose enthusiasm was now about as damp as some of the stores loaded into the ships. One effect of this *ennui* was that difficulties proliferated. It was forecast that every sort of trouble might be expected after October: the weather would deteriorate and Tymbou airfield would be out of action; wind-strengths would make it dangerous to drop parachute troops; Limassol road-steads would be unhealthy for shipping, and the sea would be too rough for the landings. In the event, all these predictions proved unfounded or surmountable. None the less, it turned out to be yet another plan for the wastepaper-basket. Three days after it had seen the light of day, the *Winter Plan* was dead but a further ten days were to elapse before Stockwell was to know why.

CHAPTER SEVEN

COLLUSION

IN PARIS another group of Frenchmen were concocting yet another set of plans, a major variation on *Musketeer Revise* of which even Beaufre, let alone his British colleagues, was barely aware. They were for a Franco-Israeli invasion of Egypt, with Britain taking part as well if her Government could be induced to do so.

During 1955 and 1956, Israel's circumstances were such that many of the country's leaders, including Ben-Gurion, who in early 1955 had returned from his self-imposed retirement and was now again Prime Minister, believed that the only hope for Israel's survival lay in a pre-emptive war against the Arab states. Their country's problems were economic and military and both equally desperate. Egypt had not only placed a total embargo on cargoes passing to or from Israel through the Canal but had blocked the entrance to the Gulf of Aqaba by occupying Sharm el-Sheikh, which commanded the Straits of Tiran, so closing the sea-routes from East Africa and Asia, and halting the development of the Negev. The military problems were twofold: the continuing *fedayeen* border raids, and Egypt's new weapons from Eastern Europe. Israeli men, women and children were being murdered in the ceaseless round of burnings, minings, ambushes and bombings, half a dozen or more of which could occur in a single day; Israel retaliated by efficient and powerful attacks on targets in the countries from which the raids had been mounted, a policy which had its successes, but which was costly, not only in soldiers' lives but in Israel's reputation abroad. Even more serious was the threat from the newly equipped Egyptian armed forces. However ineffective the Egyptians themselves might prove to be when it came to fighting and servicing the modern weapons, there was a clear danger that the Russian advisers in Egypt might man the equipment themselves when war broke out. The all but defenceless Israeli cities were less than half an hour's flying time away from the Ilyushin bomber bases. A country the size of Wales, at one point only twelve miles wide, and with a population of less than two million people, could hardly hope to defend itself from the combined armies of Jordan, Syria, Lebanon and Egypt, whose leaders had declared their intention of wiping Israel off the map.

The Israeli General Staff anticipated that the Egyptian armed forces would take six to eight months to absorb the communist weapons which had started to arrive in November 1955. War might be expected, therefore, at any time from the summer of 1956 onwards and Israel's urgent need was for weapons to counter the Russian aircraft and tanks. Since 1953, there had been close political collaboration between France and Israel, and France was now to give proof of her friendship with the delivery of twenty-five Mystère IVA fighters in April 1956, a welcome reinforcement for the Air Force, which possessed only a hundred or so obsolete jets and piston-engined relics of the War of Independence. Britain also agreed to let them have six Meteor night-fighters and France promised some AMX light tanks but the latter were no match for the Russian T34s or the British Centurions with which the Egyptian army was now equipped.

The nationalisation of the Canal increased this flow of equipment to Israel. The day after Nasser's speech, the Israelis asked the French to increase their arms shipments and in Paris on 7 August the request was agreed. Without delay, the French started to send Israel as much equipment as they could spare, but two major limitations were her own serious shortages and the strain on her merchant fleet caused by the requisitioning of shipping for *Musketeer*. Present at the meeting in Paris where this was discussed were Maurice Bourgès-Maunoury and Shimon Peres, then Minister and Director-General of Defence of their respective countries, together with General Ely the French Chief-of-Staff and Barjot. Like Monnet and Pineau, Bourgès-Maunoury was a Resistance veteran, the famous *Polycarpe*, a vigorous and determined politician who saw the Suez affair in very plain black and white and who throughout the crisis was to provide much of the momentum for intervention. Knowledge of this meeting, at which the question of joint action between France and Israel against Egypt was probably discussed,[1] was not divulged to the British, nor were details of the increased arms shipments notified either to them or to the United States, as was required by the Tripartite Agreement of 1950 which limited the flow of arms to the Middle East. The weapons were smuggled into Israel in disguised ships and avoided the ports as far as possible,[2] but the Americans were not devoid of intelligence resources, Eisenhower recording in his diary the "rabbit-like capacity for multiplication"[3] of the Mystères. Perhaps the British would have been told more if Eden had not allegedly reacted vehemently to a suggestion by Mollet on the telephone on 27 July that the two countries should collaborate with Israel against Egypt.[4]

The Israeli Chief-of-Staff, General Moshe Dayan, did not hear about the prospects of collaboration until 1 September, when his Military Attaché in Paris signalled him the details of the *Musketeer* plans, together with the information that Barjot considered that Israel should be invited to take part in the operation.[5] With Ben-Gurion's blessing, exploratory talks were then held in Paris on 7 September, with Barjot in the chair. It was less than two weeks since the French Admiral had embarrassed Beaufre at General Keightley's meeting by suggesting that the landing should take place at Port Said rather than Alexandria, with the British carrying on alone with their original plan, if they so wished. Perhaps Barjot's mind was not quite so fuddled as his compatriot had believed.

In mid-September, when the French ministers had just succumbed to British pressure to join in the SCUA discussions and thus accept the consequential postponement of *Musketeer*, further talks took place in Paris between Peres and Bourgès-Maunoury on the possibility of their two countries invading Egypt without help from Britain.[6] To the French it must by then have seemed that *la perfide Albion* had abandoned her intention of using force against Egypt, and that there was no alternative to seeking an ally elsewhere.

Among the Israeli leaders, the driving force to involve his country with France was Dayan, whose clear mind enabled him to weigh exactly both the weaknesses and the strengths of his country's defences. The Israeli Army was only eight years old; successful though it had been in defeating the combined Arab armies during the War of Independence, it was far from being the keen instrument which was later to win world-wide admiration for its prowess. In 1952, when he took over as head of the Operations Branch of the General Staff, Dayan doubted whether his infantry could even be trusted to give an adequate account of themselves in border skirmishes.[7] In the following four years, first in this post and later as Chief-of-Staff, Dayan was to reshape not only the Army's organisation but the attitudes of mind of its fighting men. Officers learned that they had to lead from the front; it was laid down that no commander was allowed to admit he had failed in an operational task unless his unit had suffered fifty per cent casualties, a harsh rule which led to heavy officer losses but which produced results. In the previous two world wars, the ratio of casualties between officers and soldiers in the British Army had been 1:10 and even then the life of the average infantry or gunner subaltern had been short enough. In the coming campaign in Sinai, 171 Israelis were to die and seventy-one of them would be officers; in the reprisal raid against the Arab Legion fort at Qalqiliya the Israelis had sixty-eight casualties, twenty-two of them officers. It was ruthless but it bred an offensive spirit which was to win wars and save lives as well, paradoxical though this may seem.

Pineau saw a greater difference of ability between Dayan and the French generals of 1956 than between de Gaulle and Gamelin in 1940,[8] but Dayan possessed another advantage in addition to this natural ability and experience. Like his officers, he was young. Still only forty-one, in the British Army he would have been thought youthful in command of a battalion. In contrast to Dayan, with one or two exceptions the senior French and British officers at Suez were men in their mid-fifties; some like Keightley and Stockwell had been generals in the previous war and had been enjoying the comparative ease and comfort of pre-retirement appointments. Men over fifty are conscious of slackening powers, reluctant though they may be to admit the fact even to themselves. The more elderly need to recuperate to regain their powers, and in planning or running a war the choice of a time for rest is not in any man's control. As a result performance deteriorates, and although experience is a valuable commodity, in battle it can rarely replace the drive, enthusiasm and staying power of youth.

In Israel, the dividing line between military and political advice was not so tight-drawn as in some other countries. So before Peres left Israel for his mid-September meeting with the French, Dayan was in no way inhibited in suggesting to him that there should be three stipulations for Israel's co-operation. First, the initiative for the deal should be seen to come from France, so that Israel could think of herself as an equal partner. Secondly, Britain must be prevented from intervening against Israel in fulfilment of her treaty obligations to Jordan: it would, after all, be grotesque if Britain were to be fighting alongside Israel on the Canal, but attacking her in the north. Lastly, Israel was to be left in control of the Gulf of Aqaba when it was all over.[9]

This meeting in Paris brought the French and Israelis even closer together and Peres returned with the information that Pineau had warned Eden, in the course of a visit to Chequers on 21 September, that France might be compelled either to act alone or in concert with Israel if Eden were to be prevented from joining in the adventure through lack of support at home. Pineau recalled that Eden had no objection to the proposal provided that Israel did not attack Jordan and he suggested that Eden even showed interest in the idea of collaborating with Israel[10] at this meeting. Pineau's recollections do not always seem to be too accurate, but if Pineau is correct, Eden's attitude had certainly changed since his telephone call with Mollet in July. There had been the mysterious business of Colonel Robert Henriques' visit to Israel earlier in September.[11] Retired regular soldier, well-known writer and a member of an old Jewish family, Henriques had been briefed before he left England by a senior Cabinet Minister. The message which he passed on to Ben-Gurion was that Israel must at all costs avoid war with Jordan but that if Israel were to attack Egypt when Britain went to war over Suez, it would be very convenient for everyone concerned and that Britain would do her best for Israel in the subsequent peace-talks. Ben-Gurion's reply was that he had heard such promises before.[12]

The meetings in Paris continued. On 29 September yet

another Israeli delegation flew there. The members, who included Golda Meir, the Foreign Minister, Dayan and Peres, returned two days later in the specially-equipped D.C.4 presented by President Truman to de Gaulle, who had handed it over to his Ministry of Defence; from now on this plane was always available for shuttling the Israeli visitors backwards and forwards between the two countries. Travelling on this return flight was a team of French officers and officials, whose task it was to discuss further military aid and to examine the facilities which Israel could provide for the French Air Force. Such a team, as a routine measure, would also have been told to find out whatever they could about the state of the Israeli armed forces, a matter on which, Dayan noted, Ely seemed to hold considerable reservations.[13]

As this French team consulted their Israeli opposite numbers, Dayan was explaining his tentative plans for the invasion of Egypt to his senior commanders and staff officers, nearly all men still in their thirties. While the French, possibly with help from the British, attacked the Egyptian airfields and seized the Canal, he told them Israel would invade the Sinai peninsula in eighteen days' time, on 20 October. Preparations for the mobilisation of the militia would start immediately: to aid security, the mobilisation itself, which could comfortably be carried out in something under a week, would be delayed as long as possible. The campaign was expected to last for three weeks and the codeword given it was *Kadesh*, the biblical site in the desert where the Israelites had sojourned on their way to the Promised Land. All officers on courses abroad were to be brought home, on the sound grounds that they were about to acquire practical experience of war which would be of greater value to them than the theory which they were being taught at their foreign staff colleges and schools.

Israel faced two major problems. The first was the possible danger, if Jordan and Syria came to the help of the Egyptians, of having once again to fight on three fronts. The second was that without the help of the British Canberras, there would be no bombers to deal with the Egyptian airfields. Dayan was ready to accept even this danger, confident as he was that Israeli and French fighters between them could either shoot the Ilyushins down in the air or strafe them on the ground. A question mark hung also over the French use of the Cyprus bases if Britain decided not to fight. Although the French were reasonably happy that they would, in any case, have the use of these bases, alternative plans had to be made for their fighters and transport aircraft to use Israeli airfields.

The members of the French delegation indicated to Dayan that they were delighted by all that they had been shown in Israel. They seem to have been inspired by the dynamism of the young nation and, warm in their praise of the Israeli Air Force, they were happy about the facilities for operating their transport planes and fighters. Agreement had been reached on the supply of further equipment, which was to include 100 tanks, infantry armoured carriers and the various specialist vehicles needed for the advance across the Sinai Desert. But although the French were surprised by the technical excellence of the Israeli forces, they considered that Dayan's plans for the invasion of Egypt were over-ambitious. A parachute drop near the Canal, with the ground link-up over nearly 150 miles of desert tracks taking place only forty-eight hours later, was, they suggested to the Israelis, rather different from *Musketeer*. Dayan explained that the essence of the tactics of his army was to gain surprise through speed, particularly when dealing with a slow-thinking army like that of Egypt. With his commanders well forward, and backed by a simple and flexible military organisation, Dayan was confident that he could retain the initiative and keep the enemy off balance.

Throughout the discussions, there were two questions which puzzled the Israeli politicians and soldiers and to which they could never obtain satisfactory answers. How was this campaign to start and where was it visualised to end? The first of these misgivings was, of course, at the root of all the British hesitations. As Walter Monckton, the British Minister of Defence, is said to have expressed it to his service advisers when they first showed him the *Musketeer* plans, "Very interesting, but how do we actually start this war?"[14] And despite the tentative plans which had been made to occupy Cairo and the military government organisation which had been set up to cope with the subsequent problems, the French were as vague as the British in committing themselves to saying where the fighting would end. General Ely went so far as to ask Dayan whether he envisaged Cairo being taken and the latter insists that he discouraged the idea because of the serious political consequences.[15] On another occasion Ben-Gurion asked the French how they contemplated toppling Nasser if they were going to do no more than occupy the Canal Zone, so leaving the Egyptian President free to organise guerillas and invoke Russian help. The French had to confess that they did not know the answer.[16] Similar questions seem to have been raised at every meeting between the Israelis and the French. In his frequent criticisms of the "lethargy" of the allied commanders, Pineau discusses the time it would have taken to occupy Cairo and implies that it was part of the allied plan,[17] but it is hard to avoid the conclusion that the British and the French politicians never made up their minds as to what was to happen, so avoiding thinking the stages of the operation through to a logical but internationally unacceptable conclusion.

Not every French officer was enthusiastic about a bilateral alliance with Israel. When Beaufre was told officially what was afoot on 1 October, he distrusted every aspect of the involvement. As he saw it, without British help France would be invading Egypt with no bomber support and with only fifty tanks; the planned Israeli action, which added up to little more than light detachments advancing towards the Canal, would take no pressure off the French. Politically, he feared, his country would have to face a long diplomatic counter-offensive, and possibly a blockade by the USSR, the United States and the Arab countries.

A measure of the hesitations of some of the senior French officers can be seen in the scale of the operation they envisaged in collaboration with the Israelis. In Beaufre's first written directive from Barjot (*Hypothèse I*, the "I" standing for Israel) only a limited operation was called for, with the French seizing Port Said by a combined airborne and amphibious attack and at the same time reinforcing the Israeli Air Force and providing naval cover to the Israel coastline. If "necessary", the directive stated, exploitation would extend as far as Ismailia. A further directive from Ely, following hard on the heels of the previous one, was more cautious still, specifying that the French forces would "if necessary seize a hostage which might be Port Said". In conversation with Beaufre, Ely admitted that he had resigned himself to these various *Hypothèses* because he did not wish it to be said that the armed forces had scotched a politically necessary operation.[18]

So Beaufre was even more exasperated than usual when he settled down to plan *Hypothèse I*, while his staff continued to labour on the completion of the preparations for *Musketeer Revise* and the *Winter Plan* as well. Without, as he expressed it, adhering too closely to the limitations in the directive,[19] he produced a plan in which Port Said and Port Fuad would be taken by three parachute regiments, one landing from the air, one from the sea, and one by helicopter from the carrier *Dixmude*. Two of these regiments, supported by his four squadrons of tanks, would push on to Qantara, leaving two Senegalese battalions behind to hold Port Said. From Qantara, the parachutists would leap-frog down to Ismailia and thence to Cairo or Suez. If this thrusting attack should prove over-ambitious, he had a reserve in the shape of the leading elements of 7 DMR which would be landing behind the Parachute Division.

While Beaufre was trying to translate hypotheses into practical military plans, the British were involved in quite a different problem. Pineau remembers that for Eden's government the whole Middle East crisis seemed to revolve around Jordan.[20] There is some truth in this exaggeration. The peremptory dismissal of General Glubb and Jordan's refusal to join the Baghdad Pact had in no way affected Britain's treaty obligations to this small Arab kingdom—and in these post-war years Cabinets still took such obligations seriously. If Israel were to attack Jordan, Britain would certainly come to her aid. Lacking an effective air force of her own, her air defence was in the hands of R.A.F. squadrons based in Jordan, together with a small force of British troops. The main reason for moving 16 Parachute Brigade to Cyprus had been to have it ready to intervene in Jordan in an emergency. Treaty obligations to Jordan, based on the need to maintain Britain's waning influence in the Middle East, were reinforced by many ties of friendship. The British Army was proud of the Arab Legion, a force which it had created and trained, and which had proved itself, both in fighting qualities and loyalty towards its ruler, as the sole Arab army worthy of admiration. Within the Foreign

Office and among many Conservative politicians, Arab
sympathies were strong and tended to focus on the two
Hashemite Kingdoms of Iraq and Jordan, both established by
Britain and the only two independent Arab countries of any
importance not now actively hostile.

At no time had the young King Hussein's hold on his country
been quite so precarious as in 1956. Nasser's incessant radio
propaganda and underground subversion aggravated the
instability of the King's successive governments and the unrest
which was spreading among many of his officers, while the
Palestinian inhabitants of the West Bank of the Jordan lacked
both sympathy and respect for his Bedouin-based semi-
autocracy. Israel's reprisal raids to counter the *fedayeen* in-
cursions from the West Bank added to his troubles. These had
culminated in the bloody action at Qalquiliya, already touched
upon, in which 100 Jordanians are said to have died; launched
on 10 October, it took place while the Israeli general staff were
in the middle of planning for Operation *Kadesh*. A previous and
similar reprisal a few weeks earlier had resulted in Nasser,
acting in concert with King Fuad of Saudi Arabia and President
Kuwaitly of Syria (both enemies of Britain), offering sub-
stantial financial aid to Jordan, with which was combined an
unwelcome invitation to associate the Jordanian Army with
the joint but illusory Egyptian-Syrian military command.

During the course of this Qalquiliya raid, Israeli fighters had
circled over the battleground, a new and dangerous escalation
in the use of force which resulted in Hussein asking General
Keightley for help from the R.A.F. in accordance with
Britain's treaty obligations. The brakes went on. In Eden's
words, our aircraft were on the point of going up, when a wise
and rapid exchange of cautionary messages on the spot
avoided catastrophe.[21]

It certainly would have been a catastrophe for Eden's plans.
The next day, at the Security Council, Selwyn Lloyd forcibly
criticised the Israeli attack but Hussein was desperate for
something more tangible in the way of help than moral condemnation of his country's enemies, and he despatched his
Foreign Minister to Cairo. This resulted in Eden asking
Nuri es-Said to send an Iraqi brigade into Jordan to reinforce
the Arab Legion; loyal as ever to his old friend, Nuri agreed

immediately to comply. At the news, the Israelis in their turn protested. It was too much for the French. Faced with the danger of the collapse of their plans for Franco-Israeli action against Egypt they pleaded with Britain to stop the move of the Iraqi troops. Eden, alarmed though he was at the possibility that Egypt might assimilate Jordan if help were not forthcoming, so leaving an isolated Iraq as Britain's sole remaining friend in the Middle East, tried to help by asking Nuri to reduce the size of the promised force and to keep it well away from the Israeli border.

This vacillation on Eden's part, impossible to explain to the ever-helpful Nuri, invoked a protest from Nutting, who was in charge of the Foreign Office during Selwyn Lloyd's absence in New York. Eden's response was a further outburst against the Minister of State during which he shouted: "I will not allow you to plunge this country into war merely to satisfy the anti-Jewish spleen of you people in the Foreign Office."[22] It could only have come from a very sick man. The previous week-end Eden had spent in hospital, fighting a recurrence of his old illness which had raised his temperature to nearly 106 degrees.

"Save for the Almighty", Dayan confided to his diary at the time, "only the British are capable of complicating affairs to such a degree. At the very moment when they are preparing to topple Nasser, they insist on getting the Iraqi Army into Jordan, even if such action leads to war between Israel and Jordan in which they, the British, will take part against Israel."[23] The French echoed these sentiments and decided that Britain must be taken completely into their confidence before their ally became even further embroiled with the Arab kingdoms. So on Sunday, 14 October, Albert Gazier, the French Minister of Labour, acting for Pineau in the latter's absence at the Security Council, arrived at Chequers accompanied by General Challe, who was Ely's deputy. At their meeting with the Prime Minister, only a private secretary and Nutting were present. The latter, who has described in some detail what took place, listened with dismay as Challe outlined the French proposals. They were that Israel should be persuaded to attack Egypt across the Sinai and that Britain and France, having given the Israeli forces enough time to seize their objectives, should then invite both sides to withdraw

from the Canal so that an Anglo-French force could land
to protect the waterway from damage. Then, on the excuse of
separating the combatants, the allies would take control of
both Canal and installations. Challe did no more than touch on
the military execution of this plan, suggesting only that there
should be a seaborne landing at Port Said, followed by the
capture of Ismailia and Suez by parachutists.

At last Eden had been shown a way in which the war could
be started. It was the excuse for which he had been long
searching. Within minutes of the two Frenchmen's departure
with a message that their Prime Minister could expect to learn
the British reactions to the proposals within the week, he was
on the telephone to Selwyn Lloyd in New York, ordering him
to return to London without delay. Meanwhile Nutting was
cautioned to take only two senior Foreign Office officials into
his confidence, both of whom, according to Nutting, when told
about the plot, agreed that they could see no argument for
going along with such a "sordid manœuvre". When Selwyn
Lloyd arrived back from New York on the Tuesday morning,
Nutting further relates that the spontaneous reaction of the
Foreign Secretary was to reject the French proposals but his
mood seemed to have changed after he had spoken to the
Prime Minister. That afternoon Eden and Selwyn Lloyd flew
to Paris.

It is hard to avoid the conclusion that Eden had already
learned that something on these lines was being planned and
that the visit by Gazier and Challe provided no more than
formal confirmation and an invitation to take part. Then, on
2 October, Dulles made another public attack on Britain and
France, saying that his country could not be expected to
identify itself with "colonial powers" and denying that there
had ever been any "teeth" in the SCUA proposals. Possibly
believing that the time was propitious after such an outbreak,
Eden is alleged to have told his colleagues the following day
that Israel had "come up with an offer" to attack Egypt, and
so given Britain and France the chance to launch *Musketeer*.[24]

Rumours that something odd was afoot were even reaching
the British service planners. Since early October they had been
wondering what was going on between their ally and the
Israelis and, on the day following the Chequers meeting, a

member of Stockwell's staff learned from an assistant that joint action was being discussed between them, information which he had probably picked up from a French colleague. But there was no official news of any kind. It was not, in fact, until Stockwell landed at Villacoublay on his way to Malta for the start of the war that he learnt for certain from Beaufre that the Israelis were, as he put it, "in on the act".[25]

When Selwyn Lloyd returned from Paris, Nutting says that he extracted from the Foreign Secretary with a certain amount of difficulty the information that Eden had wholeheartedly endorsed the French plan at a meeting which had been attended only by the two Prime Ministers and their Foreign Secretaries, and at which no notes had been taken. Nutting's reaction was to warn his superior (whom he described as a confused and unhappy man) that he would be compelled to resign if arrangements on these lines were to go ahead. Nutting's disapproval was based not only on grounds of morality: at the discussions in New York, from which Selwyn Lloyd had been dragged away, the Egyptians had at last seemed amenable to a reasonable compromise.[26]

At the Security Council, Selwyn Lloyd had stipulated a number of prerequisites for the peaceful settlement of the dispute. These Six Principles, as they were to be known, consisted of free and open transit through the Canal, without discrimination; respect for the sovereignty of Egypt; the insulation of the Canal from politics; Egypt and the Canal users between them to decide upon the manner of fixing tolls and charges; the allocation of a proportion of these dues to development; and the resolving of disputes by arbitration. In private talks with Selwyn Lloyd and Pineau, Dr. Fawzi, the Egyptian Foreign Minister, had accepted all these Six Principles, so long as they did not involve control by an international body of the type suggested by the Eighteen Powers, although SCUA, or something like it, seemed to be the sort of thing to which the Egyptians might have agreed. It was understandable that Egypt might be willing to settle the dispute. With her sterling balances blocked, her finances were precarious. Trade with Europe was almost at a standstill. Support from other Arab rulers was little more than lukewarm, aggrieved as they were that the Canal should have been

nationalised without consultation, thus endangering oil shipments. Finally Nehru, as leader of the non-aligned nations and
acting as friend of both Britain and Egypt, had done much
during the previous two months to persuade Nasser of the need
to allow the users to have a say in the running of the Canal.
According to Nutting, Selwyn Lloyd gladly accepted these
Egyptian concessions, despite his well-justified fear that Eden
would neither welcome them nor believe that the Egyptians
were doing anything other than procrastinate. But the British
Foreign Secretary, in his memoirs, emphasises strongly that in
his view the Egyptians were doing no more than spin out the
discussions, knowing that time was on their side.[27]

Pineau's attitude is intriguing and his account of the events
does not match that of either Nutting or Selwyn Lloyd. Undoubtedly he was not as wholeheartedly in support of a war
as were other members of the French Government; a military
solution to him did not "feel right".[28] Writing a long time after
the event, he emphasises the part he played in trying to bring
about a negotiated settlement and suggests that if one had been
achieved, it would have cost him his job but the French
Government would have upheld the agreement.[29] This to some
extent bears out Nutting's comment that the unexpected turn
in the events was embarrassing because the French arrangements with the Israelis were so far advanced.[30] Eden, in
Pineau's view, would have been relieved if a peaceful solution
to the crisis had been achieved in this way.

The outcome of the Franco-British talks in Paris on 16
October was the notorious secret meeting at Sèvres. Neither
Ben-Gurion nor Selwyn Lloyd were enthusiastic participants.
The Israeli Prime Minister had partially hidden his distinctive
flowing locks under a broad-brimmed hat, but a worker on
the airfield of Villacoublay near Paris penetrated the disguise
as he stepped out of the aircraft on 22 October and rushed the
news to a reporter friend, who refused to believe it, thus
missing the scoop of a lifetime. A seventeen-hour flight had
proved a gruelling experience for a seventy-year-old man and
Ben-Gurion was utterly exhausted.

The visit had been at Mollet's invitation, and with it, Dayan
alleges, was enclosed a short note from Eden, written before
he left Paris on 16 October. In it the British Prime Minister is

said to have proposed that if Israel were to invade Egypt, Britain and France would afterwards ask both countries to withdraw their forces and further he is said to have guaranteed that if war were to break out between Jordan and Israel, Britain would not assist the former. Dayan also recounts how Eden's proposal that Israel should start the war by invading Egypt did not please Ben-Gurion at all and that his Prime Minister declared that he was not prepared to accept Israel mounting the rostrum of shame while Britain and France "laved their hands in the waters of purity".[31] To him it was an abomination to see Israel condemned as an aggressor. Equally he was worried that the Egyptian Air Force might devastate Israel while the British and French waited on the side-lines. When, just before taking off for Paris, Ben-Gurion was told that the British were refusing to modify this scenario (a term which further exasperated him), he all but cancelled the flight and only with difficulty did Dayan cajole him into a more amicable and less irascible state of mind.

The villa at Sèvres, where the meeting was to take place, belonged to a distinguished family, friends of Bourgès-Maunoury, an eighteen-year-old member of which had been shot in Algiers for assassinating Admiral Darlan under instructions from the Underground. The boy's room in the villa had been left as it was when he died but with two candles framing his photograph. Many prominent members of the Resistance, including *Polycarpe* himself, had found refuge in the house during the war.

Pineau had arrived for the meeting, driving his own car, by a circuitous route and Selwyn Lloyd had been brought from the airfield in a small car, driven by a French officer, in which he had escaped a collision only by a hair's breadth. This surreptitious gathering in such surroundings must have evoked nostalgia among the old Resistance hands of the French delegation but it was hardly a suitable setting for an international conference attended by Her Majesty's Principal Secretary of State for Foreign Affairs. Arriving at 7 p.m., accompanied only by a private secretary and Patrick Dean, Dayan remembered that Selwyn Lloyd's opening words suggested the tactics of a customer bargaining with extortionate merchants.

> Britain's foreign minister may well have been a friendly man,
> pleasant, charming and amiable. If so, he showed near-
> genius in concealing these virtues. His manner could not
> have been more antagonistic. His whole demeanour sug-
> gested distaste—for the place, the company and the topic.[32]

The Foreign Secretary found this description unflattering.[33]
But, outstandingly decent man as he was, it could be read as a
tribute that he found it difficult to disguise the disgust he felt at
the conspiratorial nature of the affair in which he had become
embroiled.

It was odd that Ben-Gurion should have become a world
statesman without ever having attended an international
conference, and this inexperience may have explained the
trouble he had in getting to the point. He appeared in-
decisive, leaving the talking to Dayan and Peres after he had
completed a long opening speech in which he tried to turn the
meeting into a forum for settling all the outstanding problems
of the Middle East. Pineau had to drag him back to the
practical problem of how Egypt was to be invaded, for from
the French point of view, if action were to be taken, it had to
be taken immediately. Army units and shipping could not be
held inactive for much longer and the weather was likely soon
to deteriorate. Politically also the moment seemed to them
opportune, with the United States oblivious to little but the
forthcoming presidential elections and the Soviet Union
embroiled with the troubles of her East German and Hungarian
satellites. But Ben-Gurion could not be budged. In no way was
he prepared to accept this allegedly British scenario, with the
Europeans playing "cops" to the Israeli "robbers", while his
country's cities were exposed to attack from the Egyptian Air
Force.

According to Dayan, Selwyn Lloyd began by announcing
that agreement with Egypt on the operation of the Canal had
all but been reached in New York. In that case, he was asked,
why was he there? The Foreign Secretary is said to have
replied that such an agreement would strengthen, not weaken,
Nasser's position, and that Nasser must go; that was the view
of the British Government and his country was ready for
military action. But it seemed impossible to reconcile the

differences between the Israeli and the British standpoints. Ben-Gurion wanted bombing to start straight away so that the Egyptian Air Force would be destroyed, while Selwyn Lloyd is said by Dayan to have insisted that Israel commit "a real act of war", which would provide the excuse for an ultimatum to be delivered to both sides to cease fighting, the bombing to start when Egypt refused to comply. Increasingly incensed with Selwyn Lloyd as the meeting progressed, Ben-Gurion was adamant in refusing to permit his country to be branded as the perpetrator of a war. Nor was he prepared to submit it to the subsequent ignominy of receiving an ultimatum to withdraw from its conquests.

Dayan relates that he produced a possible compromise in the shape of a parachute drop near the Canal which could be described to the world as another reprisal raid. As such it would be unlikely to provoke Egypt to an air attack on the Israeli cities. Nevertheless it would provide the excuse France and Britain needed to request Egypt and Israel to withdraw their forces from the area of the Canal and then to bomb the Egyptian Air Force when Egypt refused to pull back. To safeguard Israel from retaliation, France was ready to station fighter squadrons at Israeli air bases and warships off her coast but when it was suggested that these French planes might operate from Cyprus, Selwyn Lloyd is said to have killed the idea, much to Ben-Gurion's disgust.

Selwyn Lloyd's account of the affair in *Suez 1956* bears little relationship to Dayan's story. He describes Ben-Gurion, with French support, asking for a joint British, French and Israeli attack on Egypt, and recounts the manner in which he pointed out to Ben-Gurion the dangers inherent in such an operation. However, only in one respect does he actually refute Dayan's allegations. Saying in his book that Dayan had written about "the British proposals, the British plan", he denies that there had been a plan for co-operation with Israel.[34] Britain, he contends, had said at the meeting that she would not defend Egypt and she had agreed only to a French proposal that if Israel attacked Egypt, she would intervene to protect the Canal. In the plans for *Musketeer Revise*, he remarked, Israel did not figure. In a similar way Selwyn Lloyd abstained from correcting a single allegation made by Nutting.

After Selwyn Lloyd had returned to London to report to
Eden, much of the next day was spent by Peres and Dayan in
persuading Ben-Gurion to agree to an operation, the scope of
which would be large enough to satisfy the British. By the end
of the afternoon they had all but succeeded. The Prime
Minister had agreed to Dayan putting forward another
proposal which involved a mechanised brigade linking up with
the parachutists, who would drop at the east end of the Mitla
Pass, some twenty miles west of Suez. That evening Pineau
flew to London to discuss these latest Israeli ideas with the
British.[35] He may also have been anxious to ensure that the
reluctant Selwyn Lloyd had given Eden an accurate account of
what had happened in France.

In Paris, Dayan and Peres tried to relax in a Montmartre
night-club and once again the press missed a good story. As
they were leaving, they heard a startled Galilean voice exclaim
"Hey boys, did you see who just passed? Moshe Dayan and
Shimon Peres! I wonder what's up? It must be something
secret, for Dayan is hiding behind dark glasses!"[36]

Determined that this opportunity of crushing Egypt would
not be missed, the two Israelis spent the next morning removing
Ben-Gurion's remaining reservations. Much worried him. He
lacked the confidence of the French that the Americans would
stand aloof and he wanted to wait until after the presidential
elections before launching an attack, by which time Eisenhower's support for an operation might have been forthcoming.
He could well have been right. Ben-Gurion was upset too by
the French failure to discuss a general Middle East settlement
and nothing he had heard at Sèvres had in any way dispelled
his mistrust for the British, who he feared might switch sides in
mid-battle if their Arab allies were to become involved.

However, by the time Pineau arrived back from London,
Ben-Gurion had been persuaded that the risks of the plan were
acceptable. Pineau reported that his talk with Eden had been
a success and a little later Dean and the Foreign Secretary's
private secretary arrived to settle the details. At 7 p.m. on
24 October, the secret protocol of Sèvres was ready for
signature. Dayan and Pineau have published slightly different
versions of its provisions, which can be summarised as follows:[37]

1. On the afternoon of 29 October, Israel would launch a strong attack with the aim of reaching the Canal Zone the following day.

2. On 30 October, Britain and France would appeal to both Egypt and Israel to withdraw all forces ten miles from the Canal and for a ceasefire.

3. At the same time Egypt would be asked to accept a temporary occupation of key positions on the Canal by Anglo-French forces.

4. If the Government of Egypt failed to agree within twelve hours to the terms of the Anglo-French appeal, early on 31 October an attack would be launched on the Egyptian forces.

5. The Israelis were given the freedom to attack and occupy the western shore of the Gulf of Aqaba and the islands in the Tiran Straits.

6. Israel would not attack Jordan during the period of hostilities, and the British agreed not to go to Jordan's aid if, during this time, she attacked Israel.

7. All parties were enjoined to the strictest secrecy.

The expression "strong attack" was a nice ambiguous term which the Israelis could interpret much as they pleased. However, they had a free hand to gain control of the Gulf of Aqaba, one of their main war aims and their attack needed to be in enough strength to accomplish this successfully. Nonetheless Dayan had no intention of allowing his troops to get anywhere nearer to the Canal Zone than the western side of the Mitla Pass, so that there would be no question of their having to withdraw when the Franco-British "appeal" arrived, that term having been substituted for the "ultimatum" which Ben-Gurion so disliked. With the British guarantee about Jordan, the Israelis had, in fact, obtained all they wanted, even the promise of air and naval support; in a separate protocol signed by the French after the British representatives had left, the French Government agreed to station an enlarged squadron of Mystère IVAs and a squadron of fighter-bombers in Israel between 29 and 31 October, and to position two naval vessels in Israeli ports.

Selwyn Lloyd's account of the signing of this paper is sparse in detail. He says that a document was produced unexpectedly which had been typed on plain paper in an adjoining room and which recorded the elements of the contingency plan which had been discussed and the actions which could be expected to follow them in given circumstances. There had been no earlier mention of committing anything to paper and Dean signed the document merely as a record of the discussion. The contents of the document, a copy of which one assumes Dean brought back for his Foreign Minister's information, are not, in Selwyn Lloyd's account, revealed. One day, perhaps, it will be published.

Even before the two British officials had departed, Dayan had signalled his staff in Israel ordering them to mobilise the reserves and to activate a deception plan conceived to suggest that Jordan, not Egypt, was the target.

The French stayed to reflect upon the nature of their British allies. "Even to-day", writes Pineau, perhaps with hindsight, "I wonder how Eden could have thought for one moment that the Arab world would swallow such a story".[38] As for the secrecy, it was remarkable how such disparate allies could have trusted one another to abide by the alleged injunction in the protocol. As soon as the operation was over, the French started to leak details. The Israelis kept quiet until 1966.

Nutting describes how he learned about the meeting between Selwyn Lloyd and Ben-Gurion the morning after it occurred and the manner in which the Foreign Secretary reassured him with the news that nothing was likely to come of it. Such an attitude makes intelligible Pineau's flight to London. The day after the signing of the protocol, Nutting again confronted a grim-faced Selwyn Lloyd, apparently tortured by doubts[39] and reminded him of his threat to resign if the "sordid conspiracy" went ahead. On 31 October, after the despatch of the ultimatum to Egypt, Nutting did resign, having previously consulted Monckton, whose own widely expressed doubts about the Government's intentions had resulted in his moving two weeks earlier from the Ministry of Defence to the comparative sinecure of the office of Paymaster-General, a move not mentioned in Selwyn Lloyd's book.

For Eden it was a disastrous decision which was to bring a long and honourable career of service to a pitiful conclusion.

When afterwards, he both explicitly and implicitly denied that collusion had occurred, few were ready to disbelieve him, despite the evidence to the contrary.[40] Some of his most vehement opponents in Parliament had faith in him. In 1958 Colonel Wigg defended him with the words

> I have never believed in the rather crude version of collusion between Britain, France and Israel . . . I believe that the truth about Sir Anthony Eden is that he was, and remains, an honourable man.[41]

CHAPTER EIGHT

ULTIMATUM

ON 29 OCTOBER, just five days after the signing of the protocol at Sèvres, sixteen overloaded Dakotas of the Israeli Air Force flew low across the Sinai Desert to avoid the Egyptian radar. As the lumbering planes reached the eastern end of the Mitla Pass, thirty miles short of Suez, they rose to dropping height and 385 parachutists floated down, three miles away from their planned dropping zone. Two hours earlier, four piston-engined Israeli fighters had swept across the desert, level with the tops of the telegraph poles, cutting the wires with their propellors and wings, a daring and novel manœuvre. The Israelis had put nearly all they possessed into the air; of their thirty-seven Mystères, only fourteen were serviceable and a high proportion of their pilots were still half-trained novices.[1] Above the American Dakotas, old British Meteors flew cover, while a dozen of the new French Mystères patrolled the length of the Canal with the object of discouraging the Egyptian MIGs from interfering with the drop. It was the start of Operation *Kadesh*.

As the parachutists were landing, the rest of their brigade, which had earlier created a diversion by feinting towards the Jordanian border, was driving south through the Negev and into Sinai across the 190 miles of sand-choked tracks which led to Mitla. Thirty-two hours later the link-up had been made. Twice the advancing troops had overwhelmed Egyptian defensive posts, each of them manned by a couple of companies of infantry, well entrenched and equipped with heavy support weapons. Behind them the Israeli units had left two-thirds of their vehicles, either stuck in the sand or broken down, including numbers of their new French six-wheel drive vehicles which had been landed only a few days earlier but which unhappily lacked the tools to loosen the wheel nuts. There was a certain fresh, and possibly foolhardy, boldness in the concept and execution of this airborne operation, typical of the ruthless vigour of military leaders untroubled by memories of past failures.

In the words of Dayan's operation order, this parachute operation was designed to create a military threat to the Canal by seizing objectives in its proximity. It was certainly not the "strong attack" allegedly agreed to at Sèvres, nor had Dayan any intention of allowing his forces to move west of the Mitla Pass. He was determined that when Britain and France issued their "request" to Egypt and to Israel to withdraw from the Canal, there would be no question of Israeli units having to undergo such an indignity. There would, in fact, be no Israeli units there to withdraw. The Israeli leaders had also been careful to design this first phase of *Kadesh* so that it would appear to the Egyptians to be no more than yet another retaliatory raid, an operation not large enough to justify the use of their Soviet-built bombers against the Israeli cities. In thirty-six hours, when the R.A.F. was due to attack the Egyptian airfields, the way would be open for Israel to develop the full force of her offensive.

The second Israeli war aim was to "confound the organisation of the Egyptian forces in the Sinai and bring about their collapse".[2] Thus while the parachute troops were dropping near Mitla, further north other Israeli troops were attacking Egyptian border positions in the initial moves of a plan designed to destroy the six Egyptian brigades defending the Sinai and the Gaza Strip and so remove the *fedayeen* threat. The third and final of the three tasks which Israel had set herself was, of course, to open the Gulf of Aqaba by capturing the Straits of Tiran.

At 4.15 p.m. on 30 October, just as had been arranged, and just as the motor column of relieving Israeli parachutists was within striking distance of their comrades below the Mitla Pass, Britain and France issued their ultimatum. Egypt and Israel were called upon to stop fighting and to withdraw their forces ten miles from the Canal, while Egypt was required to accept what was termed as a "temporary" occupation of the Canal so as to safeguard navigation. The element of fantasy in the proceedings was emphasised by the thirty-six French Mystères and the same number of F84F Thunderstreaks, waiting at Israeli airfields ready to intervene if the Ilyushins threatened Haifa or Tel Aviv. They had arrived in Israel earlier in the week from St. Dizier and Dijon, where they had formed part of the French component for NATO.[3] Most of the jeeps, recoilless guns, heavy mortars and other equipment and supplies which had been dropped at Mitla from Noratlas transports were also French. These aircraft were based on Cyprus and operating without the official knowledge of the British Air Force Task Commander, under whose command they were.[4]

Ironic also was the sea-battle off Haifa. In the early morning and well before the ultimatum had expired, the people of Haifa, standing on their balconies in their night-clothes, watched the flashes of the guns of the French destroyer *Kersaint* bombarding the Egyptian *Ibrahim el-Awal*. This former British ship had been intercepted by the *Kersaint* while trying with a conspicuous lack of success to shell Haifa and the action ended with the disabled *Ibrahim al-Awal* being towed into Haifa harbour. The *Kersaint*, and two sister-ships, none of them part of the *Musketeer* force, had been assigned to protect the coast of Israel from just this form of attack. It was fortunate that none of her shells hit the ships of the Sixth Fleet which were waiting off-shore to evacuate American citizens, an error which might have produced awkward complications.

Although the battle had opened well, the second day of the war, 30 October, the Israeli leaders had much to worry them. Even before the ultimatum had been issued, they had learned that the Franco-British bombing of the Egyptian Air Force was to start, not at dawn as had been arranged, but twelve hours later, the delay being due to a decision that Canberras should not be risked in a daylight raid. Wary as Ben-Gurion always was of the British, this seemed to confirm his worst suspicions. In bed with an attack of influenza which had lifted his temperature to 103 degrees, his illness increased his natural anxieties and Dayan had difficulty in dissuading him from withdrawing the parachutists from Mitla.

On the whole, Dayan was confident. There were no indications that Jordan, Iraq or Syria were about to come to Egypt's aid, and it was to be doubted whether they had the capacity to do more than shell the kibbutzes and border-towns, or harass communications. The dispersed defensive positions which the

Jordanian Army had occupied along the border seemed to confirm his assumption that no offensive into Israel had been planned.

In the air, too, the war was going well. No Ilyushins had yet been seen and the MIGs were inactive. Although the parachute troops near Mitla and the relieving column had both suffered some casualties from air attack, on 30 October the Egyptians flew just fifty sorties. This figure was only doubled on the following day; during the entire seven days of the war, only fourteen air battles were fought between the two sides, in which only one Israeli plane, a Piper Cub, was shot down from the air. Even before the allied attacks on the Egyptian air bases had started few MIGs were seen. The problem was that Egypt had not many pilots trained to fly her new planes and they were of poor quality. It may have been no more than a coincidence, but in two R.A.F. training courses at Leconfield which foreign students attended, the top place in the class had gone to an Israeli pilot and the bottom to an Egyptian.[5] The number of planes which the Egyptian Air Force could put into the air was, in fact, a lot smaller than any of the estimates which had been made. By Dayan's own admission, its operational strength at the start of the war was known to be only thirty MIGs, fifteen Vampires, twelve Meteors and the same number of Ilyushins.[6] These figures are far smaller than the Israelis had quoted to the French when they were seeking help, while the British estimate of the fighting strength of the Egyptian Air Force, as published in Keightley's Despatch,[7] puts the figures as eighty MIGs, fifty-seven Vampires, twenty-five Meteors and forty-five Ilyushins, a total three times greater than Dayan's figures.

The reason for this discrepancy bears examination. Israel's intelligence was acknowledged to be excellent, as it was not difficult for her to deploy inside Egypt the facilities and sources needed to produce information of this type. So there seems to be little reason to doubt the accuracy of Dayan's figures, which, in any case, are confirmed by the inactivity of the Egyptian Air Force during the first two days of the war, before the allied bombing started to take effect. Aerial photography made it easy for Keightley's intelligence staff to count the Egyptian planes on the ground but went only a limited way towards estimating the operational strength which could be deployed

in the air. Even if the allies feared Eastern European "instructors" might fly some of the planes, it appears the intelligence
staffs had formed too high an estimate of Egypt's potential
strength. It also helped to persuade the Task Force commanders towards caution. Israel could, of course, have placed
the true facts before France and Britain but she had no incentive to do so. The greater the apparent peril from the Egyptian
Air Force, the more aid she was likely to extract from her
French allies in the shape of aircraft, naval cover and air
support.

Ben-Gurion was also troubled on 30 October by the reaction
of the Americans to his adventure, even though this did not
concern him quite as much as the allied delay in starting to
bomb Egypt. While he was reading a cable from Eisenhower,
asking him to pull back his forces from Sinai, the United States
representative at the Security Council was tabling a resolution
threatening Israel with sanctions if she did not withdraw and
urging other nations against using or threatening force in the
area.

At the request of both Britain and France, this meeting of the
Security Council was adjourned for five hours, so giving them
time to deliver their ultimatum to Israel and Egypt. The two
allies then vetoed the resolution, an act which further embittered Eisenhower, who had been annoyed enough by the
Israeli offensive starting just as he was trying to bring his
election campaign to a successful conclusion. He had a lot to
complain about. That morning his Ambassador in London,
who had been trying to extract from the British Foreign
Secretary some information on what was happening, had been
fobbed off with talk of restraining Israel from attacking Jordan
and the Ambassador had first heard about the ultimatum from
a news agency report, as did the President himself.[8] Eden had
taken the precaution of delaying his cable to Eisenhower telling
him about the ultimatum until the Israelis and Egyptians had
received it, so avoiding the danger of the President bringing
last minute pressure on him to withhold it.

Ever since the United States Administration had heard on
15 October that Israel was mobilising, what Eisenhower described as "a blackout of communications" had been imposed
by Britain and France.[9] For no apparent reason the normal

channels between America and its two European allies had dried up. In Tel Aviv, the British and French military attachés, who were in the habit of exchanging information freely with their American colleague, had suddenly stopped talking. In Washington, the British Chargé d'Affaires had nothing to say, for the good reason that he himself had no idea what was happening, no more than did British heads of mission in other capital cities. An increase in cypher traffic between Paris and Tel Aviv was in itself ominous. At first the Americans suspected that action against Jordan was being planned, as the Israelis had intended should happen. The secret was, in fact, well kept and Dulles admitted to Eisenhower that he was baffled in trying to understand the real objectives of the British and the French and that he suspected that they were not too sure themselves—a shrewd comment indeed.[10] Perhaps the C.I.A. learned more than they passed on to Eisenhower; reliable journalists have said so[11] but the evidence on this point has yet to be extracted from the C.I.A. files.

Although Ben-Gurion was suspicious of the intentions of his British partners, the Israeli Government kept its side of the bargain and accepted the Franco-British ultimatum. It was easy for them to do so. None of their forces were within ten miles of the Canal, nor was there any intention of allowing them to advance any closer to it. But, as the two allies had anticipated and planned, Egypt refused to accept their demands. To stop fighting to defend its frontiers and to withdraw its troops from their positions along the Canal would have been an abrogation of sovereignty which no Egyptian could survive, as Egypt's enemies well understood. There is also some evidence that Nasser thought Britain and France were bluffing and were trying only to ensure a cheap victory for Israel by dissuading Egypt from massing to counter the attack from the north. Afterwards, Nasser told Love that the Egyptian Government could not believe that the British were participating with Israel as such an act would be so much against their own real interests.[12] This may have been retrospective wisdom, but Nasser claimed he foresaw that an attack on Egypt could only result in Britain losing its oil, its commerce and its cultural and political influence in the Middle East, together with the use of the Suez Canal as well.

As the fighting in Sinai continued a pattern emerged which was to become typical of the campaign. Entrenched in well-fortified positions which had been designed by Egypt's post-1945 German military advisers and subsequently improved by their Russian successors, the infantry were strongly supported by Russian-made tanks, self-propelled guns and other artillery. As long as the Egyptian soldiers were happy that their line of retreat was unimpeded, they often fought quite stubbornly but when they sensed that the Israelis were infiltrating behind them, they usually decided that the time had come to go. Dayan's brigades were quick to exploit this characteristic, bypassing the strongholds whenever they could. It was the philosophy of the "indirect approach", as propounded by Liddell Hart, whose theories had influenced Israel's military leaders ever since their early days in the Haganah, in much the same way as they had the German architects of the 1939 and 1940 blitzkriegs.[13] Inferior though the Israelis were in weapons and equipment, they were stronger in numbers, and they used their limited mobility to the best advantage to concentrate their forces, sometimes to assault but more often to threaten and then overrun the dispersed Egyptian strongholds.

Two metalled roads ran across Sinai, the more northerly to Quantara and the other to Ismailia. The border posts on this central route had been captured on the first night of the war, but the assault against the main Egyptian positions was not due until the following night, after the ultimatum had been delivered and action against Egypt's airfields assured. However, in complete disregard of Dayan's orders, the local commander committed 7 Armoured Brigade into the battle twenty-four hours earlier than had been planned. This gross disobedience, involving the formation which contained most of Israel's tanks, put at risk the plan for deceiving the Egyptians as to the scale of the operation. The Egyptians checked this attack, and only after forty-eight hours of hard fighting did resistance in this central area collapse with the capture of Abu Ageigila. Here the Egyptians fought with determination and even managed to mount an armoured counter-attack. The battle is noteworthy also as being the first occasion when anti-tank guided missiles were used in war. It was fortunate that the Israelis had been able to acquire these weapons from the

French as their close air-support communications failed completely, with the consequence that the forward troops were unable to call in ground-attack aircraft to strafe enemy armour or defended positions.

The action of the commander of 7 Armoured Brigade was not the sole example of poor discipline among senior commanders—disobedience which might have had disastrous consequences for Israeli plans. When Colonel Sharon, the commander of the Israeli parachute brigade, asked for permission to advance and secure the Mitla Pass, this was refused and he was told to avoid serious combat and to send out no more than a patrol. Despite this, and without telling G.H.Q., he made a determined effort to capture the Pass, using half a battalion and supporting arms, but he met far stronger Egyptian forces than he realised were in the area. The enemy were well concealed on either side of the narrow defile and strongly supported by heavy weapons and some fighter aircraft. Only after a day's dogged fighting in which the parachutists lost thirty-eight men killed and 150 wounded was the Mitla Pass taken. It had been an altogether pointless waste of valuable veteran troops. Dayan took no action against Sharon on the grounds that the determination of the man on the spot to do what he thought right more than outweighed the defiance of orders.[14] The problem was, of course, the age-old one of reconciling initiative with discipline. Independently minded these young Israeli commanders could be, but at times they took it too far and the action of 7 Armoured Brigade might well have precipitated the bombing of Haifa and Tel Aviv.

To suggest that every Israeli formation displayed the dash and tenacity of the airborne and the armoured men would be wrong. Some reserve formations contained unfit and elderly men and none of the reservists had carried out any proper training since the last annual call-up. With units in action forty-eight hours after being mobilised, the consequences were not surprising. Some officers were too bold; others were over cautious. Some units failed to carry out their objectives—to Dayan's disgust. It is important to remember that the Israeli Army was by no means the flawless instrument which some of its propagandists have suggested. Its resounding successes were all the more estimable.

The bombing of Egyptian airfields by British Canberras and Valiants, when it at last started at dusk on 31 October, more than twelve hours later than scheduled, convinced Nasser that the allies were not, after all, bluffing. He reacted by ordering his forces fighting in Sinai to withdraw to the Canal, something which was more easily said than done. At the same time he issued instructions for the Canal to be sealed by the fifty or so block-ships which had been prepared for just such an eventuality. With the Canal unusable, the flow of oil to the West was disrupted when Syrian Army engineers blew up the pumping-stations to the Iraqi oil pipeline.

In Britain, the bombing caused consternation in many circles. To land troops in the Canal Zone so as to separate two warring armies which threatened the security of the water-way was one thing, but no mention had been made in the ultimatum about bombing. Despite the widespread dislike of Nasser and the general contempt for all things Egyptian, criticism of the Government was vociferous, not only from the Labour opposition but from within the ranks of the Conservative party and even from such right-wing newspapers as the Daily Telegraph and the Daily Mail. The national unity which should never be absent when British fighting-men are committed to action was sadly lacking. However, when on 31 October Gaitskell accused the Government in the House of Commons of collusion with Israel, few members of the general public were yet prepared to believe such an outrageous suggestion, particularly after the Foreign Secretary had categorically stated that there had been no prior agreement about the ultimatum.[15]

Except among the ever-loyal Australians and New Zealanders, Britain seemed to have few friends overseas. The day following the start of the bombing, the anticipated opposition from the United States was confirmed by Eisenhower in a forceful television speech in which he rejected that there could be one code of international conduct for friends and another for enemies. For the Soviet Union it was a fortunate coincidence that their troops invaded Hungary on 1 November to smash the anti-Soviet insurrection. As a result, eyes were diverted during the following days from the slaughter in Budapest. As the world argued about the rights and wrongs of Suez, the

Russian Army was able to crush the Hungarian uprising while attention, particularly in Asia or Africa, was focused on the misdeeds of the Western allies. Knowing that the secession of the Hungarians would lead to the end of their hold on Eastern Europe, once the Russians decided to launch their invasion they carried it through quickly and ruthlessly.

The strength of the opposition both abroad and in Britain to the bombing alarmed Dayan, who realised that time was against Israel and the allies, and that pressure to halt military action could quickly become too strong to withstand.[16] So it was fortunate that the Egyptian army in the Sinai was near collapse. In the central area, advanced units were well on the way towards Ismailia, while in the north the attack had started along the axis which led to Qantara. On the evening of 31 October the assault began on Rafah, at the south-western corner of the Gaza Strip, a labyrinth of minefields, barbed wire and fortified emplacements defended by six Egyptian battalions. By the next evening, Rafah was in Israeli hands, after a set-piece battle reminiscent of the Western Desert War, and their units were fighting their way down the road towards El Arish. This was found to be deserted, even by the Egyptian hospital staff, who had abandoned the wounded, leaving on the operating-theatre table the corpse of a soldier, his leg amputated, whom the doctors and nurses had left to bleed to death when they rushed for the ambulances. That same day, 2 November, the Egyptian Governor surrendered the Gaza Strip, with its population of 200,000 Palestinian refugees. Little was left to do there except to collect 4,000 unwanted Egyptian prisoners, bury the dead and retrieve the precious store of abandoned weapons and equipment. No one counted the Egyptian casualties. As their retreating soldiers streamed in their thousands towards the Canal, struggling through thick sand or among boulders, large numbers died horribly.

One task only remained: the capture of Sharm el-Sheikh. On 1 November, 9 Brigade, a reserve formation with an average age of more than thirty years but composed of tough countrymen, had started to move down the western shore of the Gulf of Aqaba, a 200 mile journey across country which varied from tall sand dunes to mountain goat tracks less than six feet wide, through which the engineers had to blast a way for vehicles. Two hundred trucks carried food, fuel and water for just five days. There was a chance that the Navy might succeed in bringing a few supplies into Dahib, a fishing village some fifty miles short of their destination, but otherwise these reservists were on their own. Sharm el-Sheikh was held by two Egyptian battalions, well supported by heavy weapons and occupying strongly fortified positions. If the men of 9 Brigade were held up for too long on the way, either by the country or by Egyptian outposts, or if they failed to capture Sharm el-Sheikh within the five days, there was no way back. It was a powerful incentive to success.

By the morning of 4 November, the Israelis could see their objective, having overcome minor opposition on the way, dealt with mines on the track and dragged their 25-pounders uphill over nine miles of sand dunes, an interlude which cost them half a day. On the second day Dayan, apprehensive of the hazards of the operation, had ordered the parachute brigade to move from Mitla along the Gulf of Suez and so attack Sharm el-Sheikh from the other flank but this subsidiary assault proved hardly necessary. After two unsuccessful attempts to penetrate the Egyptian positions, the first during the previous evening and the second during the night, 9 Brigade stormed home at first light on 5 November, covered by accurate heavy mortar fire and supported by fighter aircraft. Part of the Egyptian garrison had already fled, ignored by the parachutists motoring in from the opposite direction, but some of those who stayed to fight resisted quite stubbornly for an hour or so. Then the Gulf of Aqaba was open once again to Israeli shipping at a cost to 9 Brigade of ten men killed and thirty-two wounded.

But for this final battle at Sharm el-Sheikh, in one hundred hours (to appropriate the title of Robert Henriques' instant but excellent account of the campaign) the Egyptian Army west of the Canal had ceased to exist. The cost to Israel of the war was less than 200 men killed and 800 wounded, a small enough national price to pay for the removal of the *fedayeen* threat and the opening of the Straits of Tiran. Enough modern equipment had been captured to more than replace that expended in the war. The reputation of the Israelis as hard fighting soldiers who produced able generals had been reinforced, but their territorial gains were transitory. By March 1957, the Israeli forces had for a time returned behind their own frontiers, leaving Gaza and Sharm el-Sheikh not to the Egyptians, but in the custody of the United Nations Emergency Force.

CHAPTER NINE

AND MORE PLANS

MEANWHILE, AS the Israeli troops fought their way southwards, the British and the French commanders argued. In *Musketeer Revise*, it will be remembered, the French and the British respectively were to assault Port Fuad and Port Said on the east and west sides of the Canal, and then advance south with the waterway dividing them. After capturing Qantara, the British were to turn inland and seize Abu Sueir airfield, while the French crossed to the west bank and continued south to occupy Ismailia and Suez. With the whole of the Canal in allied hands and the British placed to protect it from any counter-attack which might be launched from the Delta, the two allies would be placed to mount a double-pronged offensive against Cairo, should that be necessary and permissible.

As world opinion had hardened, the French exasperation with *Musketeer Revise* had become increasingly vociferous, the "hundred ship plan" being their derisive name for it. However, now that arrangements had been made with the Israelis, they had at least the consolation that complications such as the *Winter Plan* and *Hypothèse I* could be forgotten. All their energies could be concentrated on implementing the plan which had been ready in its bulky files since 12 September.

The aspect of *Musketeer Revise* which caused Beaufre most concern and about which he says he learned with mounting incredulity, lay in the long preparatory air bombardment, in which the first forty-eight-hour phase was to be devoted to destroying the Egyptian Air Force. The second phase, which was planned to continue for as long as eight to ten days, was aimed to crush the Egyptian will to resist, the assumption being that this would then enable the allied ground forces to land unopposed.[1] However, Beaufre, the clarity of whose logistic brain was a source of admiration in both superior and subordinate, knew one true reason for this long delay. To arrive

at Port Said in time the French sea convoys had had to leave
Bône on 27 October (two days before the Israeli offensive which
was to provide the allies with their *casus belli*) while the British
convoys from Malta, that much nearer in sailing time, left on
the day of the Israeli attack itself.[2]

Beaufre landed in Cyprus from Algiers on 29 October, once
again complaining about the arrangements for the accom-
modation of his staff and the manner of his reception. His first
meeting with Stockwell, who had arrived from Malta with his
staff in H.M.S. *Tyne*, took place the following day, with the
Israeli invasion twenty-four hours old. It covered the planning
for the rapid occupation of the Canal Zone should the Egyptian
forces collapse quickly under the impact of the Israelis. Now
that the whole of the 10ᵉ Division Parachutiste had concentrated in Cyprus (three regiments had flown there in requisitioned French aircraft during the previous three days), the
need was to get these parachutists, both French and British, on
to Egyptian soil with the least possible delay. It was an unhappy
time for Beaufre. On the one hand he was engaged in often
bitter arguments with his allies, trying to persuade them to
precipitate a landing, while on the other Barjot was continu-
ally urging him to be more active.[3] As the days passed, this
concern of the French to establish an allied presence in Egypt
without waiting for the set-piece seaborne invasion resulted in
a multiplication of fresh plans and modifications being prepared
and then abandoned.

The date of the arrival of the invasion fleets off Port Said,
conditioned by the operating speeds of some of the transports
and by the insistence of the Allied naval commanders on the
need for the convoys to be accompanied by slow-moving mine-
sweepers, could be no earlier than 6 November; as a consequence this was the date fixed for D Day. According to Beaufre,
it would have been 10 November if he had not succeeded in
hustling his allies to cut their timings.[4] Following a preliminary
bombardment of the beach defences at H hour, which was to
be thirty-five minutes after sunrise, two Royal Marine commandos were to land in front of Port Said and three French
Marine commandos at Port Fuad. Both of these assault groups
were to be supported by tanks. Thirty minutes later, a British
parachute battalion was to jump at Gamil airfield, to the west

of Port Said, followed shortly by a regimental jump by the French at the southern end of Port Fuad. The bridges at the southern outskirts of Port Said, the capture of which was the key to the advance along the causeway, were to be taken by a helicopter assault in which the third of the three Royal Marine commandos was to be lifted direct from H.M.S. *Ocean* and H.M.S. *Theseus* on to its objective. This was an original use for helicopters: never before had they been employed for a direct assault on to an enemy position.

Once the assault groups were established ashore in the gateway ports, follow-up forces were to land from the sea, two parachute battalions on the British side and a further parachute regiment on the French. With these parachutists would be more tanks, bringing the numbers up to about one hundred. These forces were then to break out to the south and advance side-by-side along the Canal.

This copybook plan was based on an intelligence picture which exaggerated Egyptian strength in about the same degree as it misread the terrain. It also had curious omissions. The two lightly-armed British parachute battalions which were to come in by sea were to lead the advance down the causeway. There was everything to be said for outflanking the Egyptians if the defences of the causeway were as strong as the intelligence staffs had suggested, with infantry and rocket-launcher positions every fifty yards, and the Canal Company's signal stations converted into heavily fortified strong-points equipped with anti-tank guns and self-propelled artillery. However, with the causeway bounded on one side by the Canal and on the other by the marshes and lagoons of Lake Manzala, deployment to either flank was not possible. The alternative was a parachute operation to the rear of the Egyptian defenders, somewhere in the general area of Qantara but no provision for one was made in *Musketeer Revise*. Perhaps the shortage of British transport aircraft was a factor, there being insufficient to lift even a full battalion and the anti-tank guns needed to support it. Again, it may have been the fear that the relief forces might be delayed. Whatever it was, the plan to advance on a narrow front along a bare causeway against a succession of heavily defended positions seemed to lack guile. In any case the French with their complete parachute division and forty-five large

Noratlases certainly had the capacity to drop behind the Egyptians but it is possible to sense a reluctance to allow the French to have a major role in the operation. Certainly Beaufre believed this to be so.[5]

Even though Beaufre himself had some reservations about dropping parachutists deep into areas strongly held by the Egyptians,[6] as soon as he arrived in Cyprus and even before he had talked to Stockwell, he and the French airborne commanders were thinking in terms of a rapid deployment of the three French parachute regiments, with the first dropping on Port Fuad, the second the following day on Qantara and the third either on Qantara or further south the day after that. They were anticipating the need for the variant to *Musketeer Revise*, in the shape of a rapid occupation of the Canal Zone by an airborne and amphibious operation, mounted from Cyprus as the slow sea convoys wended their way from Algiers and Malta towards the Eastern Mediterranean, an operation which could take place if the air bombardment should cause Egyptian resistance to crumble. The trouble was that the British were to insist that such an operation was practicable only if the opposition was negligible, while the French, rather more sceptical about the ability of air bombing to do the job for them, were to see in it a way to persuade the British to move in as soon as the air bombardment began. In this way, so the French argued, the occupation would be under way before world opinion was mobilised, while the Egyptians, caught off their guard, would not have time to block the Canal or to demolish its installations.

While Beaufre's ideas ran ahead of the British plan and foresaw a parachute force either in or approaching Ismailia forty-eight hours after the initial drop on 5 November, those of Massu and his staff were more ambitious. He saw the objective as the occupation of the whole of the Canal Zone and envisaged an operation *Verdict* which would accomplish just this. But he was aware that in face of what he called the monolithic inertia of the British, nothing not geared to the elaborate seaborne plans, so long prepared, was likely to be agreed. He said that, to the British, *Overlord* was the model and they chose to pay no attention to the French experience in Indo-China.[7]

Following this line of thought, which Beaufre and his

airborne commanders had annunciated on 30 October, the planning staffs started the next day to prepare what was to be known as *Omelette*. To be put into effect only when Egyptian resistance seemed likely to be negligible (that magic word), *Omelette* specified British and French parachute drops at Gamil and Port Fuad, with the assault supported by naval gunfire if such proved to be necessary. Further French drops would take place, first at Gamil if reinforcements were needed and on the following two days at Qantara and Ismailia. The remainder of 16 Parachute Brigade would be rushed in by sea to hold Port Said until the main convoys arrived several days later.

As the Task Force Commanders continued to argue throughout 31 October and 1 November, the speed and depth of the Israeli advance was increasing, as was the pressure from the French Government, exercised through Barjot, to get some allied troops into the Canal Zone by some means or other. Not until 2 November could Stockwell be persuaded to agree to *Omelette* being launched and then only if they could be sure there would be no opposition. As Beaufre so bitterly demanded, how could one be sure?[8] Stockwell's attitude, however, deserves much sympathy. Ten years later he protested that had they known the Israeli intentions, they could have planned the operations accordingly.[9] Isolated as the senior commanders were by a Cabinet which denied to them any knowledge of its political aims and subterfuges and left to pick up what scraps of information their allies might let fall, it was little wonder that they were reluctant to take risks.

Arguments about *Omelette* flared and while the invasion fleets steamed slowly towards their destination, modifications to *Musketeer* (as it was now to be called), were in train. Because anti-aircraft defences had been detected in the area, the helicopter attack by 45 Royal Marine Commando on the southern exits from Port Said was dropped. In many ways this was a pity as this use of helicopters represented the sole spark of originality about the operation, but with so little data available on the effectiveness of anti-aircraft fire against helicopters the caution was perhaps understandable. In the event the Commando did land by helicopter but only on beaches which had already been cleared of the enemy. In place of this helicopter assault, a daring French parachute operation was substituted, the landing of some 500 men on to a small triangular dropping zone largely surrounded by water and carried out from less than 450 feet, nearly 200 feet below the minimum dropping height as defined by the rule book.

A second modification to *Musketeer* was rather more fundamental. As it was at last apparent to all that the state of the east bank of the Canal and the absence of exits from the south end of Port Fuad precluded a French advance on that side of the Canal, both forces would have to use the common axis on the west bank, although some small detachments of French troops were to move in amphibious craft along the Canal itself. To satisfy the *amour-propre* of both participants, it was decided that 16 Parachute Brigade, with a regiment of tanks under command, would lead the advance but that Massu would be in command of the break-out as a whole and would control the subsequent attack on Qantara. The plan supposed that the British in Port Said would be ready to move before the French, crossing over from Port Fuad. It did not altogether please Massu, any more than did the restraints he felt the Allied system of command placed upon him. To Massu, the matter was simplicity itself. One appointed a commander, defined his objectives, allocated to him the necessary resources and left it at that. In Massu's words, the commander then set up his shop and ran his business as he himself thought best.[10]

After the morning meeting on 2 November, at which Stockwell agreed to prepare for *Omelette*, Beaufre had left by helicopter to check on the state of readiness of his parachute regiments. On his return from their base, Barjot surprised him with a signal from General Ely, which had been delayed in transit for nearly twenty-four hours and which demanded that an allied force should be landed in Egypt within twenty-four hours in view of the Egyptian rout in the Sinai. Ely's insistence that the assault force should include some tanks was singular: all were loaded into the ships which were making the slow passage from Algiers and Malta and no power on earth could persuade these ships to sail any faster. With Barjot breathing down his neck for quick action, that evening Beaufre claims that he demanded that *Omelette* should be mounted forthwith, without waiting for an assurance that the landing would be unopposed. But Stockwell remained intractable, his main argument, according to Beaufre,[11] being that air photography had revealed that the Egyptians were reinforcing Port Said and the Canal Zone, a strong indication that there was a determination on their part to resist. These reinforcements were, in fact, defeated troops pulling back from Sinai.

Beaufre saw fit to complain to Barjot that a higher échelon should have been needling Stockwell rather than the latter's subordinate.[12] This seems to be a reference to Keightley and is one of the few comments which has been made public by a senior participant on the role played by the Commander-in-Chief. One senses a rather Olympian figure who went perhaps too far to avoid interfering with his Task Force Commanders. It is a pity from the historical standpoint that he never saw fit to reveal more than such bare facts of the operation as were set out in his official despatch.

Undaunted by the opposition to *Omelette*, the French returned to the attack next morning with yet another plan, christened this time *Telescope*. This was a modification to *Musketeer*, in which three parachute battalions would be dropped twenty-four hours in advance of the seaborne assault instead of simultaneously with the main landings. After a lively discussion which produced a number of changes, the British agreed to detailed plans for *Telescope* being prepared, but the French were left with the impression that the allies were far from convinced of the need for it. This was confirmed that evening at dinner, when Stockwell told Beaufre that he had persuaded Barjot to drop *Telescope*. Furthermore, Stockwell had received a query from London asking about the consequences of delaying *Musketeer* for a further forty-eight hours.

In actual fact, Barjot had been deceiving Stockwell and his acquiescence in dropping *Telescope* was the consequence of negotiations which he was carrying out to remove his parachute troops from the allied command so that they could be made available for independent French action. Of this Beaufre was unaware.[13] The French had been driven to such a pitch of exasperation by what they saw as British caution and obstinacy that they had once again the previous evening discussed with the Israelis the possibility of mounting an operation against Port Said on 4 November, without help from the British but with the Israeli Army taking part by capturing eastern

Qantara. Dayan was only too pleased to co-operate and suggested in his turn that the French might move into Egypt by way of the road from El Arish to Qantara,[14] not that he minded the British joining in if they so wished. Ben-Gurion, the shrewder politician, saw no way in which a French force engaged in separating Israelis from Egyptians could do so by advancing through Israeli lines. However, the Israelis were to hear no more about this fanciful proposal.

The query as to the consequences of delaying *Musketeer* stemmed from the political turmoil in Europe and in North America. In every way Eden's situation was worsening. The bombing had started, on 31 October, and Nutting had resigned although the fact had still to be made public. This bombing, combined with the refusal of the Government to give an assurance that it would abide by any decision of the General Assembly of the United Nations, had led to such a deplorable scene in the Commons that the sitting had had to be suspended. A resolution in the General Assembly on 2 November calling for a cease-fire had been passed by sixty-four votes to five with only Australia and New Zealand voting with Britain, France and Israel. Five old friends and allies, together with Laos, abstained. To Eden's disquiet, the Government of the United States, and not that of Soviet Russia or one of the Arab countries, had taken the lead against the allies in the Assembly.[15] A certain smugness in the American attitude was reflected in a speech by Vice-President Richard Nixon who pronounced himself satisfied that his country had for the first time in history shown itself to be independent of Anglo-French colonial policies. Only Canada, one of the abstaining countries, had suggested anything constructive. This was for the creation of a United Nations military force to police Israel's frontiers, a proposal which Eden was now ready to accept under certain conditions. After consulting Pineau, the British Government announced the next day that the two allies would cease military action as soon as the Egyptians and Israelis agreed to accept such a force. However, they stipulated that limited detachments of Anglo-French troops should be stationed between the combatants until the force arrived and that it should remain until an Arab-Israeli settlement had been agreed and satisfactory arrangements made for the operation of the Canal.

Nevertheless, the two allies did not wait for the United Nations to reply to their proposals. The idea for the forty-eight-hour postponement of the launching of *Musketeer* was dropped no sooner than it had been made. Shortly after telling Beaufre that *Telescope* was to be abandoned, Stockwell was called to the telephone from the dinner table to learn from Keightley that orders had been received from London to launch the main operation. *Musketeer* was to go ahead as planned on Tuesday 6 November, except for its parachute component which would now drop twenty-four hours in advance. That night, Head, now Minister of Defence, together with Templer, the C.I.G.S., flew to Cyprus to confirm the decision and to press upon the military commanders the need to restrict the weight of the preliminary bombardment so as to minimise civilian casualties. After three months of planning, it was perhaps a little late to emphasise this vital facet of the operation. The two visitors added a further rider which, in view of the deteriorating political situation, hardly needed stating. Any operation undertaken was to be limited to the Canal Zone. Cairo was out.

It was an end at last to the indecision which had bedevilled political and military planning, and the sudden "lunatic" reactions to events, the adjective used by Beaufre to describe the subterfuges and vacillations of his superiors.[16]

CHAPTER TEN

THE AIR WAR

THE SIGHT and sound of Canberra bombers taking to the air and heading south towards Egypt startled the allied troops camped among the orange and olive groves of Cyprus with the abrupt knowledge that all their prolonged preparations for battle had, after all, been to some purpose. It was the same at sea. Doubts whether the British and French Governments really meant business evaporated when, during the early evening of 31 October, the air plots of the allied fleets sailing towards Port Said began to show large rectangular raids flying south-east from Malta.

Although the Egyptians had been warned on the radio to keep away from areas which had been earmarked for bombing, a praiseworthy and successful attempt by the British to lessen civilian casualties, the pilots of the leading Canberras were helped on their way by the well-lit cities and airfields illuminated below them. Only when the first bombs fell were the lights extinguished with the realisation that the British and French had not been bluffing after all. But the voices on the radio which had warned them to take cover had also exhorted them to rise in revolt against their rulers. This advice they ignored.

The first targets for the British bombers were the airfields near Cairo, together with Kabrit and Abu Sueir in the Canal Zone.[1] Included in the objectives was Cairo West, one of the main Ilyushin bases, but orders to cancel this strike arrived from London when the planes were already airborne, to the consternation of Keightley and the staffs concerned. But the reason had been sound. News had just been received that American civilians were being evacuated to Alexandria by way of a road which ran close to the target airfield.

Although the original aim of these bombing raids had been to destroy the Egyptian Air Force so as to prevent the cities of

Israel from being destroyed, they were also an essential preliminary to *Musketeer* itself, or so it seemed at the time to the
planners. The need to ensure air superiority before launching
an amphibious operation was a fundamental lesson which had
been learned in battles ranging from Narvik to the Pacific,
and revised once again in Korea. No more attractive target
could present itself to an effective air force than an invasion
fleet sailing slowly along its coast, unless it was airfields such
as those in Cyprus, jam-packed with transport and bomber
planes and there was no available intelligence to suggest that
the Egyptian Air Force was anything else but capable of
retaliatory strikes. The air war had to be won first and night
bombing raids were the proper way to start. There was a third
reason also for these raids—the vain hope of some politicians
and members of the Air Staff that the "aero-psychological"
offensive would bring about Egypt's collapse and with it
Nasser's disappearance. As Liddell Hart later expressed it, the
theory "fitted in with, and fostered, the arguments of the more
cautious of the Army planners".[2]

Throughout that night the raids followed one another,
with twelve airfields attacked by the Canberras and the new
four-engined Valiants, which had entered operational service
only the year before. These gigantic planes (or so they seemed
to be at the time) were not allowed to carry bombs any larger
than 1,000 lbs, yet another measure to avoid too many Egyptian
casualties. The result of high-level bombing with such comparatively puny weapons might well have been anticipated. The
following morning, photo-reconnaissance by Canberras and
French RF-84Fs revealed pitted runways and still blazing
installations, but few damaged planes. Afterwards Keightley
suggested that the plan had been merely to damage runways
and discourage the Egyptian aircraft from taking to the air.[3]
Even if this was the case, the attacks did not achieve their aim.
During the night twenty Ilyushins and twenty MIGs, flown
by Russians and Czechs and destined for delivery to the
Syrian Air Force, had been escorted to Syrian and Saudi
Arabian airfields by a further twenty Egyptian MIGs. Another
twenty Ilyushins escaped to Luxor in the far south.

The R.A.F. bomber crews sighted only two Egyptian
fighters during the entire night, although the next morning

a MIG did damage a reconnaissance Canberra. Concern that fighters piloted by East Europeans might attack the bombers had proved to be unfounded, while the anti-aircraft fire which burst far below the British aircraft had produced little more than a fine display of pyrotechnics. It was hardly surprising that the opposition had been so ineffective. Even if the Egyptian pilots had been experienced or better trained, or even if Russians and Czechs had flown some of the aircraft, Egypt had not yet developed the complicated infrastructure of warning systems, operations rooms and sophisticated communications needed to ensure the interception of night intruders.

With the rate of progress during the first night so slow that some felt the new Egyptian planes might become obsolete before they were destroyed, a heavy programme of low-level daylight raids was begun the next morning, using both carrier-based aircraft and land-based ones from Cyprus. There was no shortage of planes. The R.A.F. had succeeded in cramming an impressive number of squadrons into very limited spaces. Two squadrons of Canberras and one of Valiants had moved from the United Kingdom to Malta in mid-September. Towards the end of October, two more Canberra and three more Valiant squadrons joined them; at about the same time a further nine squadrons of Canberras arrived in Nicosia, making a total of seventeen bomber squadrons in the two islands. At the start of *Musketeer* there were also a couple of squadrons of Hunter fighters at Nicosia, together with four of Venoms and one of Meteors at Akrotiri. To these must be added the seven squadrons of Transport Command (not very large ones) which had been assembled at neglected Tymbou, where the French Noratlases and a squadron of Thunderstrikes were based also. With the British Shackleton maritime patrol aircraft, light Austers and the British and the French photo-reconnaissance planes, a total of thirty-eight squadrons had been fitted into only five bases including the recently completed Akrotiri, Tymbou (little more than an emergency landing ground a few weeks earlier) and the small Hal Far in Malta, which could take only a couple of squadrons.

There were also the naval aircraft. Eighteen strike squadrons had been embarked aboard the three British and two French carriers which were approaching Egypt from the west, but a lot of scratching around had been needed to find the ships. Of the three fleet and eight light carriers of the British fleet, only two were operational in July, the large and new H.M.S. *Eagle* in the Mediterranean and the light carrier, H.M.S. *Bulwark*, employed on "Trials and Training" in home waters, but without an air group aboard. Five ships were in dockyard, either being modernised with angled decks, or undergoing extended or routine refits. Of the rest, three were in reserve and two, H.M.S. *Ocean* and H.M.S. *Theseus*, were in use as floating training establishments and were not capable of handling aircraft. After these two ships returned from the quick trooping trip which they had made to Malta and Cyprus in the early days of the emergency, they seemed destined for an extension of this unglamorous chore, when metal bunks were fitted for the comfort of the soldiers and *Ocean* was rigged out as a hospital-ship. However, plans change. In late September, oxy-acetylene torches were at work cutting out the new bunks and helicopters were being taken aboard preparatory to working up for 45 Royal Marine Commando's airborne assault.

In early August, *Bulwark* sailed to join *Eagle* in the Mediterranean, after embarking three squadrons of the new Mark 6 Sea Hawk, a single-seater ground attack/fighter which had entered service two years before, and which was armed with four 20 mm cannon and could carry either twenty-five rockets or a couple of 1,000 lb bombs, or a combination of the two missiles. *Eagle* carried Wyverns, Sea Venoms and an older mark of the Sea Hawk. The first-named was a single-seater torpedo/strike plane, powered with a piston engine, whose career had been chequered; she had first flown in the late forties, but had not come into service until 1953, the result of problems in engine design. For all that and despite her slow maximum speed of only 456 mph, she was more than to prove her worth during the subsequent operations. The Sea Venom was a two-seater, all-weather strike/fighter, also armed with cannons, bombs and rockets, another aircraft which had come into service in 1954. More Sea Venoms and Sea Hawks had been embarked in H.M.S. *Albion*, the third carrier of the squadron, whose refit had been rushed through and which had arrived in the Mediterranean during the third week of September with just enough time in hand successfully to complete her work-up. Aboard the three carriers was a total of seventy-three Sea Hawks, twenty-five Sea Venoms and nine Wyverns, as well as Dragonfly helicopters and Skyraiders and Avengers for early warning and anti-submarine work. Embarked in the two French light carriers, *Arromanches* and *Lafayette*, were a further fifty or so aircraft, mostly piston-engined American Corsairs, armed with four 20 mm cannon and capable of carrying two 2,000 lb bombs or ten rockets. The Corsair had been a popular plane with the United States Marine Corps and had been used with great success in Korea but it was now sadly obsolescent.

The first strike of forty of the Royal Navy Sea Hawks and Sea Venoms swooped down on the airfields around Cairo just before dawn on 1 November. Simultaneously, R.A.F. Hunters and Venoms were strafing the Canal airfields. No piston-engined aircraft took part in these opening attacks, but as the day progressed and the sky stayed empty of enemy planes, Wyverns joined in against a coastal airfield and French Corsairs attacked the Egyptian Navy, sinking an M.T.B. and leaving a destroyer in flames.

The previous night, the small Egyptian Navy had suffered yet another loss. In the Red Sea, the cruiser H.M.S. *Newfoundland*, in the company of a task force of British and French ships, had encountered an Egyptian frigate which was en route to Sharm el-Sheikh, shadowing some merchant ships. After a sharp action, in which the out-gunned Egyptian frigate fought back bravely, hitting *Newfoundland* twice and causing six casualties to her crew, she capsized and sank. A prepared block-ship in Lake Timsah proved more difficult to destroy. After surviving one attack by a dozen Sea Hawks, she was holed during a second strike but the Egyptians managed then to manoeuvre her so that she blocked the waterway as she sank. It had been a very expensive way of doing the Egyptians' work for them and in any case proved to be rather pointless in view of the subsequent orgy of sinking of block-ships.

Despite damage to *Eagle*'s starboard catapult, which had failed during flying training just after she left Malta, the strikes continued in relays throughout the day, pilots averaging four sorties each. Overhead, combat patrols of Sea Hawks protected the ships from an Egyptian counter-blow, while Skyraiders and Avengers, together with R.A.F. Shackletons from Malta, kept watch around the fleet. That night, the bombers of the R.A.F. returned to the attack and the next morning the two navies continued their destructive work, with the Hunters and Venoms from Cyprus now confined to flying top-cover over the fleet. By 0800 hours that morning it was all but over. Worthwhile targets were now hard to find and, except for the twenty Ilyushins which had taken refuge at Luxor, the Egyptian Air Force had been eliminated.

When the plans for this air offensive had been laid, little or no thought appears to have been given to the many hostages held by the Egyptians. Despite the prior warnings which had been given about the places to be attacked, despite the limitations on the size of the bombs, the avoidance of non-military targets and all the other restrictions which hedged the operation, there could be no way of avoiding some casualties among innocent Egyptian civilians and a measure of damage to civilian property. Even if there had been no such incidents, Nasser's efficient propaganda machine would have invented them. Consequently, and remembering the horrors in 1952 when Europeans had been burned alive in the Turf Club by a mob whose provocation had been far less, it is perplexing that so little heed appears to have been paid to the fate of the British and French subjects still in Egypt. Although 4,000 holders of British passports had already left, there were still some 2,000 citizens of the United Kingdom still in the country, together with about 10,000 colonial subjects. There were also the employees of the Suez Contractors, marooned in their bases but still going about their daily work, even to the extent of continuing to ship munitions out of the base to Malta and Cyprus, something which the Egyptian Government chose to ignore so as to avoid giving the British the excuse of provocation.

The Embassy had, of course, warned the United Kingdom citizens to leave the country. As for the Maltese, Cypriots, Gibraltarians and others, some of whose families had lived in Egypt for generations, consciences could perhaps be salved by the thought that they had chosen to live in a country where violence by xenophobic mobs was always a possibility, rare though such incidents had been. But the 470 men working for the Suez Contractors were another matter. The British Government was directly responsible for their safety and it was fortunate indeed that in the event none of them did lose their lives or even suffer serious injury.

No evidence has yet been produced to suggest that any thought was given to evacuating these men before the bombing started.[4] After receiving news of the Israeli invasion on 29 October, the acting chairman of the company who was on the spot sent a signal to Cyprus through the Embassy asking for eight Hastings to be sent to Abu Sueir to fly them all out but no reply was ever received.[5] Even though they were happily ignorant that the British and French intended to bomb and then invade Egypt, the managers still made attempts to get their people out either by car through Libya or by ship but without success. On the evening of 31 October, most of the men were at home, either getting ready for bed or relaxing after a normal day's work, when armed police hammered on their doors. Hustled into buses as flares from the Canberras floated down over Abu Sueir, they were driven away to internment. There they stayed until just before Christmas, ignored or forgotten except by their employers and families, living in great discomfort and neglect, conditions caused more by the inefficiency of their gaolers than by Egyptian malice.

In neither Eden's nor in Selwyn Lloyd's memoirs, nor in any other account of the Suez affair written by a major participant, has a word been said about the peril which faced these men. At the very least the danger in which they stood should have been a major factor among the arguments used when the question of a quick airborne assault on the Canal Zone was being discussed. On the evidence so far available, it seems to be a distasteful story. Even when these men did at last reach home, they were to face months of frustration while civil servants argued about compensation for their lost possessions. Only in 1958 were the final claims from individuals settled.[6]

With the Egyptian Air Force no longer a threat either to Israel or to the allied invasion fleet, both the carrier and the shore-based pilots were able to turn their attention to strafing other Egyptian military targets. This series of low-level attacks was at first directed against Almaza, where a large number of troops and vehicles were concentrated, and on Huckstep Camp, where more than 1,000 armoured and soft-skinned vehicles

parked in tidy rows provided ideal targets on the afternoon of
2 November for the bombs, rockets and cannons of the Royal
Navy Wyverns. Since the start of the allied attack, as during the
Second World War, the Egyptians had fought their anti-
aircraft guns capably, and in the customary way shooting
improved with practice against live targets. Their first success
that day was to shoot away the undercarriage of a Sea Venom,
which the badly wounded pilot just managed to land on
Eagle's deck with a badly injured observer aboard.

The next night there was nothing for the bombers to do, as
there were no targets left which could be attacked without
endangering lives and property. During daylight, most of the
strike aircraft were now directed against the many armoured
and other military vehicles moving about the roads of the
Canal Zone. Because the Egyptian drivers had learned that
the allied pilots were under orders to go to considerable lengths
to avoid harming civilians, the crews of military vehicles were
often seen to take to their feet at the approach of allied aircraft,
while civilian drivers continued on their way apparently
unperturbed. When airfields were under attack, crowds of
spectators could be observed watching the show from the
safety of the perimeter. The drivers of other military vehicles
learned the trick of tucking themselves in among the still thick
civilian traffic, knowing that by so doing they were safe from
attack, tactics which resulted in unprofitable sorties and which
imposed serious nervous strain on the allied pilots. But as
Keightley all but admitted,[7] there were really too many aircraft
for too few tasks.

Apart from the continuing attacks on road traffic, on
3 November the defences of Port Said were hit hard, with the
offensive strikes of *Eagle* concentrating on Gamil Bridge, a solid
causeway west of the town, and the only road link with the
Delta other than the twin roads and railway running south to
Qantara. It proved difficult to damage. Although a number of
direct hits were obtained in a series of dive-bombing attacks,
success was only achieved and a third of the causeway destroyed
by Sea Hawks swooping in at a low level and sticking their
bombs into it like darts, the fuses being set so that the planes
had just enough time to get clear before they exploded. During
these attacks, anti-aircraft fire shot a Wyvern down into the

sea, from which the pilot was hauled out an hour later by a helicopter which had flown seventy miles to find him.

One target which has not yet been mentioned is Cairo Radio, the source of the virulent and successful propaganda which daily swamped the *suqs* of the Middle East and North Africa. It was a matter of direct concern for Bernard Fergusson, who had been struggling so hard to build up a psychological brick from a rather unlikely collection of straws.[8] The security which had cloaked and which had certainly hampered the planning for *Musketeer* was such that on 28 October Fergusson's seniors were reluctant to reveal even to him that the operation was to take place after all—something which he, like everyone else concerned, had by then decided was indeed improbable. That night, however, as he lay awake in his bed in London listening to the continuous aircraft noise overhead, he realised that they were bombers on their way to the Mediterranean. Two days later in Cyprus, he was told that the attack on Cairo Radio had been deleted from the bombing programme because of the fear of causing casualties to civilians in the densely packed city. As he put it, "Suddenly, somebody somewhere lost his nerve—it may have been a collective somebody".[9] It was a pity. With Cairo Radio off the air, Sharq al-Adna, the British Station in Cyprus, was to have come up on the same wavelength but with a different variety of propaganda, which depended for its success upon the audiences not being misled by the Palestinian accents of the announcers into thinking that they were being harangued by Jews rather than Arabs. The consequence was that Radio Cairo was left unharmed to make the best possible use of the weapon provided by the allies—the cold-blooded bombing of Egypt—a task to which the announcers brought every exaggeration in their armoury.

It was not until 2 November that the thought occurred to the staff in Cyprus that *they* in London might be under the illusion that the transmitting station was alongside the broadcasting studios in Cairo, whereas in fact it was in the middle of the desert, fifteen miles outside the city. The doubts were confirmed. There had been a misunderstanding and permission was immediately given to take out the transmitters. That afternoon, after the Egyptians had been given the usual warning to keep clear of the target, a force of Canberras, protected by top-cover of French fighters, attacked the transmitting station. But the bombing could have been more precise and two days later transmissions were resumed, but at a rather weaker strength.

Fergusson had developed misgivings about the staff of Sharq al-Adna, all of whom, from the Director downwards, he found to be deeply sympathetic to the Egyptian point of view. These doubts were confirmed the morning after the first bombs were dropped. An urgent signal from the Foreign Office asked him whether he realised that his station was at present broadcasting a short and frequently repeated message to the effect that the staff were heart and soul in sympathy with their fellow Arabs and that they dissociated themselves with what had been broadcast the night before. Fergusson knew how to deal with this sort of insubordination. A Royal Corps of Signals major, escorted by a small party of infantrymen, was sent to remind the staff which side they were on and the announcers soon returned to their microphones, once again warning the Egyptians that Nasser had betrayed their trust and that retribution was fast approaching them.

A major weapon in this aero-psychological campaign was the dropping of leaflets from bombers. This, it was fondly hoped, would persuade the Egyptians to see the error of their ways and so allow the allied forces to land without opposition. However, despite the shortage of bombing targets and the apparent surplus of aircraft, Fergusson found the R.A.F. reluctant to drop the leaflets, pleading that they were far too busy to do so. The reluctance was understandable: no one wants to risk lives and valuable aircraft on such pointless exercises. The result was that although hundreds of thousands of leaflets were dropped on Cairo and other Egyptian cities, many more were consigned to the incinerators. Some were appeals to the Egyptians to see sense and some dire warnings of the retribution awaiting them for the sins they had committed, but others were brilliant cartoons by Ronald Searle. He was a friend whom Fergusson had hijacked to help despite his lack of sympathy for the operation, sentiments which were shared by many other people who did their best to bring the operation to a successful conclusion whatever reservations they may have held.

The Peace Seekers: Eden and Dulles just before
the London conference on Suez – 16 August, 1956 (*Popperfoto*)

Where it began: Egyptians in Alexandria listen to Nasser announce
the nationalization of the Suez Canal – 26 July, 1956 (*Popperfoto*)

The Peace Process: Robert Menzies during his visit to Colonel Nasser and Mahommed Fawzi, Egyptian Foreign Minister – September, 1956 (*Popperfoto*)

The Allies: French and British leaders meet in Paris, 16 October 1956. (L–R, Selwyn Lloyd, Guy Mollet, Anthony Eden, Christian Pineau) (*Popperfoto*)

The Airborne Objective: Gamil airfield at Port Said
with the sewage farm in the foreground (*Airborne Forces Museum*)

The Airborne Landing: 3 Para arrive at Gamil Airfield –
5 November, 1956 (*Airborne Forces Museum*)

The Airborne Battle: Colonel Paul Crook (CO 3 Para)
and his wireless operator move to the command post –
5 November, 1956 (*Airborne Forces Museum*)

The Opposition: A captured dug-in Russian SU-100 self-propelled
gun guarding the exits from Gamil airfield (*Airborne Forces Museum*)

The Response: Sunken ships block the entrance
to the Suez Canal at Port Said (*Imperial War Museum*)

The Seaborne Landing: Approaching troops study
the burning oil-tanks of Port Said (*Airborne Forces Museum*)

The French Battle: Swing-bridge on the road South out
of Port Said, taken by the French in a daringly low-level parachute jump –
5 November, 1956 (*Imperial War Museum*)

Looking for Action: French armour in the streets
of Port Said (*David Hodson*)

Port Said: The waterfront after the battle,
with command ships, an aircraft carrier
and (L) the de Lesseps statue (*Airborne Forces Museum*)

The Refuge: The Casino Palace Hotel on the Port Said
waterfront, damaged by Allied shellfire and converted
to a first-aid post (*David Hodson*)

After the Battle: The Generals inspect French troops.
(L–R, Generals Stockwell, Beaufre and Keightley) (*Imperial War Museum*)

Where it Ended: Troops of 2 Para dug-in at El Cap,
7 November, 1956 (*Popperfoto*)

The air forces had just one more task to complete before the landings took place. The twenty Ilyushins which had escaped to Luxor on the first night needed to be eliminated. A number of night raids had failed to destroy them but on 4 November Thunderstreaks from Lydda, fitted with long-range fuel tanks, attacked them with rockets and cannon. After five minutes over the target, the French pilots turned for base, leaving behind twenty charred hulks and an enormous cloud of thick oily smoke mushrooming over the devastation.

These French fighters operating from Israel were a cause of embarrassment to the two allies. All British and French aircraft taking part in *Musketeer* were distinguished by five stripes, three yellow and two black, and when a photograph was published of what seemed to be a Mystère of the Israeli Air Force wearing these stripes, there was an uproar at Westminster.[10] Here indeed was proof of collusion. Proof it could have been but a correct conclusion may have been drawn from faulty data. When the Mystères of 2ᵉ Escadre returned to France, it was noticed that their national markings had been obliterated hastily and badly by something else. Possibly the photograph was of a French Mystère carrying Israeli markings rather than an Israeli plane wearing the allied recognition stripes.

A British commander told Hugh Thomas that Barnett, the Air Task Force Commander, knew nothing about this operation until it was too late to do anything about it.[11] If the informant is to be believed, Barnett must have been turning a tactfully blind eye to the activities of the French. He could hardly have been unaware that the French fighters were operating from Israel under the direction of his French subordinate, Général-de-Brigade Brohon, who was wearing a couple of hats and one of them not in public. For as well as being Barnett's deputy, Brohon was also in command of the French squadrons in Israel and responsible for the supply drops to the Israeli Army. According to the French reporters, the two Brombergers, whose sources of information were sound, Israeli liaison officers were operating on Akrotiri airfield, a few yards away from the operations room.[12] This could well have been so. There were few British officers about who could have distinguished an Israeli in French uniform just by the quality of his French accent.

The problems of language, different logistic systems and separate organisations can produce irksome difficulties when land forces of different nationalities have to be integrated. With air forces, everything should be simpler, but nothing was simple about *Musketeer*. There were grounds for discord everywhere—in the grossly overcrowded airfields, some shared between the two air forces, in the political uncertainties which bedevilled the planning of the bombing and in the difficulties for the French in having to try to conceal some of their affairs from their allies. However, the two commanders had been well chosen and made a sound team. Barnett was a quiet and practical New Zealander, precise and imperturbable, qualities which appealed to his allies. Brohon, only forty-four years of age, was a fine pilot and an intellectual. He also spoke excellent English, understandably so, as he had passed through the R.A.F. Staff College and flown in night bombers over Hitler's Germany, after escaping from Vichy in a British Lockheed. The able manner in which the two air forces were integrated and led may in part have been due to Barnett having used Brohon as a true deputy, leaving the Frenchman in Cyprus to direct air operations in his name while he himself accompanied Stockwell in H.M.S. *Tyne* as a member of the Task Force Commander's Committee.

This is not to say that everything in the air war went as it should have done. On the face of it, the results looked impressive. The British and French Air Forces destroyed a total of 260 Egyptian planes on the ground, most of them during the first thirty-six hours of the battle. Only seven allied strike aircraft were lost from anti-aircraft fire or by accident, together with three air-crew, two French and one British, all naval pilots; the Egyptians, of course, claimed more, successes which were readily accepted at home because jettisoned fuel tanks look very like crashing planes. But it had taken forty-four squadrons of allied strike aircraft thirty-six hours to eliminate the Egyptian Air Force with no fighter opposition and anti-aircraft fire which at the best was no more than moderate. In contrast, at the start of the Six Days' War on 5 June 1967, Israeli fighter-bombers destroyed 300 Egyptian aircraft in under three hours.

The British bombers were, of course, restricted by the size

of the bombs they were allowed to use and the airfields which they were forbidden to attack. Nevertheless, most of the Egyptian planes were destroyed by cannons and rockets, rather than bombs, mainly by naval strike aircraft. In fact, the high level bombing by Canberras and Valiants did little worthwhile damage. Possibly this could have been foreseen: however precise the attack, small bombs scattered in limited numbers over large airfields were not likely to hit well dispersed aircraft.

The carrier forces seem to have been a little out of practice, the inevitable consequence of a long spell of peace. An experienced naval pilot[13] has recalled that no aerial photographs of targets were available at briefings, nor did the pilots know the type or number of the Egyptian planes they might expect to find waiting for them; they were merely allocated an airfield or other target, given the map reference and told to hit whatever might be around. Plenty of photographs were being taken, both by high-level reconnaissance and the low-level Sea Hawks but intelligence could not cope with interpreting and distributing the flood of material. Little was left of the excellent organisation which had operated so well during the previous war and subsequently in Korea.[14] The training of the aircrew also seems to have been a little rusty, many attacks being made at too high an airspeed and too steep a diving angle, with consequent loss of accuracy.

For all that, the allied air forces accomplished their task efficiently and economically, conserving the lives of their aircrew. What was rather more difficult, they avoided killing too many Egyptians, particularly civilian Egyptians. Serviceability was excellent, and errors few; only one sad and costly mistake marred the subsequent landings when naval aircraft strafed some Royal Marines, the sort of error which is hard to avoid in the tricky business of close air support.

Stockwell has said in a newspaper article that both he and the other Task Force Commanders had always been keen to launch the assault forty-eight hours after the first air strike.[15] There was, in fact, an astonishing degree of unanimity afterwards among the participants that the political consequences of failing to land as soon as possible could have been foreseen, with world opinion, exacerbated by the bombing, hardening against the

Allies. The primary reason for prolonging this attack after the Egyptian Air Force was eliminated was the deluded hope that the aero-psychological stage might produce an Egyptian collapse. Useful though the strafing of roads and depots and the cutting of communications was to be, their effect on the ability of the Egyptians to resist was no more than marginal. In the same way, although it was important to neutralise the anti-aircraft defences of Port Said before the transport planes dropped their parachutists, this could have been done by naval strike aircraft just prior to the drop without introducing an element of unjustifiable risk into the operation.

CHAPTER ELEVEN

THE AIRBORNE DROPS

I<small>T IS</small> now necessary to jump back a few days to the British
and French troops waiting or working in Malta, Cyprus,
Algiers and Britain.

By the end of October most of the servicemen in Malta, who
were crammed into camps which seemed to fill every scrap of
spare land in the island, had decided that the whole affair had
been a waste of time. As the months moved into autumn, the
weather deteriorating, the odds which betting men were laying
against a war ever starting had lengthened: some officers who
had been borrowed from their specialist duties were even
returning to their proper jobs. So on 28 October, when everyone
was summoned from bars, cinemas and Sunday lunch parties
to prepare for yet another "training exercise" it was hardly
surprising that many of the rather disillusioned troops felt that
they were being mucked about to no good purpose. Some of the
more perspicacious realised that something odd was happening,
but the attitude of most was epitomised in the remark heard by
Douglas Clark, a gunner captain recalled from the regular
reserve to work as a Forward Observation Bombardment
Officer to direct naval gunfire ashore. "If", protested a Royal
Marine, "they can't arrange a bloody exercise without us
having to work all Sunday afternoon to get ready for it, it's
time they let *me* have a go."[1] The inevitable consequence was
that some of the preparations were completed in a less than
wholehearted fashion. For example, some articles of equipment
which would not be needed on a short training exercise, such
as a full operational scale of radio batteries, were not even
packed by some units.

This secrecy which covered the launching of the operation
was necessary for political rather than military reasons. As the
Sunday afternoon in question was the day before Israel was to
invade Egypt, it was hardly possible at that stage to tell the

troops that they were on their way to the Suez Canal. However, some commanding officers had been told the truth and some had disobeyed orders and dropped the necessary hints to a few key subordinates.[2]

Stockwell had landed in Malta two evenings before on his way to Cyprus and only during the course of that journey had learned from Beaufre, whom he had met when he touched down *en route* at Villacoublay, of the arrangements which had been made between Israel and the leaders of their two countries and the consequent need to speed up the preparations for the invasion.[3] From Stockwell's statement it would seem that no one, either inside of outside the Government, had felt fit to take him into their confidence.[4] It was on his own initiative, he says, that he arranged with the Royal Navy for *Exercise Boat-hook* (a communications and loading rehearsal by a fortuitous chance already planned) to be used as an excuse for loading the assault force, so cutting by two or three days the time required to get the troops from Malta to Port Said. The French 7 DMR and 10ᵉ Division Parachutiste were already at sea and the French fleet had sailed from Toulon.

After the Malta troops had been embarked, difficulties arose in briefing the officers and men for the coming fight because of the way units had been split between different ships according to when and where the men and vehicles were to be landed. When at last they were out of touch with land and Clark, who was landing with the Royal Marine Commando Brigade, was able to tell his gunner teams that the unexpected had happened, unfeigned delight followed unbounded surprise. This was typical: it was not that these young national servicemen and the older reservists were spoiling for a fight because they had become bored with hanging about, but because they saw the quarrel with Egypt in quite simple terms: the Canal was vital to British interests, Nasser had appropriated it and their job was now to get it back and remind the Egyptians that their country was not one "to be messed about with". From the moment they heard what was in store for them, grumbles and discontent were forgotten in the last-minute preparations for the coming battle. But it both puzzled and aggravated them to learn from the B.B.C. news bulletins that so many politicians and others at home were critical of the business upon which they were engaged. It was a new experience for British troops to learn, just as they were about to go into action, that they lacked the wholehearted support of their fellow-countrymen and understandably they bitterly resented it.

In Cyprus the loading did not run smoothly and for those responsible for embarking the troops and vehicles it was to prove a frustrating few days during which the inadequacy of Famagusta and Limassol as harbours was amply confirmed. 16 Parachute Brigade Group (less that part which was to be dropped at Gamil), various gunner, sapper and other miscellaneous supporting and administrative units, together with what many people viewed as a rather bloated Force Headquarters had all to be loaded into the troopship *Empire Parkeston*, a number of L.S.T.s and a collection of hired merchantmen. Most of the troops got aboard in good order, but last minute changes to the *Musketeer* plans wrecked many of the complicated loading tables. Substitutions such as a sapper bridging unit for a battery of guns and irritations such as the disembarkation of the already loaded vehicles of H.Q. 16 Parachute Brigade (which was now to land by air instead of by sea) produced conditions so chaotic that at one stage the carefully planned system did collapse. One of the many unfortunate consequences of this breakdown was that stores for one parachute battalion arrived just four hours before it withdrew from Port Said.[5]

Once aboard their ships, bewildered regimental officers were faced with problems of reconciling the briefing of their troops with the need for accounting in a proper peacetime manner for the ships' stores with which their soldiers had been entrusted. In one instance this culminated with a harassed O.C. Troops insisting that each overburdened soldier, as he staggered towards the ship's rail and the scrambling net below, should let fall into the waiting hands of a member of the crew the pillow-slip on which his head had rested for two days and which he had borne up from the mess-deck clenched in his teeth.

Other problems were more serious. The last-minute changes of plan which had so confused the loading in Cyprus had produced different problems for that part of the assault force already on its way from Malta. A consequence was that Brigadier Madoc, who was in command of the Royal Marines, had to call his unit commanders aboard his ship to learn of the changes of plan caused by the decision to land the parachute troops twenty-four hours in advance of the seaborne assault and the relegation of 45 Commando from their helicopter assault to a reserve role. It was a little reminiscent of Nelson summoning his captains to confer in his flagship.

The repercussions of changes such as this echoes all the way down the line. For gunners like Clark, busy with bombardment tables, amendments began to arrive at hourly rather than the more normal daily intervals. The final blow fell during the last hours before landing, when everyone who could was trying to get a little sleep before the 2 a.m. reveille. First came a signal that no gun of a calibre larger than 4·5 inches was to be used, a decision which eliminated all the cruisers from the bombardment programme. All the plans now had to be re-written to transfer these tasks to the destroyers. As the revised programme was being checked, the changes were capped by yet another signal. There was to be no bombardment at all. Again a "collective somebody" in London had lost its nerve. By then, the parachutists had been in action for over twelve hours and the commandos knew that they would be fighting for the beaches in the morning. No officer could contemplate ordering his men to land unsupported on a defended shore but happily a solution was to be found in semantics. What was to have been a naval bombardment became naval gunfire support, something which had not been forbidden and everything was left as it was. Clark recounted this incident[6] and, if his memory was not faulty, one can but wonder at senior officers allowing an order such as this to reach the troops, whatever the political pressures may have been and however well-intentioned the thinking behind the orders. Officers about to take their men into battle should not be vexed by futile instructions which can be evaded only by subterfuge. Whoever subsequently briefed the Minister of Defence appears to have been unaware that these final orders were, in actuality, a non-event: on 8 November, the House of Commons was assured that "the preliminary bombardment which would undoubtedly have caused considerable damage and civilian casualties" had been avoided because the airborne troops had dealt so effectively with the strong points and emplacements.[7]

By 5 November, the men aboard the Cyprus convoy could see on the horizon the forest of masts of the fleets approaching from Malta and Algiers. It was a fine sight that Monday evening and one unlikely to be seen again, with every type of vessel from giant battleship to chartered merchantman spaced out across the ocean. And these three fleets were not the entire total. For the past few days the Carrier Task Force had been operating some fifty miles off the Egyptian coast while *Theseus* and *Ocean*, laden with Royal Marines and helicopters, were also on their way from Malta which they had left two days before. Further away still was the convoy from the United Kingdom carrying 3 Infantry Division, the follow-up formation.

There were also other warships sailing these seas. The truth about the orders given to the American Sixth Fleet has still to be published but it certainly played an odd part in the affair. Instead of confining itself to evacuating United States citizens from Egypt and elsewhere in the Middle East and keeping a safe distance from the allied fleets, it seemed to be intent on getting in their way. That night searchlights of the American ships suddenly illuminated the blacked-out allied fleet. It was an inexplicable act. The British ships rang to action stations and the Americans were signalled in blunt nautical terms to get out of the way.[8] Ships of the Sixth Fleet shadowed *Theseus* and *Ocean*, steaming on a parallel course. American planes made dummy attacks on a French cruiser and allied destroyers detected a submarine shadowing the main British convoy; apparently able to intercept British orders to engage a hostile vessel, it surfaced hurriedly, hoisted a large Stars and Stripes and then sailed at speed through the fleet, receiving as it did so a signal to come and join the party, an invitation which it refused with good grace.[9] With the allied commanders kept in ignorance of what the Sixth Fleet was doing but only too conscious of the political standpoint of their erstwhile allies, they could never quite disregard the possibility that the Americans might think fit to intervene. Although the Americans have strongly denied any intention to embarrass the British and French, it has never been explained whether they were deliberately getting in the way, and, if so, what their motives were.

Meanwhile, back in Cyprus, the British and French parachute troops were making their preparations for battle. At
midday on 29 October, the 3rd Battalion The Parachute
Regiment had returned wearily from an operation against
EOKA in the Paphos Forest: the following afternoon the men
were starting to load their kit for what they were told was an
airborne exercise, a subterfuge which deceived nobody. The
next four days were to be a nightmare as they struggled with
the unfamiliar task of preparing to go into battle by air,
coping with a hot, dusty wind which covered everything
in the camp, including the kit which they were trying to pack,
with a sandy film as cloying as cocoa powder.[10] To add to their
troubles, the limited time to prepare and to adapt to their new
role was cut short by the decision to bring forward the parachute landings by twenty-four hours—an act apparently
motivated by a political need to have troops on the ground in
Port Said before the Security Council met in New York on that
Monday morning. But soon after midnight on 4/5 November,
3 Para were cramming some breakfast down their throats
before driving to the nearby airfield where the Hastings and
Valettas were waiting for them. Here they received the usual
warning that the appearance of the green light constituted an
order to jump, a routine precaution to ensure that the evidence
would stick at the subsequent court-martial of anyone who
decided not to do so and in no way connected with a press
report that the parachutists, disagreeing with the politics of the
operation, might refuse to carry it out. Needless to say, this was
a suggestion which caused some wry amusement.[11]

For the red-bereted Frenchmen of *2ᵉ Régiment de Parachutistes
Coloniaux*, the routine had been much the same, except that
each man had been handed a leaflet at 2300 hours that evening telling him to be proud of the vital mission with which he
had been entrusted, and assuring him that "France and the
World have their Eyes on you". One of the recipients decided
that the exhortation contained too many capital letters.[12]
Certainly it did little to relieve the fears of some of the young
paras of 2 R.P.C. as they flew towards Egypt, scared not only of
what awaited them but scared of being scared, fears which
would vanish only at the moment when they would fling
themselves out of their aircraft.

The parachute drops which were to take place twenty-four hours before the seaborne assault made very little sense except in political terms. In the earlier *Musketeer* plans, 3 Para was to capture the airfield at Gamil thirty minutes after the Royal Marines landed from the sea. At the same time a *coup-de-main* party of 2 R.P.C. was to seize the two vital bridges at Raswa, across which ran the roads and railway from Port Said to Qantara. To the east other *paras* were to seal off Port Fuad. In the new plan the objectives were the same but the troops were to drop a day ahead of the seaborne invasion. It provided all the risks of an airborne invasion without any of the consequent gains. The two units would neither reap benefit from the naval bombardment which was to support the seaborne landings, nor would they receive support from the artillery and tanks which were to come ashore in the early assault waves. And they would have to fight alone for twenty-four hours. Fortunately for them, the Egyptians lacked both the ability to concentrate their forces against the attackers and the will to do so. It is difficult to establish just what they had in or near to Port Said; reports vary but the most likely estimate is that there were one regular and two National Guard battalions, as well as coast and anti-aircraft artillery, together with about four of the Soviet SU 100 self-propelled guns which had arrived in the town the day before. Dogged, if not at times tenacious, though the Egyptian resistance was to prove, it was hardly to be expected that National Guard units would be capable of holding out against the best airborne troops in the world, let alone counter-attacking them.

The objective of 3 Para, the Gamil airfield, only just merited the description of airport. It was a strip of land running between the surf-edged sea and the brackish Lake Manzala, never more than 800 yards wide and consisting of a pair of runways and a simple control tower. At the sea's edge ran the road to the Delta, severed now by the attack of the Fleet Air Arm on the causeway bridge. Between the airfield and Port Said lay first the town's sewage farm, surrounded by half-drained marshland and then a series of cemeteries which reflected the diverse creeds and cultures of its inhabitants. Nearer still to Port Said were several blocks of high flats and the coastguard barracks and then on the edge of the town

proper an area known as Shanty Town, whose inhabitants were
to suffer most from the invasion.

This long thin objective of Gamil airfield demanded a long
thin plan and so the troop-carrying aircraft flying into the
barely risen sun each carried elements of all of the three rifle
companies engaged in the assault. This allowed the men of
A Company to leave the aircraft first, secure the western
end of the objective and at the same time check whether the
causeway was impassable. Next out was C Company with the
task of assembling in the centre as the battalion reserve, while
last jumped B Company on the sewage-farm side of the airfield,
ready to push eastwards after it had been captured. Apart from
the supporting weapons which the battalion took with it (and
these amounted to no more than four medium machine-guns,
four 3-inch mortars and the six recoilless anti-tank guns
borrowed from NATO stocks), there was a troop of parachute
sappers to clear mines and demolitions and two air contact
teams to direct the fire of the supporting aircraft and naval
guns (when the latter came within range). Jumping also was
Brigadier "Tubby" Butler (a lithe, slim man), the commander
of 16 Parachute Brigade, together with his small tactical staff.
Butler was commanding both the British and the French units
which dropped on 5 November but separated as he was from
2 R.P.C. by Port Said and bad communications, there was
little he could do to influence the actions of the French
contingent.

Tubby Butler was that rare type of British officer to whom the
French took instinctively and Massu gives the impression that
he would not have been displeased to have had him as one of
his subordinate commanders. His lively gestures, his quick mind
and power of decision made some French draw parallels with
an exceptional rugby three-quarter, while others were reminded of the bounce and power of the roles played in the
thirties by James Cagney.[13]

To drop 3 Para on Port Said strained the resources of R.A.F.
Transport Command. Neither had there been the opportunity
for any type of rehearsal. In the event, the performance of the
twenty-six aged Hastings and Valettas failed to match the
expectations of those who had prepared the flight plan, with
the result that some of the pilots had to feather their outer

engines to avoid drawing ahead of the main body, while others had to pile on maximum boost to keep their place in the dropping order. The least loved feature of the unloved Valetta was the deep wing spar which bisected the cabin, over which the over-burdened men had to climb to reach the exit door. It was a slow business getting out and in one case another run had to be made to release a single man. The pilot did well to carry out this second circuit, straining again into the rising sun through a makeshift vizor to pick up the smoke flare which a low-flying Canberra had dropped a few minutes earlier to mark the dropping zone.

Although the lack of good intelligence about the strength and dispositions of the Egyptians had resulted in the briefers exaggerating their numbers, it still surprised the men of 3 Para to see red tracer arching towards them as they floated earthwards. Fortunately for them, it is an even more frightening experience to see a cloud of several hundred parachutists descending upon one than it is to be shot at in the air when the adrenalin is flowing freely. Apart from that, men hanging from parachutes lack freedom of action, while those on the ground can make themselves scarce and unless they are of exceptional staunchness this is what generally occurs. It says much for the Egyptian soldiers that they fought for as long as they did, but within thirty minutes of landing 3 Para had cleared the airfield, which they found had been held by about a company of infantry defending a couple of concrete pill-boxes and a number of trenches dug along the beach and the airfield perimeter.

This is not to say that events moved particularly quickly. There was no way they could. Before the British parachutist could start to shoot back at his enemy, he had to unpack his weapons from the container which was attached to his leg and released as he descended, to dangle on a rope below him. It took time to rid himself of his collapsed chute and then to recover and unpack his personal container. Even then it was difficult for him to move quickly. With their enormous loads— 100 lbs in the case of the medical officer—it was virtually impossible to run for more than a few yards. Captain Cavenagh described the scene:

We lurched to our feet and headed for the control tower once again. After a few yards our running degenerated into jogging and then we frankly walked. Looking around, it was just like Frensham Common all over again. Innumerable figures were strolling across the scene. Each was carrying too much weight to move any faster. Bullets were cracking all over the place, mortar bombs began to fall on our right and from time to time great balls of fire tore along the length of the runway overhead. These were the missiles fired by a rocket projector somewhere on the outskirts of Port Said. Amid all this the Toms ambled about their appointed task.[14]

Not only their aircraft and equipment but some of their weapons left a lot to be desired. The Sten sub-machine gun in particular was an unreliable piece of armament. Its habit of jamming had cost many lives in the past, something which had apparently been forgotten by 1956 as the men of 3 Para were under the impression that it had been a success in North-West Europe and that the problems which they encountered were merely due to sand. It was galling indeed for them to discover that the Egyptians were armed with much more modern and efficient weapons and even more so to know that they had been compelled to leave behind in Cyprus so much of the arms and equipment which had finally come forward to replace their outdated Second World War material.

With the airfield cleared of enemy by 0800 hours it was possible to start the advance towards Port Said. Defending the narrow peninsula along which the British troops had to move were more infantry positions, supported by mortars; the Russian rocket projectors already mentioned, known to those on the receiving end as Stalin Organs; and the SU 100s dug in as strong points. B Company, who were to take the sewage farm, had not only to contend with the Egyptians and with the labour of moving through marsh and thick reeds but also an attack by two French fighters whose pilots mistook them for the enemy, failing to appreciate that they could have moved so far so quickly. Fortunately the men found shelter from the cannon and machine-gun fire under the concrete walls of the foul smelling sewage tanks and lost no more than their fragrance and the regard of their friends in other companies.

Although the aircraft-carriers had not worked previously with the Parachute Brigade, co-operation could not have been better. Most of the day a cab rank of twelve to sixteen British aircraft and six French Corsairs was waiting above the troops and fire was put down when it was needed, often only 100 yards or so ahead of the men being supported. When trouble was encountered later in the day from the coastguard barracks, a solid modern building against which rockets and cannon had little effect, Wyverns dealt with it by dropping 1,000 lb bombs with delayed action fuses. During this strike, the leader was shot down by anti-aircraft fire but the pilot was fished out of the sea almost at once by a helicopter.

Despite the help from the air, 3 Para saw quite a lot of unpleasant fighting during the day's grim games of hide and seek with snipers among the headstones of the cemeteries and few prisoners were taken. In these attacks and during the subsequent thirty-six hours, the battalion lost four men killed and thirty-six wounded, the low ratio of the former being a tribute to the rapid evacuation of the wounded by air and the work of the surgical team which had dropped with the battalion and started work even before the fighting on the airfield was over. Among the first of the injured to be carried to the dressing station was Peter Woods, B.B.C. newsreader, then a war correspondent. He had carried out his first parachute drop with courage that morning, but he had damaged both his ankles in the process.

The helicopters which started to run a regular service between the carriers and shore from mid-morning onwards brought in medical supplies, an additional doctor and more radio batteries. Later water, together with cigarettes and beer (the gift of the ships' companies to the parachutists) were landed. Soon after the first helicopter left, a French Dakota landed on Barjot's instructions to check whether the airfield was usable. It is hard to understand why helicopters, Dakotas and possibly other transport aircraft could not have been used to bring in reinforcements, particularly those of 45 Commando which were ready at hand. The old maxim of reinforcing success seems on this occasion to have been completely forgotten.

The French force, dropped to secure the bridges at Raswa

and the adjoining waterworks, faced a challenging task. Not
only was their objective reported as being heavily defended,
but the dropping zone was small in the extreme. It is not easy
to drop a stick of parachutists with accuracy on a triangle of
land with sides little more than 300 yards long; to do so with
any hope of success involved the planes flying in at a height of
450 feet or so, almost 200 feet less than the accepted minimum.
There was hardly time for the parachutes to open before the
men hit the ground but for all that, the drop was a complete
success: fifteen minutes after the British landed at Gamil, 500
Frenchmen were also on the ground. With them was a small
party of British airborne sappers and eight men of the Guards'
Independent Parachute Company, their task to help the
French clear the bridges of mines and charges and to patrol
down the roads towards Qantara to check whether they were
blocked by the Egyptians.[15] It was an experience which gave
these British soldiers a healthy respect for French methods and
for their fighting qualities, although they fell into the common
error of assuming that all the French were veterans of Indo-
China with innumerable operational drops to their credit. This
was possibly the consequence of talking to English-speaking
officers and senior N.C.O.s, most of whom had indeed seen a
lot of fighting. For their part, the French were puzzled by *Les
Gardes*, who neglected to wear steel helmets and who brought
their feet together with such a show of force and precision when
they delivered a message. However, they were not all impressed
by the weight of equipment which their British allies dropped
with and which they were carrying on their own backs.

Like 3 Para, the men of 2 R.P.C. floated down amid the din
of battle. About forty Egyptian soldiers who were entrenched
on and around the dropping zone had been starting their breakfast as the Noratlases arrived overhead. Others were dug in
around the reservoirs and bridges. But the difference between
the two landings was that the Frenchmen were in action, firing
back at the Egyptians below them, even before their feet
touched the ground. Their rifles and sub-machine-guns, fitted
with folding butts, were not in separate containers but tucked
under the straps of their parachute harnesses. However, although the troops had landed in the right place, many of the
jeeps and anti-tank guns had come down on the Egyptian

side of the two bridges or in the water, their positions marked by their parachutes floating like immense water-lilies on the surface.

Helped by the broken nature of the dropping zone, which provided a little cover during the anxious moments of assembly into fighting units, the two *coup de main* companies were soon heading for the bridges. As the men on the right flank fought their way through the trees which bordered the reservoirs, Leulliette, an N.C.O. of 2 R.P.C., noticed the body of one of their sergeants gazing down on them, hanging by his parachute from a palm frond, his blood dripping slowly into the sand below. Ten yards away a small Egyptian lay lifeless in a bed of flowering roses.

To the chagrin of the French, the right-hand bridge was blown up before they could reach it, but the other, across which ran both the main road and the railway, was captured intact. Wearing red berets like those of their French assailants, some of the defenders died bravely, firing from behind huge steel girders, one in particular at the entrance holding out for a quarter of an hour before he died. Then *les paras* stormed across, with the British sappers following. As they passed the dead Egyptian, flies were already gathering in black circles around his eyes.

With the bridge taken—it had not even been prepared for demolition—there was still much to be done. Snipers littered the area, while tanks, guns and mortars harassed the French from positions in the town and across the Canal in Port Fuad. These the Corsairs tackled. All morning the sky had been full of allied aircraft waiting for the contact teams to guide them down on their targets. Overhead circled also General Gilles, the French airborne commander, in a Noratlas which had been converted into a map room and communication centre, from which he was able to speak both to the headquarters afloat and to Colonel Chateau-Jobert, the commander of 2 R.P.C., a small swashbuckling warrior with a pointed beard and balding head. It was a command technique developed in Indo-China. Even though the Egyptian Air Force had been eliminated and the anti-aircraft fire was inaccurate, "It was not", as Gilles later observed, "a situation from which to contemplate a ripe old age." But it gave Gilles the best view and the highest radio aerial in Port Said, fortunately so as the British radio sets were once again being temperamental.

Meanwhile two jeeploads of British guardsmen and sappers had been some way down the road towards Ismailia, disregarding a warning not to press too far because of the real danger that a roving allied plane might mistake them for Egyptians. The road proved to be clear. There was no sign at all of the Egyptian section posts which they had been warned were spaced out at every fifty yards (less pessimistic intelligence sources did put them at an interval of 500 yards). In fact, the sole sign of the enemy was a hut containing 1,200 lbs of explosive at the six kilometre point, near which the road had been prepared for demolition, but the occupants of the hut had fled leaving their half-eaten breakfasts behind them.

At 1345 hours, the second lift arrived, 100 reinforcements at Gamil for 3 Para, together with heavy equipment and supplies and some 450 men of 2 R.P.C. under Lieutenant-Colonel Fossey-François. General Gilles, reading the battle with his single remaining and Olympian eye, delayed briefing Fossey-François until a few minutes before he and his men dropped. There had been two choices, either to reinforce the bridges if there had been continuing trouble there, or to seal off Port Fuad, so silencing the flanking fire from across the Canal. The successful capture of the larger bridge made the second choice possible.

Except for pedestrians or camels, Port Fuad was effectively an island. Dropping within sight of their comrades across the water, the French made good use of the last few hours of daylight, first to seize the salt works so as to secure their flank and then to take the police barracks, which fell in a sharp and bloody action. Although Beaufre had warned Fossey-François not to push his troops into such a position that they might be at risk from the next morning's seaborne assault, everything had gone so well during the first ninety minutes, that the Colonel decided to exploit his success. Seeking out the local police chief, he persuaded him to co-operate in the hope of avoiding the loss of life and destruction which would be inseparable from a seaborne invasion. Soon the French had eliminated the last pockets of resistance in the town and Corsairs had left blazing a convoy of military vehicles which tried to escape across the ferry. By 1645 hours the French were in control of Port Fuad and armed Egyptian police were patrolling in company with Allied detachments around suburban streets so French in atmosphere that the invaders felt quite at home.

As at Raswa, many of the Egyptians in Port Fuad had fought stubbornly. Sixty died and few prisoners were taken, wounded or otherwise, a sad reminder that the longer defenders resist, the less their chance of saving their lives by surrendering. 3 Para may not have been too gentle when they captured the cemeteries but the French had come straight from the Algerian *bled* where both sides looked on prisoners as either hostages or sources from which information could be extracted. For either an Algerian or a Frenchman, capture was often to mean a lingering end instead of quick death in the heat of battle. If Leulliette is to be believed, the French spared few lives in the early assaults and at times the killing degenerated into sadism.[16] One consequence of this ferocity was that the Egyptians learned that it was a mistake to provoke the French to violence: during the subsequent occupation, the British in Port Said rather than the French in Port Fuad were to become targets for stones and snipers' bullets.

Faulty though the radios often were, other communications continued to work. Nobody had thought to shut down the telephone system, with the result that the resourceful Chateau-Jobert succeeded, at about 1300 hours, in contacting Brigadier El Moguy, the local Egyptian commander, with a proposal for a cease-fire. The Egyptians at first rejected the idea but as the afternoon wore on with more civilians dying in the fighting and all suffering from thirst (the consequence of the French at Raswa severing the water supply), they thought again. Contacting Chateau-Jobert again through Colonel Rashdi, the local chief of the political police, El Moguy arranged to meet the allied commanders. Just after dark, a party of four officers arrived at the waterworks; waiting for them were Chateau-Jobert, together with Butler, who had flown over by helicopter from Gamil.

El Moguy was very much of the old school, a plump, moustached and dapper officer, whose English manners reflected the many army training courses he had attended in the United Kingdom. Whether he really wanted a permanent cease-fire, or was simply playing for time, as he subsequently protested, is still a matter for argument. However, it mattered little as the rather sinister Rashdi soon took over from him. When Butler proposed that the Egyptians should surrender and lay down their arms, this was immediately rejected, Rashdi warning the two allied officers that arms were even then being distributed to the civilian population. However, a temporary cease-fire was arranged to last until 2130 hours. Just before it was due to expire, Butler asked over the telephone for an hour's extension so that more wounded could be evacuated to the carriers by helicopter, but that was the end of it. Soon the shooting started once again.[17]

In Port Said the consequences of this cease-fire were slight, but for Eden they were to be troublesome. Butler reported the news to Gilles and from his aircraft the message went to Stockwell in H.M.S. *Tyne*, from him to Keightley in his Cyprus headquarters and then to Whitehall and Downing Street, all within the hour. The outcome was a little like the party game in which a circle of children pass a message from mouth to mouth to see how it changes as it goes. By the time the news reached the Prime Minister, Brigadier Butler's emphasis that the cease-fire was unlikely to stick had disappeared. To deliver this much needed and welcome news, Eden broke into a Commons debate in which the Government was being lambasted about the wording of one of the leaflets which had been dropped on Cairo and which warned Egyptian soldiers that their villages and homes would be destroyed if they did not evacuate—a far cry, as Aneurin Bevan protested, from military action to separate the Israeli and Egyptian armies.[18] The Conservative benches erupted with joy when Eden told them that surrender terms were being discussed and that a cease-fire had been arranged but, as he later admitted, he had made a mistake.[19] Within the hour, Radio Cairo had denied the report. Only the prorogation of the House saved the Prime Minister from humiliation.

Keightley's despatches include a categoric statement that "surrender terms were agreed and the Egyptian forces began to lay down their arms . . ." and go on to blame the "subsequent tribulations suffered by Port Said on the local commander being overruled and instructed to continue the battle".[20] Eden, writing three years later, when he should have been in possession of the full facts, declared that he was convinced that this reversal of action was prompted from further afield.[21] Nothing had, in fact, been reversed and no surrender terms were ever agreed. It is even possible that El Moguy never consulted Cairo about the cease-fire.[22] Later he insisted that his object had been only to get the water flowing once more and to gain time for guerilla resistance to be organised. In these two aims he succeeded, but it did not save him from subsequent disgrace at the hands of his own people.

Many Egyptian soldiers had already discovered that safety lay in discarding their boots and covering their weapons and equipment in the all-enveloping garment of the civilian *galabiya*, a ruse which helps both to explain and to justify some of the allied troops being trigger-happy. But as Rashdi had warned the two allied parachute commanders, civilians were being armed. Police in lorries had toured Port Said handing out new Czech weapons, some still in their packing grease, to anyone who cared to take them—patriots, criminals and small boys as well. By the afternoon these weapons were in use, some for a little desultory sniping, some to shoot other small boys, some to pay off old scores but some just tucked under the bed for a rainy day. To the subsequent fury of the police who had helped to distribute them, other weapons fell into the hands of prisoners from the Port Said gaol, who owed their escape to the damage inflicted on the building by an allied rocket attack.

Following the trucks from which these weapons were being distributed were loudspeaker vans proclaiming that the Russians were speeding to the aid of Egypt and that atomic bombs were already falling on Paris and London. Although there is no sound evidence to suggest that the Russians helped to organise these actions, their consul in Port Said, Anatoly Tchikov, was certainly not being idle. There are a variety of accounts of his driving around Port Said helping to distribute arms and exhorting the people to resist their attackers, but most have been plagiarised. Tchikov was a close friend of Rashdi and spoke Arabic well and it would have been in keeping with his character to demonstrate in such an energetic fashion Soviet solidarity with the Egyptians. El

Moguy was not at the time a free agent, but he did afterwards insist that Tchikov took no part in distributing the weapons and that the announcers in actual fact had a free hand to say what they wished over the loudspeakers.[23] This may well have been so. So far as can be discovered, no eye-witness of Tchikov's activities was ever produced.

Throughout the subsequent occupation, Tchikov was to make good use of his diplomatic status to move constantly around the Egyptian part of Port Said and whatever he may have been doing, he was certainly not persuading the Egyptians to forgive and forget. In the end his behaviour became so aggravating that he was given a permanent escort of British soldiers, who followed him about in a pair of Land Rovers whenever he set foot outside his front door. It was, a senior British staff officer explained to him, merely for his own protection.

Nevertheless, that night of 5 November Russia did, for the first time, intervene directly in the conflict. Separate letters were delivered to Eden, Mollet and Ben-Gurion from Bulganin, the Soviet Premier, the texts of which had already been made public over the radio. The letter to Eden contained the warning that the Soviet Government were "filled with determination to use force to crush the aggressors and to restore peace in the East." There was also some vague talk about rockets.[24] The threat, couched in the most undiplomatic language, came as a surprise. For the first five days of the conflict, Soviet comment both at the United Nations and over the radio had been comparatively restrained, more so in fact than that of the United States, but at last it seemed to have dawned upon the Russians that the Americans were genuine in their opposition to the French and British action. It must have been hard for them to believe their good fortune: their enemies had split. It was also the opportunity they so badly needed to divert attention from what was happening in Budapest.

For all that, the Russians did not go so far as to give direct assistance to the Egyptians. If a document shown to Love in the Egyptian military archives is to be believed, Khrushchev did that same day inform the Egyptian Ambassador in Moscow that Russia could not offer material help because of geographical obstacles and that it was for Egypt to strengthen her will to resist.[25] After all, in 1956, there was little the Soviet Union could do: there were no Russian ships in the Mediterranean and with Egyptian airfields under continuous allied attack, any assistance which could be brought to bear would have had little more than a marginal effect. Neither Eden nor Mollet took the Russian attempt at intimidation too seriously, although it did revive the fear that "volunteers" might interfere. But, in any case, the allies were now committed to landing; they could hardly have halted the invasion fleet and left the parachutists to their fate.

From the military standpoint, the situation in both Port Said and Port Fuad at the end of the first day's fighting looked promising. Resistance in Port Fuad had been overcome. To the south of Port Said, the more important of the two bridges at Raswa was intact and in French hands: the road leading south was open and apparently undefended. Furthermore, with their control of the waterworks, the French had Port Said in a stranglehold and all their successes had only cost them ten men killed and thirty wounded. To the west, the British held Gamil airfield, but 3 Para was not strong enough to occupy Port Said on its own and was now running out of ammunition. Patrols had reached the edge of the town but had then been withdrawn to the eastern side of the sewage farm, where the company holding it was to spend a malodorous night devoured by mosquitos. There had been no point in consolidating positions further east at a possible cost of more casualties, as a withdrawal would have had to have been carried out the next morning to avoid the effects of the naval bombardment.

In Dayan's contemptuous phrase, "after a lengthy incubation, two chicks had finally burst through".[26] If, however, the success of these two chicks had been quickly reinforced by air, the whole of Port Said might have been in allied hands that first evening, but there was a strange absence of determination, or perhaps just an obstinate insistence that the seaborne landing should take place as planned: a proposal from Beaufre to reinforce his troops at Raswa was refused on the specious grounds that there was no air cover available, even though the second drop was, at the time, taking place less than a mile away.[27]

In the event, it mattered little. What was to happen the next day was to be a total irrelevance.

ALLIED LAND FORCES: *Operation MUSKETEER* (Principal Units Engaged Only)

5 November 1956

3rd Bn Parachute Regiment (Br) : parachuted PORT SAID (Gamil Airfield)
2e Régiment de Parachutistes Coloniaux (Fr) :
(i) parachuted PORT SAID (southern exits)
(ii) parachuted PORT FUAD

6 November 1956

40 Royal Marine Commando (Br) :
42 Royal Marine Commando (Br) : assault-landed PORT SAID beaches
C Sqn 6 Royal Tank Regiment (Br) :

Commandos Marine (Fr) :
1er Régiment Etranger Parachutiste (Fr) : landed PORT FUAD beaches

45 Royal Marine Commando (Br) : helicopter-landed PORT SAID

2nd Bn Parachute Regiment (Br) : landed PORT SAID. Advanced EL CAP

6 Royal Tank Regiment (less C Squadron) (Br) : landed PORT SAID. A Squadron advanced EL CAP

Note—This table is intended to show only the principal "teeth" units engaged in the assault upon Port Said/Port Fuad and should be read in conjunction with the maps. It omits a number of support units (both British and French), such as artillery and engineers, which played an essential role in the operation. Nor have those elements of 3 Infantry Division, which relieved the British assault units and maintained the occupation of Port Said in difficult and uncomfortable circumstances, been listed although they are noted in the text.

CHAPTER TWELVE

THE ASSAULT FROM THE SEA

As FAR as the British were concerned, the plan for the second day's fighting was comparatively straightforward. At Port Said itself, 40 and 42 Commandos were on 6 November to assault the beaches in the first wave, their dividing line being the small pier which lay in front of the Casino. Supporting them was a squadron of waterproofed Centurion tanks of 6 R.T.R.; in reserve was 45 Commando, helicopter borne and ready to land where most needed. On the right the task of 42 Commando was to push south through the town in order to join up with 3 Para, which would be resuming its advance from the sewage farm. 40 Commando on the left was to move through the business and shopping areas which flanked the Canal to link up with the French at the inner basin bridge, securing on their way the Abbas Hilmi Basin where the rest of 16 Parachute Brigade was scheduled to land later. Then 2 Para and 6 R.T.R. would drive south down the Canal towards Qantara.

For those aboard the allied invasion fleet, Tuesday 6 November brought an early start. Clark, the gunner captain, who was supporting 42 Royal Marine Commando and who had crawled out of his bunk at 0200 hours with a mouth still sour from the surfeit of cigarettes smoked as he had pored over the bombardment tables an hour or two before, was rather less than enthusiastic about the naval fare served to him for breakfast—a large plateful of kidneys swimming in thick gravy with boiled potatoes and onions on the side. The sudden conversion of the wardroom into an operating theatre as he was eating, with a white-coated surgeon laying out blood-plasma and instruments, completed the ruin of any remaining appetite.

A little later, standing upright in his Buffalo amphibian and watching the approaching shore, Clark was greeted by an impressive display of the destructive power of high explosive—the bombardment, or support fire as it had now been christened.

Half a mile away, rolling clouds of grey smoke from the blazing Casino building and a line of beach-huts effectively concealed the shore-line. Flashes in the murk marked the places where more shells were exploding. Overhead, the naval fighters screamed earthwards and proliferated destruction. Only about one-tenth of the potential of the naval guns was being used but the 4·5s of the destroyers and the guns and rockets of the aircraft were quite enough to neutralise the two-mile stretch of beach. The 15-inch guns of the French *Jean Bart* and the 6-inch guns of the cruisers would have been an unnecessary addition. Clark described the Buffaloes as waddling through an "inferno".[1] Stockwell called it "saturation fire".[2] The original plan had certainly over-insured.

The Buffaloes were a mere 100 yards from the shore when the jet fighters made their last run along the beaches, a little too close for the ease of mind of the men in the assault craft and the result of a slight error in timing. However, when the machines crawled up the beach just before 0700 hours and green-bereted Royal Marines jumped out, only the occasional shot smacked into the armoured sides of their vehicles. The Egyptians had not stayed to suffer the bombardment, but had withdrawn into the houses behind. For the present, the only danger facing the attackers came from the stocks of Egyptian ammunition exploding in the flames of the beach-huts.

The first of the waterproofed Centurions of 6 R.T.R. waded ashore a few minutes late, as the two commandos were closing up towards their first objectives, the line of buildings fronting the beach. When it came to discarding the waterproofing of the tanks it was found that the explosive bolts which held the material in place had rusted. Sledge-hammers had to be brought into use and it was thirty minutes before the two leading troops were on their way to support their respective commandos. Scattered among the buildings and dressed now like their comrades of the previous day in the all-enveloping *galabiyas*, the Egyptian soldiers were sniping at the Royal Marines from every street-corner and making good use of the disinclination of the British to fire at what seemed at first sight to be civilians. In the early stages some marines were even a little chary of using force to break into houses in which snipers might be concealed, but they soon managed to get the better of such inhibitions. Equally many of the Egyptian civilians felt little fear for their invaders, whose characteristics they knew so well from the past. Clark describes how they were soon swarming around the Royal Marine posts, asking for food and medical aid.[3]

Despite opposition by snipers, 42 Commando had by 1000 hours traversed the boulevards and squares to reach the gasworks on the outskirts of the town, the final objective which had been set them. On their left, 40 Commando had edged along the waterfront, passing in turn such familiar land-marks as the de Lesseps statue, Simon Arzt's famous store and the Canal Company Offices. Again, most road junctions had to be cleared of snipers and a detachment of police had to be overcome at their Port Station, for which they fought sturdily. From Gamil, 3 Para, who had helped the Marines to land by enfilading the beaches with their medium machine-guns, were once again pushing into the town.

No area could be considered safe just because troops had passed through. Parties of troops on foot, and unarmoured vehicles, provided attractive targets to Egyptians in first-floor windows, and it was too easy for snipers to lie low and come up firing half an hour later. To have cleared every building would have taken far too long and occupied far more men than were available and it would also have resulted in more civilian deaths and damage to property.

It soon became clear that the reserve, 45 Commando, would be needed to help speed up the clearing of the city. Their arrival was not without incident. The first helicopter carrying the commanding officer, who was flying ahead of his men with his personal staff so as to reconnoitre the ground, found its landing ground obscured by smoke and set off to find somewhere else. The Sports Stadium, lying to the west, seemed suitable and here the pilot landed his passengers. Perhaps the Egyptian defenders of the Stadium had been nonplussed by the sudden arrival of the helicopter, for they waited before it had disembarked its load and taken off before opening fire at it.

Made clear that something was wrong by a bullet nicking his finger, the pilot returned to the Stadium and the Royal Marine party scrambled back on board. The helicopter, now with thirty-two bullet-holes in it, went in to land its passengers once more, this time in the shadow of de Lesseps statue on the waterfront and the pilot radioed the other score or so aircraft, which were orbiting the carriers about eight miles away, to start the lift. In two and a half hours, the complete commando, together with its stores, had been landed. It was the first unit to have flown into action in rotary-winged aircraft, and a strange sight it had been. The helicopters had not been built for the purpose. The Sycamores could carry only three military passengers, all sitting on the floor. The centre one hung on to his two companions, whose legs hung out on either side; this anchor man balanced on his knees six mortar-bombs (a load of sixty pounds), while the other two were each encumbered with a three-foot 106 mm anti-tank gun shell.

It was sad that the fates had not been appeased by the escape from the Sports Stadium. As the assembled commando was preparing to move off into the town, a Fleet Air Arm Wyvern was called down from its cab rank on to an erroneous map reference, the point where the headquarters of the commando had just gathered. One marine was killed and another fifteen wounded, including the commanding officer and his intelligence officer, more casualties than the commando was to suffer in the whole of the subsequent fighting. The same aircraft then continued on its way to do more damage among Brigade Headquarters and 42 Commando further along the road. It appears that the air contact team with the commando had not been given control of the strike: had it been, the fatal error would not have occurred.

Dawn brought a series of aggravations to the men of 3 Para. First they were strafed by a MIG, the only hostile plane to be seen that day; the men on the ground had watched it approach, confident that it was either British or French until a stream of green and white tracer bounced along the runway and they saw its Egyptian markings. Next, breakfasts had to be abandoned uneaten when C Company was moved at short notice back to the cemeteries. But aggravation hardly does justice to the feelings of a group listening to one of their radios, the frequency of which had been switched to catch the B.B.C. news. After a report about the "heavy fighting" in which their battalion had been involved, the announcer went on to describe the frenzied uproar of the previous evening in Parliament when the rights and wrongs of the fighting had been debated. Behind the listening soldiers lay the shrouded bodies of two of their friends, killed the day before and awaiting a plane to fly them to Cyprus for burial.[4]

After once again clearing the cemeteries of enemy, by 1000 hours the men of 3 Para had winkled the last remaining snipers out of the flats and coastguard barracks which the Wyverns had shattered the day before. Ahead of them the road now forked at the outskirts of Port Said, with its northern branch continuing towards the beaches over which the commandos had landed and its southern running along the edge of the close-packed houses and the narrow streets of Arab Town. At the fork in the road lay the Ophthalmic Hospital, with the miserable *bidonville* of Shanty Town and a police station nearby. Here 3 Para met more opposition and lost more men wounded. An Egyptian machine-gun set up among the hospital buildings was the cause of the terrified inmates being caught in the cross-fire of the battle. Shanty Town, ignited at one end by a shell from a destroyer and at the other by a recoilless anti-tank-gun, exploded into flames and in the course of the day burned itself to the ground. Along the side of the Manzala Canal, the sole escape route from the crowded streets of Port Said, a mass of refugees streamed south, among them many Egyptian soldiers dressed indistinguishably from the civilians. This was as far as 3 Para got that day. There was little or no point in penetrating the rabbit-warren of Arab Town.

Meanwhile, the rest of 6 R.T.R.'s Centurions and the other units of 16 Parachute Brigade, which together formed the break-out force, were still afloat in their transports, waiting to be called forward to land. The L.S.T.s and troopships which had brought them from Malta and Cyprus were to have sailed into the Abbas Hilmi Basin to off-load about an hour after the commandos had landed but this was no longer possible. Between the Basin and the mouth of the Canal lay the block-ships sunk by the Egyptians, an effective barrier to anything of the draft or beam of the troop-carrying ships. The naval task force responsible for port operations consisted of two destroyers, two mine-sweepers, a survey vessel and a couple of tugs. The Port Commandant-designate was aboard and he was now faced with the problem of using the rather more rudimentary facilities at the seaward end of the Canal for berthing and off-loading. After some delay while the mine-sweepers finished the job of clearing the sea ahead of the assault waves, the landing-ships began to off-load at the fishing harbour, the quay nearest to the open sea. As they did so, diving teams were still busy searching for mines. It was soon discovered that the height of the sea-wall near the burning Casino was such that landing-ships could unload there too and this permitted the next squadron of Centurions to be landed without further delay. The task of this squadron was to join the French at Raswa but an unfortunate decision to deploy the tanks across the golf links led to their being bogged down in the soft going. Extracting them led to further delay and it was some hours before they could be assembled in front of the French position. Here they picked up a small party of *paras* and they then started down the road to the El Tina station on the way towards Qantara.

As the day progressed, 40 Commando met increasingly stubborn resistance. After it had captured the group of offices belonging to the Canal Company, the next objective was a complex of warehouses and at the Customs' Warehouse the Egyptians fought stubbornly. Although Centurions were brought up to engage the defenders at point-blank range, they managed to kill two British officers and wound a number of marines before being overrun. But the main Egyptian resistance in this area was centred on Navy House, a massive stone building, previously the headquarters of the Royal Navy. Here the 130-strong Egyptian garrison put up a very fine fight indeed. It soon became clear that the building could be stormed only at heavy cost, so the now exhausted commandos were pulled back out of harm's way and the Fleet Air Arm was ordered to finish off the job, despite a slight twinge of sentimental regret among some of the senior ranks of the Royal Navy at having to destroy an edifice which for so many years had been closely associated with the Senior Service. During the afternoon and early evening, successive strikes of fighter aircraft dived upon Navy House. It seemed impossible that anything could survive the cannon fire and rockets, but the next day, when the fighting was over, twenty survivors emerged from the building. Inside lay thirty of their dead.

On the other side of the Canal, the French were having a comparatively quiet time. Not until 0500 hours that morning had confirmation been received in the *Gustave-Zédé* that Port Fuad was firmly in the hands of 2 R.P.C. This meant that the French seaborne landing would be unopposed and the preliminary naval bombardment was able to be cancelled. Due to signal delays there were then some very anxious moments before the shelling (which was due to start at 0600 hours) was countermanded. In the event, "overs" from the British guns firing at Port Said fell in Port Fuad, much to the consternation of the men of 2 R.P.C. who assumed that their own ships were firing at them. This danger from "overs" had been anticipated; it was one of the reasons why there had been opposition to the idea of capturing Port Fuad ahead of time.

Except for some sporadic sniping, the only fighting that day in Port Fuad was at a police post a mile to the east of the town which the Foreign Legion captured at 0800 hours at a cost of two men killed. The seventy-two Egyptian defenders were either killed or captured and a quantity of useful stores taken, including half a dozen anti-tank guns.

At Raswa, on the other side of the water, 2 R.P.C. were much more busy. The sole surviving bridge which they held was the main escape route from Port Said, and there were a lot of Egyptian troops intent on using it, including some who were ready to fight to do so. Time and again during the morning small parties of infantry, sometimes supported by tanks and self-propelled guns, attacked the French, who had little difficulty in holding on to their positions with the help of air strikes but lost quite a few men in doing so.

During lulls in the fighting, *les paras* were sent to collect the 'chutes which still littered the open ground behind their positions on which they had landed the previous day. To the French, the parachute was a valuable piece of equipment, to be retrieved and used again, while to the British it was expendable after an operational jump. When the French naval officer who was in charge of the air contact team attached to 3 Para and a close friend of the battalion, saw a soldier sawing at his 'chute with a jack-knife, he was moved to protest at such wanton destruction merely to line a slit trench. "You know how much a parachute costs," he demanded. "Yes, sir," came the reply, "Ninety pounds."[5] In only one eventuality did the French neglect to recover their chutes. On the dropping zone at Raswa lay two silk cocoons, one white and one green. By tradition, *le para* was buried, not in a coffin, but in his parachute.[6]

Around 0900 hours both Stockwell and Beaufre heard from their respective commanders in Port Said and Port Fuad that the Egyptians wanted to surrender.[7] Accordingly, about an hour later, a launch left H.M.S. *Tyne* carrying the two generals together with the Sea and Air Task Force Commanders to receive the Egyptian capitulation. As the launch entered the outer harbour, fires still burned from the early morning bombardment, a pall of smoke from the blazing oil tanks covered the town, and a British Centurion could be seen in action ashore. However, instead of landing its very important passengers at the fishing harbour, where L.S.T.s were unloading tanks and equipment, for some unexplained reason the launch carried on towards the offices of the Canal Company, which the Egyptians were still defending. Stockwell described what followed: "As we were milling around off the town in a motor launch, looking for somewhere to land, we were smartened up by an Egyptian light machine-gun, which put a series of bursts around us, one hitting the wooden bridge where we were standing. This brought the comment from the Admiral 'I don't think, General, they are quite ready to receive us yet!' " Fortunately no one was hit and the launch quickly beat a retreat to the fishing harbour. As Beaufre reflected with sardonic amusement, if the Egyptians had held their fire, the valuable party could have been taken prisoner as it landed. With some justification he felt that the incident hardly inspired confidence.

The four senior officers then set off on foot into Port Said. Finding their way to the headquarters of the Royal Marine Commando Brigade, they borrowed a jeep and drove to the Italian Consulate, where, they had gathered, the Egyptians were waiting to surrender. In charge there they found Count Vicente Mareri, who was said to have been the moving force behind these negotiations.

The Italian Consul appears to have been the one person in Port Said to have taken the threat of invasion seriously, even after the allies started to bomb Cairo and the Canal Zone. In the usual manner, some of the more wealthy had left but most people took little notice of what was happening, despite the belligerent warnings which were being broadcast over the radio. The afternoon before the airborne troops landed, the waterfront cafés and promenades were crammed with the usual Sunday crowds when fighters swept down to blast the anti-aircraft and coastal guns along the harbours and jetties. The fire was so accurate that only military installations were hit, but even after this display of guns being flung in the air some cafés stayed open and some shops carried on business.

Mareri, who had seen the Japanese invade Shanghai and witnessed similar horrors in Saigon, had stocked his Consulate as a refugee centre for the Europeans of the city, turned the Italian school next door into an improvised hospital and had planned to move as many families as possible from their scattered houses to whatever protection the diplomatic immunity of the Consulate might provide. When the parachutes floated down at Gamil and Raswa, Italian, Greek and French families hurried through the din of the fighting and struggled at the doorway to get in. For the rest of that day Mareri toured Port Said, ferrying Europeans of all nationalities to what he hoped might prove to be a place of safety for them. That evening there were bullet holes in the windscreen and roof of his car, but hundreds of people were sleeping in the Consul's offices, corridors and garage.

There are a variety of accounts of what the four allied commanders found at the Consulate after they had clambered over the recumbent bodies of these refugees. Beaufre described how they discovered the Egyptian Governor slumped in a chair, exhausted and unhappy, and lacking the means to arrange a cease-fire but he named the Governor inaccurately as Brigadier El Moguy. Others say the Egyptian brigadier was a prisoner of the Royal Marines at the time, having been captured by them earlier that morning (there was quite a lot of confusion about the identities of the various Egyptian military and civilian leaders in Port Said). Stockwell states that they merely hung about for a time without anyone turning up, a statement which is repeated in Keightley's despatches. Keightley blames the continuation of the fighting on the failure of the Egyptians to come to the rendezvous, but there was now little chance of any cease-fire sticking without the approval of the Egyptian Government and this was hardly likely to be forthcoming in the face of the propaganda value of the French and British having to fight their way through a densely inhabited and peaceful city. Mareri's efforts to bring about a cease-fire were clearly doomed from the start.

CHAPTER THIRTEEN

EXPLOITATION

WHEN STOCKWELL and Beaufre returned from the Italian Consulate to the Commando Brigade Headquarters, having separated from their naval and air force colleagues, they learned for the first time of the link-up between the tanks of 6 R.T.R. and Chateau-Jobert's parachutists at Raswa. Beaufre was aggravated also to discover that his squadron of A.M.X. tanks, which had been landed with the leading elements of his amphibious group during the morning at the fishing harbour, had been commandeered by Stockwell to protect the Commando Brigade Headquarters. This was quite a legitimate act on the part of the Task Force Commander but a trifle tactless in view of the rather delicate relationship between the two allied commanders.

Beaufre now left Stockwell and carried on over to Port Fuad to meet Massu who had come ashore to take command of his airborne division. Borrowing a craft from their amphibious group, the two French generals then sailed down the Canal to visit Chateau-Jobert, on this occasion keeping well clear of the Canal Company Offices. Butler joined them by helicopter at Raswa, where Beaufre co-ordinated the orders for the next phase of the operation, the exploitation to Qantara, something which Stockwell had already done in Port Said. It was all a little complicated with the Army Task Force Commander issuing orders to the British component of his force, and his Deputy doing the same to the French units. The complications might have been less if it had not been necessary to deploy both British and French units along the single road for the break-out towards Qantara, but because of it national susceptibilities had to be considered. There were also too many generals and other senior officers milling about ashore.[1]

It was arranged that Butler would be in charge of the

advanced guard of troops from his own brigade and that these would consist of 2 Para with supporting troops under command, including the Centurion squadron already at El Tina. In overall command would be Massu, travelling with the main body, following Butler's troops along the road with elements travelling along the waterway in amphibious craft. Standing by in Cyprus was the third battalion of 2 R.P.C., ready if need be to be dropped at first light at Qantara. Also in Cyprus was the whole of the third regiment of Massu's division, the *1ᵉʳ Régiment de Chasseurs Parachutistes* (1 R.C.P.), available to assault Ismailia when the Noratlases returned from Qantara. Butler's objective was the Abu Sueir airfield for which he would make as the French thrust towards Qantara.

Afloat some miles offshore, 2 Para had been waiting for some time to get into battle. Not until shortly after noon (more than nine hours after reveille) did the *Empire Parkeston*— a Harwich–Hook-of-Holland ferry—together with her accompanying L.S.T.s, start to creep towards the shore. As the soldiers watched from their disembarkation stations, the whole of Port Said appeared to be in flames. From the oil tanks along the Canal to the blazing huts of Shanty Town, a thin pall of smoke drifted from right to left across the skyline. Around them were countless ships and craft of every size and shape and overhead little helicopters were fussily ferrying their loads backwards and forwards between the aircraft-carriers and the shore.

As the ships edged into the Canal mouth, the noise of battle could be heard—odd bursts of machine-gun fire passing overhead and the dull crump of mortars and anti-tank guns reverberated back from among the buildings. Above naval fighters screamed, wheeling and darting in and out of the smoke, firing their rockets from what seemed to be masthead height into Navy House, half a mile behind the funnels and superstructures of the sunken blockships poking out of the water. Ahead, the Casino Palace Hotel was not in the same state as some of the returning travellers remembered it from more tranquil days and nights.

Because the leading L.S.T. to touch the wharf some hundred yards to the south of the de Lesseps statue had difficulty in lowering its ramp, the passengers of the *Empire Parkeston* were the first ashore. They scrambled down the nets which draped the ship's sides into the waiting lighters, an uncomfortable feat for fully laden infantrymen, despite being fit and well trained. By the time everyone had collected ashore, the light was fading fast, incongruously so, as watches suggested it was no more than mid-afternoon, the consequence of fighting the war in G.M.T. rather than in local time,[2] and when the battalion set off into Port Said, led by the Guards Independent Parachute Company in their Champs, no one whose advice was sought was quite certain where either the commandos or the Egyptians might be found. In small groups, keeping close to the buildings, the men doubled across road intersections, jumping or stepping over bodies, debris and piles of boxes of Czech self-loading rifles, most of them empty but a few still intact. They were little hindered by the shooting which seemed to be going on all around them, but it was 1930 hours (local time) before they had all concentrated at Raswa, where the occupants of the leading Champs had at first found difficulty in persuading their allies that they were British and not Egyptian.

With hindsight, it does seem to have taken rather a long time to start this exploitation towards Qantara. The previous day the patrol of the Guards Independent Company, which had dropped with the French, had ventured at least six miles down the road without finding any opposition. That same morning they had returned to set up a road-block some nine miles from Port Said, where throughout the afternoon, they had collected a miscellaneous bag of Egyptian soldiers, sailors and policemen, some more effectively disguised than others. Only towards the late afternoon did a properly organised Egyptian patrol approach them, which the guardsmen, who showed a laudable reluctance to kill if they could possibly avoid doing so, warned to return by the way it had come when it was thirty yards away. The Egyptians complied.

Massu's reproaches in this respect are bitter. He could not understand why Gamil airfield, once cleared by 3 Para, was not used for rapid air reinforcement of the bridgehead gained; he could not understand why 2 Para, once ashore, were not ferried to the waiting Centurions of 6 R.T.R. at El Tina by the available helicopters instead of laboriously making their way on foot through the snipers of Port Said. But above all he saw the greatest fault as the failure during the afternoon of D+1 to parachute the French regiments, waiting by their aircraft in Cyprus, on Qantara and Ismailia.[3]

A little later the first squadron of 6 R.T.R. drove through the road-block, the French parachutists mounted on the backs of the tanks. Despite an attempt by the Guards to wave them down to pass on the news that the road ahead was clear, the tanks trundled blindly on to fight a futile battle against an empty pill-box some half a mile down the road, much to the amusement of the guardee spectators. At El Tina, a little further on still, the tanks halted for good, having been ordered to venture no further because they lacked adequate infantry support.

Back in Port Said were a dozen or more of the large amphibian Buffaloes in which the leading wave of Royal Marines had come ashore. If these craft had been moved to Raswa under tank protection and there joined by 45 Commando, which could have landed safely on the French dropping zone, a balanced force would have been available strong enough to reach the outskirts of Qantara before nightfall. Also if the subsequent reports about the absence of Egyptian troops in the area were correct, the troops might well have reached Ismailia. Naval strike aircraft could then have crushed anything which tried to delay the armoured column, or the amphibians could have bypassed pockets of resistance to take the enemy in the rear.

To have pushed on in this manner might have delayed the cleaning up of Port Said but there were other units waiting offshore which could have been landed and used for this purpose, among them 1 Para, the third battalion of Butler's brigade. In any case, there were plenty of French troops already ashore, in Port Fuad alone the equivalent of several battalions with little or nothing to do except deal with a few snipers. The landing-craft were small enough to bypass the sunken ships blocking the Canal; embarked in these and travelling in the lee of the tanks, the Frenchmen also could have been in Qantara by nightfall if they had started in good time.

There were two difficulties. First, there was little sense of urgency except among the British and French airborne and commando leaders. Secondly, no one was really in control of the battle. The task of coordinating an advance such as this, with so many unknown factors, was not at all simple. Stockwell had reserved to himself the decision to order the breakout, but for much of the day he was out of touch with his fellow Task Force Commanders and all his subordinates except Butler and Madoc. A lieutenant-general loose ashore in such circumstances without a proper staff, transport or communications is like a conductor standing in the middle of the orchestra pit with his hands tied behind his back.

In the event the delay in exploiting the success of the landing did not matter. Although none of the allied commanders in the Mediterranean had yet been told anything, they had nothing to gain from occupying the rest of the Canal Zone. That morning in London at 0945 hours the British Cabinet had already decided that the fighting must be stopped. Sadly, many more people were to be killed before this could be achieved.

Eden had not been alarmed by Bulganin's empty threats, but he was now dealing with other pressures more difficult to contain. Ever since the ultimatum had been delivered to the Israelis and the Egyptians, he had been assailed daily in Parliament by an opposition frustrated in its search for the collusion it suspected. Against these penetrating attacks Eden and his ministers could defend themselves only with tendentious half-truths. Although his majority in the House was safe enough, he knew that he had lost the support of some of the more influential members of his own party. Nutting had resigned, Monckton had left the Ministry of Defence in circumstances which have not been sufficiently explained and Sir Edward Boyle at the Treasury was also about to leave the Government. The Prime Minister's Press Secretary, William Clark, was about to resign. Nutting had only with difficulty prevented a number of senior Foreign Office officials from taking a similar course and at one stage all three of his junior ministerial colleagues appeared to be on the point of walking out with him.[4]

But the main factor in the Cabinet's decision to halt

hostilities was neither Soviet posturing, the insults of the Opposition, a divided Conservative Party nor international disapprobation. A run on the pound had started, at the time an apparent calamity, not the regular occurrence which the country was later to accept with resignation. After a sound financial start to the year, reserves had begun to fall during September. The momentum accelerated until 279 million dollars vanished during November, a paltry sum in today's currency but at the time fifteen per cent of the country's gold and dollar reserves. Withdrawal of sterling balances by Nationalist China and India contributed towards the losses but there was also heavy selling in a number of markets, including Wall Street.

American aid and support was needed if the pound was to be prevented from falling further and with the Canal blocked and the Syrian pipeline severed, oil would have to be bought with hard currency if British industry was not to collapse. But it is difficult to persuade one's partner to provide loans if one has ignored his advice and admonitions.

For months Eisenhower had been pleading with Eden to show restraint, always in a civil and friendly fashion. The bombing of Egypt had, however, enraged him and this annoyance was compounded by the ignorance in which Britain and France had kept his administration since the Israelis had mobilised. By the time they attacked Port Said, the President had lost all sympathy with his two European allies. In his view, they were endangering world peace, not for their stated aim of ensuring the safety of the Canal but merely to discharge a vendetta against Nasser. And, of course, it was the eve of American Presidential election. Nonetheless, his attitude towards the Russian threats was as robust as Eden's, even though there was a certain amount of panic in official circles in Washington. But some Americans, while sharing their President's attitude, were puzzled by the British decision to halt their advance so suddenly. "To the amazement of many Americans, including myself", wrote Murphy, "when the operation seemed about to achieve its goal, Prime Minister Eden decided to quit short of the objective".[5]

Perhaps Eden quit because he no longer possessed either the will or the physical strength to carry on. He had set out to destroy Nasser but with world opinion so solidly behind him, the Egyptian President seemed more firmly in control of his country than ever. Physically the Prime Minister was all but finished even though he had displayed remarkable resilience for a man who at his age four weeks earlier had been running a temperature of 106 degrees. Back at his desk forty-eight hours after the attack, he was to keep going, but all the time the illness was sapping his strength.

Divided as the British Cabinet was in its decision to stop the war, the French were to prove a little more difficult to bring into line. As soon as the Cabinet meeting was over, Eden had telephoned Mollet who asked for time to consult his colleagues. After discussing the possibility of finishing the job themselves, the French ministers were obliged to accept the inevitable. But the events left a lasting bitterness, and was yet another proof of the historic truth that Albion was not to be trusted. During the next twenty years memories of Suez were to do much to influence French attitudes towards their partners in NATO and E.E.C.

Before the Cabinet had met that morning, Macmillan, the Chancellor of the Exchequer, had telephoned Washington to ask for financial help. From the reply he received it was clear to him that this would be forthcoming only if a cease-fire was put into force before midnight.[6] The Americans would then support a loan of 500 million dollars from the International Monetary Fund, would defer interest payments due to them that year and support borrowing within the United States against the backing of Britain's 1,000 million dollars' worth of securities.

The country had now to be told. Despite the reservations and opposition from so many quarters to the Government's actions, most people had been persuaded of the need to invade Egypt, and there was no way of persuading them now that it had all been a mistake and that the fighting had to be stopped as soon as it had started. It was a grim decision for the Cabinet to have to take, and in many ways a brave one.

In some circumstances it is often easier to allow mistakes to agglomerate rather than to admit error and make a change of course. The pity was that the Government decided to try to justify its decision on the grounds that there was no purpose in fighting on when the war between Israel and Egypt had ended.[7] It was a specious excuse when everything except for the concluding battle at Sharm el-Sheikh had ended even before the allied troops had landed.

There was a way of easing the humiliation of such a volte-face. That evening, when the Prime Minister announced the cease-fire to the House of Commons, he could say that the Cabinet had made the decision on the assumption that a competent United Nations force was being prepared and that he had proposed that Anglo-French technicians should start straight away to clear the obstructions from the Canal so as to open the waterway. The raising of such a U.N. force had first been mentioned by Eden in the House on 1 November. The following day at the United Nations, Lester Pearson, then Canadian Minister for External Affairs (who later received the Nobel Peace Prize for the part he played), developed the idea. It received support from the Norwegians and others, and two days later the General Assembly accepted a Canadian resolution requesting the Secretary-General to submit a plan for a United Nations Emergency Force; the next day, 5 November, he was able to report that already Colombia, Norway and New Zealand had offered troops and his recommendations were accepted that a United Nations Command should be formed and preliminary administrative preparations be made. The Prime Minister's announcement first stupefied the Commons and then evoked the over-enthusiastic response customary at such emotional and highly-charged times. Only a group of Tory backbenchers stayed stubbornly glum when their leader claimed that the fighting could now stop because the aims of the allies had been achieved.

The troops at Port Said were also stupefied but not quite so jubilant. During the late evening, the first news about the cease-fire had arrived by way of the spare radio sets which had been tuned to the B.B.C. It was an odd way of hearing that the war they were fighting was over, hardly conducive to confidence in the higher command. For most, the gratification of learning that their hope of surviving the following day had improved was nullified by the frustration of stopping before the job was finished and the knowledge that all their effort and all their losses, few as they may have been, had been wasted. As usual, the French were sure of betrayal; it was worse even than Indo-China, *les paras* fulminated.[8] Many of the servicemen were certain that it could not possibly be a general cease-fire but no more than a local truce to save civilian lives in Port Said; after all there had been talk enough of cease-fires during the previous thirty-six hours.

At 1900 hours the official order reached Keightley's head-quarters that a cease-fire would be timed for five hours later at midnight G.M.T. It was some time before Stockwell heard about it. Stranded ashore in the dark, after the helicopter had flown home to roost (as he put it), he was obliged to hitch a lift back to H.M.S. *Tyne* from the Royal Marine coxswain of a landing-craft. No sooner were they clear of the breakwater than they ran into a heavy sea. It was pitch dark and *Tyne*'s position was four miles offshore. Then the steering gear broke and the pumps failed. But fortune favoured them. The first ship they hailed was *Tyne*, and under way at that. A false alarm from Cyprus that pseudo-Egyptian Soviet submarines were on the prowl had caused the Admiral to order his fleet to disperse and lights to be extinguished. Not surprisingly, Stockwell found the Admiral a little tetchy about his inexplicable and prolonged absence. A few seconds later Stockwell's Chief-of-Staff appeared, carrying a signal which read simply "Cease-fire at midnight".[9]

Stockwell's deputy had a similar experience. Beaufre's launch took an hour to reach the *Gustave-Zédé*. After clamber-ing up the pilot's ladder in a sea so rough that his signaller was nearly drowned, he was presented with a signal just received from Barjot telling him that a cease-fire was in prospect for 1900 hours, the time at which the signal had been handed to him. This he ignored, assuming that it referred to the abortive cease-fire which they had been trying to negotiate ashore. He was soon disillusioned . . . by a B.B.C. broadcast, not by his immediate superior. It was a further five hours before the message from Stockwell reached him to provide official confirmation of the B.B.C. announcement.[10]

Battles will go awry if commanders absent themselves from their headquarters for too long and the risks are compounded if they take their deputies with them. With their communications unreliable or non-existent as well, they can be a positive liability to their own side. At Port Said that evening the danger was not of losing a battle but of not stopping one in time. If the fighting had not been halted, the fighting troops might at least have suffered less frustration and exasperation.

Meanwhile 2 Para and the Guards Independent Company were pushing down the Treaty Road towards Qantara at the best speed they could muster, having taken leave of the French at Raswa at 2030 hours. The causeway along which they were travelling ran from Port Said to their objective like an arrow-shaft, forty-five kilometres long and some 200 metres wide. Alongside the banks was the Canal Company's Road; apart from the occasional signal station, its only landmarks were the signs warning cars to use dipped headlights to avoid dazzling the pilots of the ships. Next to this road was the Sweet Water Canal, Port Said's water supply, where lurked the freshwater snails which carried the liver-fluke parasite, the source of the debilitating bilharzia. A single-track railway had been laid next to the Sweet Water Canal; then came an open strip of sand and scrub. Finally, on the edge of the vast and impassable salt-marshes, was the second or Treaty Road, the axis chosen for the advance of the British parachute battalion group.

Using some of their few Champs to ferry the leading troops and the rest to carry their mortars and heavy machine-guns or to tow the borrowed NATO anti-tank guns, the parachutists made good progress to El Tina, where they found the Centurion squadron leaguered for the night and unaware that a cease-fire had been ordered. In the absence of precise instructions, their commanding officer, who had joined the squadron with his regimental headquarters, had decided against pushing on in the dark with no more than a few French *paras* to support him. Tanks share with cats the enviable quality of curling up and making themselves comfortable in the dark and there was some brisk discussion between the two C.O.s before everyone got moving again. In fact it took an hour, despite the sense of urgency of the officers of the parachute battalion whose orders from their brigadier were to push on as quickly as possible so as to reach Qantara before time ran out at midnight (or 0200 hours by the local reckoning).

Motoring on, with the leading company now mounted on the backs of the tanks and the rest of the battalion carried in a heterogeneous collection of lorries which the Brigade staff had commandeered in the city, the only indications that they were at war were the occasional burnt-out Egyptian vehicles by the roadside, the absence of lights and the road craters caused by the allied naval aircraft bombing. For those who knew this road of old, it even conjured up memories of driving home to one of the Canal garrison towns after dining late and well at some Port Said restaurant or club.

But the cumulative delays of the day prevented the troops reaching Qantara within the time-limit, however much this was somehow or other stretched. Just before the end of the causeway, the advance stopped at the small fishing village of El Cap. Soon dawn broke and the unusual defensive position which political circumstances had forced upon the troops was clear to everyone. Even though the causeway did bulge slightly at this point, it was so narrow that it was only possible to hold the position on a two-platoon front. To the rear stretched the rest of the battalion and supporting troops, with the tanks and trucks spaced along the road, unable to leave the hard shoulders for fear of sinking in the ooze. Weary soldiers struggled to dig slit-trenches in glutinous and evil-smelling mud. Surely, everyone thought, this anti-climax could not be the sole result of so much planning and preparation. Cease-fires there had been before and there seemed to be little reason why this one should not end at any moment, with MIGs swooping along the line of parked vehicles.

The war had ended. The anti-climax, after so much effort and courage had been wasted, had much the same effect on everyone concerned—*poilu* and Royal Marine, general and air marshal. The former, of course, accepted what had happened rather more philosophically, accustomed as they were to being messed about in incomprehensible fashions, but some of the more senior were moved to protest. As Stockwell put it, they were on the verge of complete success and when they were just about to reap the reward for the months of preparation and effort, they were thwarted of their prize.[11] He made the best of it. Butler made a public protest about his frustration, an unusual step for a senior British officer. Eighteen months later Massu told Randolph Churchill that the great remorse of his life was that he had not disregarded his orders and marched to Cairo, or at least to Ismailia.[12] Perhaps it was a portent for his ill-starred future. Even Beaufre, who wrote that he felt that he had been hit by a blow in the stomach, wondered whether he should disregard Stockwell's cease-fire orders. Matters were complicated as he had received in quick succession two telegrams from Barjot, both barely comprehensible. The second one ended with the words "As regards exact timings, greater flexibility is permissible in relation to movement than to cease-fire". These "carefully worded and useless" instructions seemed like a bad joke to Beaufre, but after further thought he decided that to seize Qantara on his own initiative would provide no more than fleeting satisfaction and might even result in a shooting match with the British troops who lay astride the road. Then he remembered the Soviet ultimatum and he realised that prudence, not rashness, was required of him.[13]

OCCUPATION

ON 7 NOVEMBER, the morning after the cease-fire, the main problem facing the allied troops in Port Said and Port Fuad was to restore to normal the life of the two towns, to clear the blockships from the mouth of the Canal and to get the port working once again.

At first sight it was far from encouraging. Although all was quiet in Port Fuad, in Port Said the Royal Marine Commando Brigade, with the help of 3 Para, was still busy clearing up a few remaining snipers. Many of the Egyptian civilians and soldiers who had died in the fighting still lay where they had fallen, the hospitals were crammed with wounded and injured and the water, electricity and sewage services were out of action. Food shops were shut. In the short length of the Canal that lay between Port Said and Port Fuad, the Egyptians had sunk a considerable number of vessels, mostly the dredgers, floating cranes and tugs needed for the operation and maintenance of the waterway. Troops disembarking at Casino Quay could see the upper works of these ships lying on the bottom of the Canal, blocking the passage of all but the smallest craft.

The two allies, who had brought with them civil affairs organisations set up for the purpose, gave immediate help to the Egyptian authorities striving to bring the city back to normal. Army engineers assisted in restoring the water and electricity supplies. The streets were cleaned up and the dead collected and buried. Food, water and medical supplies were distributed from army stocks and in both permanent and makeshift hospitals, British and French doctors and orderlies worked without respite to help the Egyptian staff cope with the influx of casualties.

The largesse of arms which had been so widely distributed in Port Said had to be collected. Some were found by search parties, tucked away in hiding places ready for future use but the scale and severity of the searches was limited by the need to avoid provocation. Reporters were now everywhere, hunting for good stories. Many of the arms had been merely abandoned in the streets by citizens anxious to rid themselves of such embarrassments and some were even handed to friendly-looking journalists; 45 Commando alone collected fifty-seven lorry-loads of assorted weapons and ammunition to be dumped into the sea.

At El Cap, the air of unreality and anti-climax remained. That morning, after months of anticipation and training, the men of 2 Para found themselves barely blooded (as dashing infantry commanders liked to express it) and stranded in the desert with Qantara some four miles away but unattainably beyond their reach. Confirmation of how easily the town could have been captured was soon established. Their first visitor from the south was a puzzled Swedish reporter who had driven from Cairo to garner a story. "I cannot understand why you've stopped here", he commented, "there isn't a single Egyptain soldier in Qantara, and the only one I saw in Ismailia was a fat officer getting into his car and driving frantically towards Cairo". There was no way of explaining matters to him.

Accurate though the reporter's information may have been the Egyptians soon remedied the matter. Later that morning the crews of the forward troop of tanks were servicing their vehicles when a crowd of some fifty Egyptian civilians approached them from the south. Suddenly rifles were fished from beneath *galabiyas* and the Egyptians opened fire, wounding a sergeant. This allowed the British troops to break the injunction which had been imposed upon them not to use their weapons and one of the tank's crews loosed off a few rounds from their Browning machine-gun, killing two of the Egyptians.

It was clearly time to take a closer look at the Egyptian reaction to the presence of the British troops on the causeway. A helicopter was summoned from Port Said and the commanding officer, accompanied by one of the authors, set off to try to peer over the massive railway embankment ahead, which dominated their position and blocked their view down the causeway. As the helicopter climbed the two officers could

see groups of vehicles in the Sinai Desert over to the east which
they correctly assumed to be the forward elements of the
Israeli army, halted by the cease-fire. Then, when they were
high enough to look over the embankment, Egyptian infantry
could be observed lining its crest, from which every detail
of the British positions was revealed: in the bowl behind, military vehicles were dispersed, with more moving up from the
direction of Qantara. Because of the restriction which prohibited any flying south of the British front-line, the observers
were reluctantly obliged to return. As the helicopter's rotors
stopped, solicitous figures pressed forward to disclose that
during their leisurely flight along the embankment the
Egyptians below had been loosing off with every weapon they
possessed. No sign of damage could be found on the helicopter, nor had the passengers been at all aware that the
shooting had been taking place.

Among the welcoming party was the French major who
had been attached to the battalion in Cyprus. He was now
anxious to borrow a helicopter to visit a friend whom he
described as the French liaison officer with the Israeli armoured
forces across the Canal. While the existence of such a person
would at the time have been denied vigorously, the officer to
whom the request was made does not recall that the implied
information came as any sort of surprise. However, in loyalty
to the political ethic of the operation the French officer's
simple social wish was not gratified.

Both the amount of material damage which had been
inflicted upon Port Said and the number of Egyptians who had
been killed in the fighting were to become the subject of
acrimonious dispute. Many servicemen and reporters remembered widespread damage along the waterfront and the
devastation at the western end of Arab Town. However, when
the flames had died away and the glass and rubble had been
cleared from the streets, the damage looked far less serious.
The exception was Shanty Town whose luckless inhabitants
had seen their acre of flimsy shelters reduced to blackened
embers. A series of graphic photographs, taken by an enter-
prising reporter, had suggested to the world's press that this
pitiful destruction was typical of the city as a whole but except
for Navy House, the police barracks, the Custom House, and

the warehouses of the inner basin—all places where fighting had occurred—the damage was in the main confined to shell-holes in the buildings which faced the beaches where the commandos had landed. As General Burns was to comment, when he arrived in Port Said to command UNEF, the damage was not very great, certainly by the standards of the previous war.[1] The restrictions which had been placed on the scope of the bombardment had proved to be wise after all.

A well-documented report[2] by Sir Edwin Herbert, the President of the Law Society, estimated that 650 Egyptians had died in Port Said, 900 had been wounded and detained in hospital, and a further 1,200 or so had been slightly injured; these figures were exclusive of losses in Port Fuad, where he estimated that about 100 people had been killed. Of the killed and wounded he thought it improbable that more than twenty-five per cent were civilians.

An earlier investigation into the Egyptian casualties was carried out by Sir Walter Monckton and although his integrity was in every way beyond reproach, few foreigners could readily accept that someone who had until recently held the office of Minister of Defence in the British Government was capable of bringing the proper qualities of independent judgement to bear on such a task. They were wrong. However, the consequence was that Herbert was sent out to report further; his judicial honesty was the equal of Monckton's, but he lacked the stigma of having been a member of the Cabinet which had been responsible for the invasion.

As was to be expected, the Egyptians exaggerated the casualties in the same way as they had the damage. There were other suggestions that Herbert's figures may have been on the low side but Brigadier Fergusson, who accompanied Monckton during the first enquiry, thought that they could well have been in excess of the actual total.[3] Burns mentioned a figure of 1,000 but quotes no source for his information.[4] Even though Herbert was able to spend only four days in Port Said and was impeded by the understandable reluctance of many Egyptians to be open in their evidence, his investigation was thorough and his figures are unlikely to be far out. Whatever the figures may have been, the lives of these men, women and children were as much wasted as those of the allied servicemen who died in the battle—sixteen British and ten French, with a further ninety-six and thirty-three wounded.[5]

Taking into consideration the care which had been taken before and during the assault to avoid Egyptian casualties, their losses might be thought high. But in his report Herbert emphasises that the steps taken to protect the interests of civilians had jeopardised British lives and increased British casualties. All that can be said is that few other countries would have been prepared to risk the lives of their own servicemen in such a way by reducing the naval bombardment to one tenth of what had been thought to be necessary, by broadcasting their operational plans in order to help civilians keep out of the way and by forbidding the bombing of military objectives in order to avoid hitting civilians and their property.

Despite the damage and the casualties, the attitude of many of the people of Port Said towards the invaders was at first far from unfriendly. In the past many of them had depended upon the British services for a living, with the result that old employees turned up looking for jobs in the fond belief that their previous masters were back for at least another seventy years. Children were as ready as ever to accept sweets and chocolates; in no time at all street vendors were starting to hawk their traditional wares. When the time came to pay the troops, shops took down their shutters to reap the welcome harvest.

Some shops opened rather more quickly than others. The French *paras* showed considerable zeal in getting goods moving. On their own initiative they forced the famous Simon Arzt departmental store and other shops to open their doors but neglected to assemble the sale staff before doing so. Nor did they have the cash to pay for their purchases. Before their commanders clamped down upon them, the British troops looted a little too, as troops always will in such circumstances but the French were in quite a different league, shipping vehicles and other bulky articles which they had "liberated" back to Cyprus. The inhabitants of Port Said themselves wasted little time in emptying houses and flats vacated by wealthy owners and it was only too easy for the invading forces to be credited with these activities as well.

Among the French loot was a quantity of Czech and other

weapons which subsequently fetched a good price from EOKA in Cyprus. Consequently when 3 Para themselves arrived back in the island, the Red Caps were waiting on the quayside to frisk the men, much to the rage of their commanding officer. Disgusted at this slur on his soldiers, on his own responsibility he marched them back to the camp unsearched. A few day later, the medical officer of the battalion discovered a selection of captured carbines and sub-machine-guns tucked away under the bandages and shell-dressings in his medical panniers, the stores having arrived back under the protective cloak of the Red Cross.[6] There was no question of the soldiers planning to sell the weapons to the terrorists, whom they were known to dislike more even than the politicians at Westminster. It was merely their normal acquisitive instincts coming to the fore.

With the troops at last on shore, the planners might well have expected some respite from their toils, but it was not to be. As Stockwell succinctly expressed it, he was faced with three choices—to go forward, stay put or get out.[7] Nor could the possibility be disregarded that at any moment the allies might find themselves fighting an opponent rather more formidable than the Egyptians. Two days after the cease-fire there was, in fact, a scare that the Russians were about to bomb the Fleet, with the result that quite a lot of jumping up and down took place, as one of the senior officers involved later put it.[8]

To cope with the possibility of the allied advance continuing, the planners had to withdraw 16 Parachute Brigade back to Cyprus (where a sizeable French airborne force was still waiting to go into action), to prepare for further airborne operations and to land 3 British Infantry Division in their place. At the same time stocks of ammunition, fuel and other material needed to support offensive action had to be offloaded. On the other hand, to stay put and perhaps occupy Port Said indefinitely involved providing a few basic comforts for the troops and the stores needed by Civil Affairs to keep life going in the city. Against this a withdrawal might be ordered at very short notice indeed, a contingency which required that the troops and stores ashore should be reduced rather than increased. These three conflicting requirements were seemingly irreconcilable, particularly as the ships waiting offshore were loaded tactically with a view to a continuing build-up of the invasion force. However, somehow or other staffs coped and they did so with conspicuous success.

The units of 3 Infantry Division, which had sailed from the United Kingdom on 1 and 2 November, had joined the mass of shipping anchored five miles off Port Said nine days later. 29 Infantry Brigade disembarked on 11 November to relieve Butler's parachutists but it was another two days before 19 Brigade could land, the delay being due to a lack of space alongside the crowded quays and the long-anticipated deterioration in the weather which prevented the troops being transhipped into landing-craft. This latter brigade then took over from the commandos, who moved into reserve prior to returning to Malta. The third brigade of 3 Infantry Division was still in the United Kingdom together with the divisional artillery, waiting to be flown out to the Mediterranean if they were needed. There they would have picked up their transport and guns, loaded into ships so many months before.

It suited all concerned that the parachute units and the commandos should be replaced by 3 Infantry Division. The General Assembly of the United Nations among their many resolutions about the emergency had passed one demanding the withdrawal of the allied "shock troops", an expression foreign to the British military vocabulary. Possibly the French did not even notice the resolution. In any case, their "shock troops" remained in Port Fuad, while their units still afloat sailed back to Algiers where other work was awaiting them.

When ships which had been loaded for so many weeks eventually off-loaded their cargoes at Port Said there were some unexpected surprises. At the fishing harbour a senior staff officer one day noticed a 3-ton lorry, so overladen that its rear springs were all but concave and stuck fast on the ramp. "Who the bloody hell are you", he enquired kindly, "and what are you doing?" "I, sir", responded a voice of much dignity, "am the mess-sergeant of Her Majesty's Life Guards, and I have with me the officers' mess silver and champagne".[9] In early August, H.M.G. had announced in words which seemed to echo Palmerston that The Life Guards and the 1st Battalion The Grenadier Guards were to move from Windsor for an undisclosed destination. But when the former was removed from the order-of-battle because there was no role for an armoured car regiment at Port Said as there might have been at Alexandria, there was no means of extricating the mess truck and other vehicles from the vessel into which they had already been loaded. The fate of the champagne is unrecorded but if its existence in Port Said was widely revealed it could hardly have survived the free-booting activities of the French, whose commissary had condemned them to exist on vinogel, a plastic substance alleged to be indistinguishable from certain sorts of wine after being mixed with water and drunk from an opaque vessel.

By the time 3 Infantry Division landed, the likelihood of any serious fighting had receded almost to vanishing point in the minds of the soldiers sitting in and around Port Said. Nevertheless the expansive nature of allied intelligence persisted. On the day set for the relief of 2 Para by the first elements of 29 Infantry Brigade, a tracked Bren carrier was seen approaching from the north at high speed, weaving and jinking across the scrubby waste, its occupants prudently tucked below the rim of the little armoured vehicle. When it drew up, its most senior passenger raised his nose above the parapet to enquire whether it might not be safer for his men to be brought forward in small packets in the intervals between the shelling. It was a few moments before the amused parachutists were able to take the proposal seriously.

Despite some frantic night-firing by the Egyptians, who clearly knew nothing of any cease-fire, the few days spent by 2 Para had been passed in relative tranquillity. One day an ambulance-train went through, to return the following day laden with wounded, while just before the relief an unlucky pair of journalists, one American and one French, apparently determined to discover what was happening on the other side of the bund, drove through the forward positions without stopping. Both were killed by the Egyptians further down the road.

Life for the British troops sitting in and around Port Said during the forty-six days of the occupation was to prove tedious, uncomfortable and only at times dangerous. It was to be thankless and unrewarding work. The individual battalions of 3 Infantry Division were dispersed into company areas, where the men were housed in abandoned or requisitioned blocks of flats, sometimes lacking furniture and frequently devoid of both heat and light. Those few regulars who had fought in Korea had learned how to make life tolerable in much harsher conditions and were able to pass on their wrinkles to their mates. But, as usual, the French philosophy was rather more practical and clear-cut: the spoils of war belonged if not to the victors, at least to those who had been left in possession of the field. This allied to a native ability to make good use of any material which might be found lying about (anyone who has seen the difference in the results achieved on either side of the Channel in that element of a recruit's basic training known as "mess-tin cooking" will bear out this statement) mitigated some of the discomforts and frustrations of the occupation. In any case, Port Fuad was a rather more salubrious spot than Port Said.

Provided with what amounted to no more than a loose brief to attend to the problems of law and order, these individual British infantry companies deployed around Port Said had little contact with other units, or even with the rest of their own battalion. The daily round was dreary, guard duties alternating with patrols and sleep; distractions such as canteens did not exist, while Egyptian cafés were out of bounds. The presence of the soldiers in the area did much to reassure those European civilians still living there and helped also to preserve their property from unwelcome attentions. Among their more tiresome duties was to protect the civilian police as they distributed essential commodities such as paraffin to the inhabitants of Port Said. Queues would often collapse into riot and the soldiers would themselves have to take charge. In such circumstances, co-operation with the Egyptian police soon became surprisingly effective, even though the precise authority under which the temporary forces of occupation were operating was never clearly defined.[10] From day to day the morale of the civilians and hence their passivity or hostility towards the soldiers, fluctuated unpredictably, fuelled as it was by Radio Cairo. It was a little difficult for the possibly phlegmatic Northern soldiers to understand the volatility of these Egyptians, when an isolated incident at a street corner could so easily develop into mob action. But they managed to cope with such situations in their normal equable manner as they continued to maintain the *status quo* until the United Nations Emergency Force should be ready to take over their task.

CHAPTER FIFTEEN

WITHDRAWAL

GENERAL BURNS, to whom Dag Hammarskjold, the Secretary-General, had entrusted the command of this United Nations Emergency Force, was a Canadian and had for the previous two years been in charge of the United Nations Truce Supervisory Organisation, a force of some forty or fifty officers responsible for holding the ring between Israel and her Arab neighbours. As Burns discovered when he visited Cairo on 8 November, the Egyptians were not lacking in reservations about both the tasks and the composition of his proposed command. It did not help that the United Nations had failed in the not simple task of providing a clear statement of its purpose and Nasser was concerned that the troops might stay indefinitely in Port Said and take over the protection of the Canal and the maintenance of law and order—in short, develop into a force for the international control of the waterway as Britain and France had originally envisaged.

In discussing the composition of the proposed UNEF, Burns was upset to discover that Nasser held pronounced views on the subject of which countries would be prohibited from providing contingents. Australians, Pakistanis and New Zealanders were not acceptable, nor were Canadians, despite the lead they had taken in setting up the force. The difficulty was that Canadians were not only subjects of Her Majesty the Queen but they also wore the Queen's uniform, which happened to be almost indistinguishable from that worn by the British. Nor did it help that the first unit earmarked for the force held the proud title of the Queen's Own Rifles.[1]

Burns was under considerable pressure to establish his troops in Egypt as quickly as possible so as to forestall the arrival of any "volunteers" from the Soviet bloc. Korea was fresh in everyone's mind and there was widespread fear that the forces of the West, once again acting under the flag of the United Nations, might find themselves dragged into a conflict with the Communist countries of Eastern Europe in a repeat of the earlier affair.[2] The consequence of this was that units started to assemble more quickly than arrangements could be made to supply, maintain and accommodate the men. When Burns inspected advance parties of the Norwegian, Danish and Columbian contingents, staging in Naples on 14 November (by which time Nasser had finally agreed to accept United Nations' troops on his territory), nobody was yet sure what the troops were to do or how they were to live when they landed in Egypt. It was hard for anyone to comprehend these UNEF infantrymen being capable of more than mounting ceremonial guards and it appeared that if they were not to starve they might have to live off the land.

Fortunately Egypt and the two invaders between them produced, at least in the early stages, the support needed to enable UNEF to operate and both sides did so with a genuine show of goodwill. This was not surprising to the British for they were accustomed to working smoothly in tandem with the Canadians, and Burns and Keightley had been fellow corps-commanders during the Italian campaign. The result was that the negotiations for the transfer of British stores and vehicles in Port Said to UNEF proceeded with barely a hitch, a Gilbertian situation as Burns commented.[3] The Egyptians were equally helpful, not only in major matters such as providing UNEF with a base at Abu Sueir but in minor ones such as producing Czech field-cookers on which the ill-equipped peace-keeping units could prepare their food.

Eventually UNEF consisted of the equivalent of six infantry battalions, drawn from India, the four Scandinavian countries, Indonesia, Colombo and Brazil. Jugoslavia sent an armoured reconnaissance unit, whose officers, inexperienced as they were in the ways of the West (and even more so of the British), were astonished to be welcomed at Port Said by an enthusiastic General Stockwell who went out of his way to be both friendly and helpful.[4]

When Nasser eventually withdrew his objections, Canada

provided the bulk of the logistical and support units, other than a medical company sent by Norway. The first of the troops—a strong Norwegian infantry company—arrived in Port Said on 21 November by train from Abu Sueir. Their welcome by the Egyptians was so hearty that the troops were all but engulfed in the crowd, despite the efforts of the detachment of Royal Military Police which had been paraded to protect them. Stockwell had his hat knocked off and in the end reinforcements had to be summoned to ensure the safe journey of the Norwegians to the camp—made ready for them by the British.

The battalion of Indian parachutists was an experienced regular unit, whose Kumoanis looked just like Gurkhas to the uninitiated and were welcomed as such by the British soldiers. On the other hand, the raw young conscripts who manned the rest of the UNEF military units were regarded by both British and French with amused but forbearing contempt. Dressed in American uniforms with blue-painted American helmet-liners, their nickname of "Bluebells" was insulting rather than affectionate. Glaswegian Scots jeered at barefooted Scandinavian eurhythmics on the beach, while equally xenophobic French *paras* were similarly insulting about the habits and appearance of the South Americans. Burns himself, in a laudable attempt to avoid looking like a British general, designed for himself a uniform in United Nations sky-blue, to the delight of the swarms of reporters who crammed Port Said, all avid for human copy.

Nasser was also able to demonstrate the strength of his position when it came to clearing the Canal. Since the maintenance of free and unfettered transit had been the ostensible political aim of the allies, it was regrettable that the consequences of their efforts were twenty vessels sunk between Port Said and Port Fuad, thirty-seven more further south and a couple of collapsed bridges too. As the Egyptians had used the ships which were nearest to hand to block the waterway, it followed that most of the wrecks came from the dredging and salvage fleet used for keeping it navigable. Consequently resources that the allies might have hoped to have pressed into service had themselves become obstacles to be cleared.

Fortunately the post-war run-down of the British services

had not obliterated the salvage fleet of the Royal Navy and, with French help and foreign charters, a respectable team was put together, all under the command of a French admiral. This salvage work had started at the very beginning of the invasion, when naval divers slid into the waters of the outer harbour as the commandos were still fighting their way off the beaches. This first reconnaissance, which established that the Egyptians had not further complicated the problem by mining the wrecks, allowed work to start on the morning after the cease-fire. A week later the first L.S.T. was able to pass through the blockships and berth in the inner harbour.

By 25 November, Port Said could handle ships of 10,000 tons, and a twenty-five-foot-wide channel had been opened to El Cap, which was as far as the Franco-British team could proceed. The Egyptians, however, still held a powerful weapon. Until such time as the allies should leave Port Said and Israel should withdraw her forces from the territory she occupied, they had no intention of allowing the Canal to be cleared further nor would they permit allied salvage teams to remain to finish the job, even though there seemed to be no one else capable of doing it.

The consequence was that the United Nations Suez Clearance Organisation (UNSCO) was set up to do the work, with an elderly retired American engineer general named Wheeler in control. Wheeler, who had worked under Mountbatten in South-East Asia and received both the KCB and the KCIE for his services, had the reputation when provoked of being "ornery". His task, as the buffer between the two allies and the Egyptians, was far from easy. It was hardly surprising that he received an abominable press in Britain and France, where understandably the popularity of Americans was at an all-time low. However, after a number of stormy interviews, a compromise was reached by which the allies would leave a part of their salvage fleet behind them when they left, operating under UNSCO, with the ships' crews dressed as civilians. Protection was to be provided by UNEF troops, also wearing civilian clothes, but distinguished by blue berets and armbands. In the event, these arrangements worked well: the crews were not molested and the Canal was cleared. The first convoy sailed from south to north on 29 March 1957, the removal of the final block-ship having been delayed until the Israelis should evacuate the Gaza strip and Sharm el-Sheikh.

Under the bitter duress of world-wide sanctions, Israel had no alternative. But she had gained something from the war, unlike Britain and France: her ships were again free to navigate the Gulf of Aqaba and Gaza could no longer be used as a *fedayeen* base. The Israelis had also consolidated their new-found reputation as a fighting people, a quality which the world had forgotten during the two millennia of the Diaspora. In future Israel was to be treated with respect.

When Eden had accepted the inevitable and halted the invasion, he believed that Port Said could be held as a bargaining counter to ensure the prompt clearance of the Canal and the enforcement of a general settlement. Little did he think that a second capitulation would quickly follow the first and that the allies would be forced to relinquish even the small toe-hold which they had seized. But the United States maintained its pressure. Eisenhower had first agreed to receive Eden and Mollet in Washington on 7 November, but to the chagrin of the two leaders the invitation was withdrawn. Instead Selwyn Lloyd travelled to New York, and without success, tried to mend the broken bridges. In a humiliating and unhappy ten days in America, he found the attitude of the State Department aggressively negative—to use Eden's phrase.[5] During the time Selwyn Lloyd was away, Eden's health again collapsed under the accumulated strain of the previous weeks and he departed for a three-week stay at Golden Eye, Ian Fleming's Jamaica house. Butler, the Lord Privy Seal, whose support for the Suez venture had never been more than luke-warm, was left in charge to clear up the mess and persuade his Tory colleagues there was no alternative to withdrawing— a task which did not help his chances of succeeding Eden as Premier when the latter was at last obliged to resign through ill-health the following January. The trouble was that the Americans extended their blackmail (as Butler put it)[6] from dollars to oil. With the blocking of the Canal and the cutting of the Syrian pipe-line, three-quarters of Western Europe's oil had been denied and the only other source was North America. The French, who had not been as susceptible to the

financial pressures as had the British and who had tried to
prolong the occupation for as long as possible in the face of
their ally's opposition,[7] were obliged also to accept the fact
that there could be no alternative to leaving Port Said in the
sole care of UNEF.

The fact that the troops were to be withdrawn was made
public on 3 December, although the exact date they would
leave was kept secret to avoid the Egyptians planning large-
scale farewell demonstrations. At that time Port Said was
reasonably quiet, despite the encouragement to violence
emanating from Radio Cairo, and the troops had been able
to relax a little. But the announcement that the allies were
to leave acted as a signal for the start of a series of deliberate
attacks against British forces. Snipers again became active,
grenades were thrown into vehicles from balconies and street-
corners, shops put up their shutters and the civilian labour
which had been taken on vanished. Designed to indicate to
the outside world that the invaders were not leaving on their
own accord but being driven into the sea, these attacks were
often well planned, apparently by professionals. Fortunately
for the British troops the subsequent shooting tended to lack
accuracy. A particularly nasty incident occurred when a
young subaltern of the West Yorkshire Regiment named
Moorhouse was abducted as he was driving his jeep alone
along a street; the consequence was an escalation of incidents
as troops searched for him and for the weapons which were
now being smuggled into the town across Lake Manzala.
Despite the increasing provocation, the troops managed to
retain their self-control until a company commander of the
Argyll and Sutherland Highlanders was mortally wounded
in a night ambush. The subsequent punitive action, in which
a troop of Centurion tanks helped the infantry, resulted in
a number of Egyptians being killed and wounded, the exact
count remaining uncertain because most were removed by
their friends. This, the sole incident of its kind, had a salutary
effect and there was little further trouble.

There were hardly any problems at all in Port Fuad. In
some measure this was due to the suburban lay-out of the
streets which inhibited bombings and similar ambushes but
there is little doubt that the Egyptians were reluctant to go

too far in aggravating *les paras*. Patrolling Foreign Legionaries rarely hesitated before opening fire on someone they suspected might be about to do them an injury. Leulliette describes how an Egyptian officer who had the temerity to brawl with his French guards was shot out of hand in cold blood.[8] Beaufre himself admitted that as soon as a minor incident took place, punishment followed at once. According to him, relations in Port Fuad between the French and the Egyptians almost verged on the cordial, in spite of the incessant propaganda, and he believed that similar methods might also have succeeded in Port Said.[9] On the whole and despite the occasional scandal, the British do avoid repressive measures. Their officers are disciplined to work within the guide-lines set by the government of the day and their soldiers do not enjoy violence for its own sake. How successful the policy has been is arguable but few regret it.

Further contingents of UNEF troops had followed the Norwegian company into Port Said, and a company of Danes was interposed between the Egyptians and the York and Lancaster Regiment at El Cap—a very delicate task indeed—so allowing the British battalion to pull back. The United Nations troops then started to take over the guard duties at vulnerable points, such as public utilities and food warehouses, and in this way by degrees they assumed the task of "maintaining peaceful conditions". "Law and order" might have been a more accurate term but to this the Egyptians took exception.[10] As the allied troops pulled back towards the docks, they handed over the town section by section to UNEF and to the civilian police who were working with the newcomers. But because these UNEF soldiers were forbidden to open fire except in self-defence, they had to establish their authority by their presence alone. This they accomplished admirably and on only two occasions were they obliged to use their weapons.

When the announcement was made on 3 December that the British and French troops were to withdraw, there were some 22,000 men ashore, with about one vehicle and two tons of stores to every four of them, a measure of the logistic problems of mounting such an invasion. Fourteen days were needed to ship out the men and equipment and half were moved during the first week of the withdrawal. With them sailed large numbers of civilians, holders of British and French passports, people born in the country whose families had often lived there for generations. Other foreigners followed later, including members of the Greek and Italian communities which had contributed so much to the commercial life of the country. The polarisation of race in what had, on the whole, been a tolerant country was an unhappy side-effect of the Anglo-French expedition.

The last allied troops to leave were 19 Infantry Brigade from Port Said and two battalions of *1er Régiment Etranger Parachutiste* from Port Fuad, together with a squadron of tanks with each contingent. The troops in Port Said were withdrawn behind a barbed-wire fence three miles long, built with prodigious toil. Behind this barrier the troops of UNEF established a buffer zone a few hundred yards wide from which everyone had been evacuated. But, despite these precautions, in the final stages of the withdrawal any Egyptian who could lay his hands on a weapon discharged it aimlessly in the general direction of the allied shipping. When the firing became dangerous, the British replied in kind but with rather more effect. Sandwiched in the middle and unable to do anything about it, the UNEF men had an uncomfortable time.

The date fixed for the final withdrawal was 22 December, frequent changes having earned it the official nickname of *YO-YO*. These delays had occurred as a consequence of the negotiations to exchange 230 Egyptian prisoners, some of them civilian, for the interned employees of Suez Contractors Ltd., life for whom had become rather less intolerable since the International Red Cross and the Swiss Embassy had been allowed access to them. Complications had been caused by the French having shipped some of their prisoners out of the country; these had to be retrieved before the Egyptians would permit the Suez Contractors' men to leave. However, on 21 December, the internees arrived at El Cap by train, where Indian UNEF troops welcomed them with hot tea provided from their own rations. On the way to the docks the men were obliged to run the gauntlet of abusive crowds, to the embarrassment of the Finnish troops who were guarding them.

Lieutenant Moorhouse's fate was poignant. An officer of UNEF, who was trying to secure his release, had at one point been led blindfold to a house and shown someone dressed in a British uniform whom he was assured was Moorhouse. The news was flashed around the world that the young officer was alive and well and his parents looked forward to his return for Christmas. But the party which waited that last day on the quayside for the Egyptians to produce Moorhouse waited in vain. It later transpired that he had died soon after he had been captured, probably suffocated accidentally by his captors when they were hiding him from a search party.

There was much in the way of both high spirits and ceremonial about the final departure of the allied ships and soldiers on 22 December. Well known are the anecdotes of the Union Jack nailed to the greasy flagstaff on the quayside (which the Egyptians sawed down) and the allied flags fixed to de Lesseps' statue (which they later blew up). The pranks of the young naval officers were possibly not very dignified but they were understandable.

For 3 Infantry Division, the Suez affair had been an unhappy period in the history of a famous formation. Arriving too late to see any proper action, the men had endured the discomforts and frustrations of the occupation without any of the compensations. The final ignominy was reserved for the division's rearguard, 19 Infantry Brigade. Arriving at Southampton on New Year's Eve, with two Scottish battalions in their number, they were greeted with the news that the dockers had no intention of unloading the ship until after the holiday. When the men did at last disembark, Her Majesty's Customs levied their due tolls, leaving few packs, kitbags or suitcases unsearched. In this way the soldiers become aware of the attitude of many of their countrymen to the service they had given.

CHAPTER SIXTEEN

HOW DID IT HAPPEN?

REGARDLESS OF their rank, the actual planning and execution of the Suez operation had been tackled with enthusiasm by the allied servicemen who took part. But some of those at the top had their reservations. Earl Mountbatten, the First Sea Lord at the time, told his biographer that it would be futile to pretend that he did not have grave doubts about the whole affair—doubts which centred upon collusion with Israel, his country's relations with America and the United Nations, its military unpreparedness and the sudden application of the brakes after a start had been made. As he saw it, Suez had been inspired by very different ideas from those which had guided him during his years in South-East Asia and afterwards as Viceroy of India.[1]

Field-Marshal Montgomery, then serving in his last active post as Deputy Supreme Commander at SHAEF, was his normal uninhibited self. In his foreword to Cavenagh's book about the drop of 3 Para, he alleged that the true story of the Suez "muddle" had yet to be told, and that when the day did come it would not reflect credit on either the British Government of the day or on the Chiefs-of-Staff.[2] Six years after Suez, during the course of one of his periodic lectures on grand strategy to the House of Lords, he recounted how Eden had summoned him back from Paris during the early stages of the planning of the operation, and that in reply to his enquiry, "What is your object?", the Prime Minister had answered, "To knock Nasser off his perch." Such an aim, Montgomery replied to Eden, just would not do, asserting that he himself would have needed to know what the political object was when Nasser *had* been knocked off his perch, because that would determine how the operation should best be carried out.[3]

Field-Marshal Lord Slim, Montgomery's successor as C.I.G.S., remarked afterwards to Menzies, "If you'd been

Prime Minister and I'd been C.I.G.S. at the time of Suez, we'd have finished the job effectively,"[4] but the man who was C.I.G.S. and who had succeeded Slim, Field-Marshal Sir Gerald Templer, has kept his own counsel. Nonetheless, there seems to be little doubt that Jacques Baeyens, Barjot's *conseillor diplomatique* was not far off the mark in saying that a good number of *"les grands chefs anglais"* were opposed to the very concept of the operation.[5] Close as he was to the inner circle of those involved at Suez, Baeyens' frank comments on the operation and the personalities are both trenchant and amusing.

There may be a measure of hindsight in the reservations which so many senior officers later expressed. Some people have also changed their minds about their attitude towards the operation, and some have even admitted it. Among them was Randolph Churchill, who in his critical biography of Anthony Eden wrote:

> If we had known with what ineptitude the campaign had been planned, if we had detected the inherent fraudulence of the Anglo-French ultimatum, if we had known of the Government's miscalculations about American reactions, if we had perceived that because of these miscalculations the enterprise would have to be abandoned in thirty-six hours, many of those, who like the author, applauded the action on the day might have adopted a very different line.[6]

Among the "many who applauded" was one of the authors of this book. Whatever Eden's mistakes and faults he surely caught the mood of the country at the time, however misplaced the enthusiasm may have been. Sixteen years later Bernard Levin was said not to remember Suez as being so divisive as tradition had it.[7] The ever pragmatic Jim Callaghan well understood that the average Labour voter did not subscribe to his party's stand on Suez, and that his party was still paying the price for this as late as the 1959 elections.[8] It is a paradox that the country might have been still more united if a Labour government had been in power; Eden expressed this well in the words:

> Left-wing governments, if they are firm in discharge of their responsibilities in international affairs, can always count on

support. Right-wing governments cannot always do so. It was perhaps fortunate that it was a Labour government which had to expose Soviet behaviour after the war and break the blockade of Berlin by the airlift.[9]

Opposition to the venture was, in fact, concentrated among those who felt an instinctive revulsion against the idea of attacking a small, weak country; among those who sensed political advantage in giving expression to such revulsion; and among those who were outstandingly perspicacious about the consequences of the action which was being contemplated. Among the perspicacious were many of the Government's senior advisers, both civilian and military, individuals such as the senior Foreign Office officials who sympathised with Nutting's stand, the ambassadors in the major world capitals whom the Government kept in ignorance of their plans and service officers close to the Chiefs-of-Staff. Such men have access to what should be and usually is accurate information—economic, military and political—and they are trained to draw proper conclusions from it. But the politician, with whom lies the final decision, can rarely avoid calculating the political advantage which will stem from a particular course of action and may therefore find it difficult to discard emotion and personal ambition. It is apposite that at one stage the Joint Planners (according to information which Hugh Thomas received from a senior officer) presented a paper which forecast with some accuracy the likely chain of events—the opposition which the action would arouse in America and the United Nations, the pressure on the pound and the enforced withdrawal. Thomas's informant accuses Eden of calling the paper in and destroying it.[10]

The senior officers of the armed forces had grounds for criticising the political leadership of the country on a number of counts. There is the allegation that the Chiefs-of-Staff were on the verge of resignation in the early stages of the crisis because they were being impelled to mount an immediate airborne operation. If this is true, it suggests that the Prime Minister must have been pressing his proposals in an over-pertinacious manner. It could be some measure of the Governments lack of realism that they should have been insistent on mounting such an operation with inadequate airborne forces and transport aircraft, without a suitable nearby base and with no follow-up forces immediately available to relieve the airborne troops; even more so, that they should have issued threats to Egypt, both explicit and implied, without the military forces to back them.

Equally reprehensible was the Government's inability to face up to the problem of what would happen once the Army was back in Egypt. The Canal Zone had just been evacuated, primarily because of the problems of maintaining the large forces needed to counter Egyptian antagonism, expressed in both civil resistance and outright terrorism. Now the servicemen were being told to return and occupy not just the Base Areas along the Canal, but possibly the rest of the country as well. This was a task quite beyond the capability of the British and French forces which could be collected for the operation, even in the face of Egyptian resistance similar to that experienced in the past, let along what might be expected in the aftermath of an invasion. With Nasser out of the way, effective leadership would have devolved upon the terrorist groups, whose reaction would have been impossible to contain without the use of repressive measures of an unacceptable degree of ferocity. Even if the old politicians excised by the Young Officers had been brought back in the baggage-train of the invaders, such men would have been only targets for the bombs and revolvers of the guerillas. The manner in which Eden and the French avoided the issue of what was to follow Nasser is a measure of a lack of foresight which was equalled only by their scant understanding of the new coherence of Arab nationalism.

The extent to which Eden informed his immediate military advisers of his dealings with the Israelis cannot yet be established. The only firm evidence on the subject is Selwyn Lloyd's statement that the Permanent Secretary to the Ministry of Defence and General Keightley were both present at the meeting of the Inner Cabinet at Chequers on 21 October, when the decision was made that the Foreign Secretary should travel to France to meet the Israeli leaders the following day.[11] Hugh Thomas suggests that the only civil servants who were fully informed of what was happening were Patrick Dean, Kirkpatrick, the Head of the Foreign Office, and Brook, the

Secretary to the Cabinet.[12] With the secret understanding affecting the military plans in the way it did, if Keightley was taken into Eden's confidence it is hard to believe he would not have insisted that Stockwell should be informed as well—or even himself told Stockwell what was happening, regardless of any prohibition.

In fact, Stockwell heard nothing from his masters about the Israeli involvement and was placed in the invidious position of picking up details from his French subordinate. Although he did not complain, it must have been equally galling for him to discover that his staff officers and junior commanders were learning what was happening from their French opposite numbers, when the information had been denied to him and his fellow Task Force Commanders. To know that one is not trusted to receive information which bears directly on one's operational plans hardly inspires confidence. Neither does it encourage one to take a chance, and Stockwell justifies his reluctance to agree to the French pressure for a deep airborne penetration down the Canal, after 29 October, on the grounds that it seemed to be unnecessary to take risks which did not appear to help to achieve the aim of the operation—the cessation of hostilities between Israel and Egypt. "Had we been given the information", he wrote, "about the intention of the Israelis and had we been allowed to use their attack to our advantage, I would have been ready to accept the risks that an airborne operation presented. I could then have launched the British and French parachutists in depth between Port Said and Abu Sueir."[13] Stockwell also mentions the need for the men who have to do the fighting to be given as clear a concept as is permissible of what they are being sent to do and why, and that junior leaders should not be burdened with the additional task of justifying to their own men "the cause of the military events".[14] As it was, however, the regular soldiers, the reservists and the young national servicemen had few reservations about what they were doing. It was enough for them that the Egyptians needed to be taught a lesson and the Canal once again made secure. Fierce though the debate had been in many officers' messes, once the operation was under way it was conducted with unswerving enthusiasm and sense of duty.

The military leaders' primary criticism of the Government was the lack of any proper object to the operations which they had been told to plan. Stockwell complained of being "bedevilled throughout by the lack of clear political aim", echoing the protest which Montgomery had made to the Prime Minister. Stockwell attributed this to the continual manœuvrings during the course of the original tripartite meetings, and to the negotiations for the Canal Users' Association and at the United Nations. He also pointed out that military action could not succeed if kept "hanging on a string",[15] particularly in a complicated operation which involved bringing forces to a state of readiness and then concentrating and moving them from a large number of divergent bases into an assault landing.

Stockwell was partly correct in blaming the extended international negotiations for clouding the issue, but the greater blame surely lay with the Prime Minister and his immediate Cabinet colleagues (and the French as well) for failing to clear their minds as to what they were trying to do. At the start, the problem which faced the Government was clear-cut. Egypt, a country seen in the West as both incompetent and untrustworthy, had nationalised the Canal. Either she would prove incapable of operating it efficiently, or she would use it as a weapon of political blackmail, or both. Even more serious was the fear that the influence of Soviet Russia, already strong in Egypt, would be extended with disastrous consequences for Western Europe's strategy and economic future. Possibly this view was based on a number of misconceptions, one being Egypt's readiness to exchange one type of colonialism for another and further, her technical inability to run the Canal. For all that, the fears were understandable. Since 1945 the Soviet Union had provided ample evidence of her intention to consolidate and expand her ring of protective client-states, while, on the other side of the world, Korea had been saved from Chinese communism only by the West making a fighting stand in which even an uncommitted nation such as India had taken part. As the Berlin airlift had also demonstrated, only the determination of the West was likely to halt the spread of the Communist empires.

Prestige was also important to a country which, in 1956,

still headed a vast empire. For seventy years it had been an article of national faith that the Canal was vital to Britain's prosperity and survival: during two wars, campaigns had been fought to protect its approaches; moreover, it had become a symbol to arouse emotion. Now, within weeks of its final evacuation, those who had protested at the folly of relinquishing control seemed to have been proved right. Weakness and conciliation did not pay after all and the general feeling was that it was galling to be messed about by the upstart leader of a small country which it had long been fashionable to deride.

This mood was reflected in the actions of a Prime Minister rather too conscious that his standing was lower than might have been expected from Churchill's nominated successor. At home his performance had been particularly poor. Strength seemed to be needed and strength was a quality which the Government in which Eden had first held the office of Foreign Secretary had failed to show when Hitler had marched into the Rhineland in 1936. It was far too easy to equate the actions of the two dictators, a facile argument to which not only the Prime Minister fell victim but Gaitskell also in the early stages of the crisis. But it was a personal affront to Eden that this Egyptian colonel should have had the temerity to challenge Britain's standing and policies in the Middle East. Disregarding Nasser's popularity in the Arab world and of the question of his replacement when he was "knocked off his perch", Eden developed this obsession to oust him, an aim which matched that of his French allies, to whom Nasser was the evil genius upon whom could be heaped the responsibility for their country's misfortunes in Algeria.

The consequence was that the Government developed two separate political aims: to occupy the Canal Zone and so guarantee freedom of navigation, and to get rid of Nasser. The first was clear enough but to sit along the Canal might not necessarily result in Nasser's removal; in fact, it might even strengthen his position. The only sure way to oust him was to occupy Cairo and possibly the rest of the country besides, having first destroyed his prestige by defeating the Egyptian Army in battle and so removing his power-base.

However outspoken the Prime Minister might be to close

associates such as Nutting and Montgomery, his aim of destroying Nasser could hardly be expressed in formal terms to the Chiefs-of-Staff. Confusion therefore arose, with the armed forces told to seize control of the Canal but the Prime Minister determined to remove Nasser regardless of the consequences to Egypt. The original *Musketeer* plans for an invasion through Alexandria would have brought the Egyptian Army to battle outside Cairo and involved allied troops entering the city. From a narrow military standpoint it was a sound plan and forces were made ready and ships loaded so as to put it into effect. Its successful completion would probably have toppled Nasser, but it would also have given the Egyptians time to sabotage the Canal and its installations. Eden realised too late that such a roundabout approach to the Canal, involving as it did an assault on the Egyptian capital, was unacceptable to world opinion, even in those countries which were sympathetic to the British and French cause, a point which should have been considered by the Government before any planning started. As it was, time had been wasted in preparing for the wrong invasion and decisions had been made which could not be reversed later because of the rigidity which was imposed by the loading of the store-ships. It was the start of a series of delays which was to culminate in troops being committed to battle to further a stated aim which had no relevance to their actual task. To tell servicemen that they were fighting to separate Israelis from Egyptians was not only a lie, but it was known or suspected to be one by many of those involved.

Although Suez was hampered by the lack of a clear political direction, other mistakes were made as well. It was the first time since 1945 that the British had been obliged to plan and mount a full-scale operation, using sea, air and land-power. Undoubtedly the lessons drawn from the war against the Axis powers weighed heavily on British thinking, particularly in the use of airborne forces, in the meticulous planning of the assault and in the build-up and logistic planning of the operation. In the event, the plan worked with few hitches of major consequence; Fergusson, in fact, with some accuracy described the operation as being "technically brilliant".[16] The planners had done their work well, but this is far from the same thing as saying that the plan was the right one in the circumstances. The problem with large-scale and elaborate projects is that once they build up a certain momentum their progress becomes self-generating and their achievement a sufficient purpose in itself—the true aim becomes overlaid or forgotten. The need for careful plans to bring superior forces to bear across a sea barrier against a determined and well-equipped army was self-evident when fighting the Germans and Japanese, but the Egyptians, as the Israelis were to demonstrate, were not such an enemy. As the French were never to stop complaining, and with justification, the British commanders were not only slow but were reluctant to take any sort of risk. Massu, who saw the British as being hag-ridden with *Overlord*, mixed guarded admiration with condemnation. The constant references to the lessons of Arnhem irritated him, while the inability to learn from the past only when one had tasted the experience for the second time, and the combination of an inventive spirit with a horror of improvisation, were his abiding memories of his British colleagues.[17]

Although the way in which British commanders conducted the operations was in some measure due to lack of political direction, senior officers had perhaps learned the lessons of the second world war rather too thoroughly. After 1943, when success seemed assured and time was not a major factor, it became an axiom that care in preparation was the only sure way to win battles, to reduce casualties and to preserve the post-war position. But after the nationalisation of the Canal commonsense demanded that if an Anglo-French military reaction was to be effective, it had to be mounted swiftly. Von Brentano, the Foreign Minister of West Germany, remarked to Selwyn Lloyd on 22 August that if force had been used within forty-eight hours, there would have been considerable world support.[18]

At the time the landing at Alexandria was rejected in favour of one at Port Said, a rapid surprise attack would have been a feasible operation. By mid-September, the two allies had four airborne brigades available, together with the aircraft to drop them in a succession of lifts. As a follow-up force there were two commando brigades with enough amphibious craft to land 100 tanks. With some squadrons of Canberras, support from carrier-based aircraft and with helicopters (which were available in both Cyprus and Algeria) to help an immediate re-supply, the Canal could have been captured and held until further forces could arrive by sea from Malta, Algeria and the United Kingdom. A major factor in the rejection of French proposals for such a plan was the fear of Eastern European "volunteers" intervening to help Egypt, and it was the intelligence failure to make a correct assessment of this threat which perhaps as much as anything else prevented such an operation being launched.

Once the idea of such a *coup-de-main* had been rejected, the decision of the Task Force Commanders to bomb Egypt for ten days (even though it was later reduced to six) was as unnecessary as it was inept. The wishful thinking that this "aero-psychological" phase, as it became known, would somehow cause Egyptian resistance to collapse and Nasser to vanish was perhaps a rationalisation of this basic *Overlord* concept. In the event only thirty-six hours were needed to destroy the Egyptian Air Force on the ground. As for breaking Egyptian resistance, the "aero-psychological" offensive succeeded only in hardening opinion against the British and French action both within Egypt and internationally. Even in *Brassey's Annual* for 1957, the *Armed Forces' Year Book*, (in the preface of which the editor railed against those who had "affected" to disbelieve the official denials that the British and French governments had preconcerted their action with Israel,[19]) Cyril Falls, the leading military commentator of the day, admitted that "One winced each morning as one read the headlines, which always seemed to include the word 'pounding', in the morning papers."[20] It has always been difficult for air staffs to accept that bombing, however ruthless it may be, is more likely to stiffen resistance than to win wars by itself. In this attack on Egypt, it stood even less chance than usual of success, with bombing confined to military objectives and the population warned to keep clear of the targets but at the same time cautioned of the dire consequences of further resistance and loyalty to Nasser.

The bombardment was, of course, part of the bargain made with Israel to protect her cities from air attack during her attack on Egypt. It is hard to understand in retrospect how those who manufactured specious pretexts for the invasion could have believed that the collusion would not become public as soon as the recriminations started. In many ways it marked a watershed in political credibility in Britain. Before 1956 all but the outright cynical were ready to accept a categoric denial by a minister in Parliament on a matter of such importance; but during the past twenty years, the public have learned to bring a wary scepticism to bear on every Government statement.

As well as the harm done to Britain's good name and that of her leaders by this conspiratorial alliance, its immediate political consequences were counter-productive. At a time when Britain and France were busy damaging Nasser's reputation in any way they could, the Israeli attack enabled him to rally his countrymen with the old battle-cry of Zionist aggression. Both at home and in Muslim states abroad, Arab and non-Arab, Algeria as well, the Egyptian leader's standing was enhanced; the exact opposite of what his enemies had intended.

But whatever errors were made, either political or military, during the autumn following the Canal's nationalisation, the primary reason why Britain failed to take the lead and intervene quickly and effectively was the lack of an effective strategic reserve together with the necessary sea and air transport to lift it.

The cause of this gap in Britain's defences was the over-stretching of her resources, but there were few who were prepared to acknowledge the fact or recognise the degree to which freedom of action had become progressively more circumscribed through the shift in relative economic strength which had begun a generation before the Kaiser's war and which the victory of 1945 had served to accelerate rather than reverse. In the subsequent eleven years of post-war reconstruction, power had been divided almost equally between Conservative and Labour governments, with Churchill and Attlee as Prime Ministers for most of the time, two men who had undergone the strains of war-time leadership but who wore the resultant prestige both at home and overseas. Despite her economic weakness, Britain had entered the war in 1939 as a great power, a country with wide imperial responsibilities, whose voice carried more weight than any other. She ended it with a reputation even further enhanced, with the rest of Europe in

ruins and with her three enemies—Germany, Italy and Japan—
all beaten. They were three nations which the British people
had seen in terms of black and white, as embodiments of evil
ideologies which had to be destroyed on grounds of self-
preservation allied to plain decency, but they were also
countries whose economies had been growing at a faster rate
than that of the United Kingdom and whose external policies
had too often manifested themselves in a way hostile to the
interests of the British Empire.

In spite of the Marshall Aid which had set much of the
world on the road to recovery, few of the recipients understood how the United States had benefited from the war to
enhance its economic strength at the expense of Britain and the
rest of Europe. In the United States itself a new awareness of
the country's power had accompanied this economic domination, together with a desire to exercise it internationally,
especially in view of the expansion of the Communist empires
and the fear of a third, nuclear war. One manifestation of this
new attitude was the increased support and sympathy the
Americans gave to independence movements working to rid
themselves of colonial masters, something which Churchill
expressed in his protest that he had not become the King's
First Minister in order to preside over the liquidation of the
British Empire.[21] This American attitude was partly the
product of idealism and partly an attempt to shield Third
World countries from the spread of communist imperialism.
Nevertheless there were few who anticipated that America
would act in a manner so hostile to its wartime allies after
Nasser had nationalised the Canal and even fewer who understood that she was prepared to exercise the economic pressure
which would result in instant capitulation. The euphoria of
the Anglo-American wartime partnership and the way in
which Britain and the Commonwealth had so readily supported the Truman initiative in Korea in 1950 did not prepare
people for what was to happen.

This lack of understanding of the changes which had taken
place in both the economic strength and the influence of their
country abroad was in itself a product of the life lived by the
British people, characterised by a lessening of vitality, a running down in energy and initiative, a disregard of the need for

change and, as an awareness of a growing loss of power began to make itself felt, an inward-looking preoccupation with domestic problems.

It would hardly have been possible for conservative organisations such as the armed forces, which tended to reflect the feelings and aspirations of the people from whom they were recruited, to have remained immune from these influences. Earlier in this book some of the mistakes made by the army in the post-war years have been considered and similar ones were certainly not absent from the other two fighting services. Many of these deficiencies stemmed from a reluctance to change, allied to a strong measure of self-satisfaction and complacency, characteristics which were to be found widely in the nation. All organisations complain of a shortage of resources, the armed forces as much as any. It is fair to question whether, during the decade after the war, the fighting services had in fact wisely spent their budget and if this was not a major reason why no proper strategic reserve was available in July 1956.

What the end-result of successful intervention would have been is quite another question. Possibly if a Slim and a Menzies had been in harness the invasion could have been carried through to a militarily successful conclusion and the ignominy and futility of the enforced cease-fire avoided, but sooner or later Britain and France would have been obliged to depart.

As it was, the abortive invasion consolidated Nasser's authority, not only as head of the Egyptian state but also as the leader and the inspiration of the Pan-Arabic world. Throughout the crisis his personal conduct had been marked by an unexpected dignity and restraint, qualities which he had earlier commended to his countrymen in the words

So we are strong. Strong not in the loudness of our voices when we wail or shout for help but rather when we remain silent and measure the strength of our ability to act.[22]

The strength of the Arabs lay also in their oil, something which Nasser had also foreseen.[23] The West had proved the extent of their dependence by making clear how the threat of cutting supplies could be used as a weapon to blackmail. It was a lesson which the Arabs were a little slow to learn but when they eventually did, it had near-disastrous consequences not only for Europe but also for the economies of many emergent nations dependent on Arab-owned oil. Above all, perhaps, the political defeat of the British and the French (which was magnified by an able propaganda machine into a military defeat) helped to give the Egyptian masses a pride in their new-found independence and confidence in their rulers. This, despite the many difficulties with which they had to cope, not least of which was a continuing and grinding poverty, has led to Egypt becoming the most influential country in the Middle East, one with the courage to expel her Russian advisers when the time became ripe, the wisdom to re-establish friendly relations with Britain and France, and the courage to seek a peaceful settlement with Israel.

In France the *débâcle* was felt most by the armed forces. Mollett and his colleagues in the Cabinet incurred little blame for what had happened, criticism being deflected towards what was seen as the bullying tactics of the Americans and the weak and vacillating behaviour of the British. In any case, the up-surge of the revolt in Algeria and the subsequent disloyalty of the armed forces, which threatened the country with a military dictatorship, provided France with more immediate worries. Her military, angry at the failure of the operation and at the enforced evacuation, saw the cause in the pusillanimity of allies. Disillusion with the Anglo-Saxons and particularly with the dominant Americans led on to France's eventual withdrawal from NATO and her adoption of an independent nuclear deterrent.

The after-effects of a concussion can be far more serious than the hurt felt at the time and so it was with the blow to the pride of the British after Suez, accustomed as they had been to success and authority. Before Suez, Britain had been second in strength and influence only to America and Russia, but within the next generation she was to surrender the rest of her Empire, and with its loss the self-confidence of her people evaporated. No one would have dared to prophesy that twenty years after Suez it would become fashionable to equate Britain with Portugal and Greece—two other countries which had slid into decline when they lost their empires—or that she would earn the contempt of her friends for her economic weakness. The link between Britain's present troubles and the blow to the self-esteem of her people brought on by Suez may be circum-stantial, but it was from 1956 that the decline accelerated.

What the Government and the people had concealed from themselves was their vulnerability and in the end it was the brutal exploitation of this by the Americans which brought the Franco-British action to an ignominious halt. The under-lying strength, in economic and therefore in military terms, which was needed to sustain such an operation was simply not there. The self-will and the self-deception which had animated the whole British approach to the Suez crisis was stripped away and an opportunity for honest self-analysis presented itself. It was not taken.

AFTERWORD

WITH neither official approval nor official encouragement, we began to write this book barely more than half way through the thirty-year period of embargo on the release of Public Records. At the time we both believed in different degrees that our country had made a serious error of judgement in undertaking the Suez operation, that the nature and extent of the error was being deliberately concealed from the public, and that as much as could be discovered of the true story should be published.

In the years since the book originally went to press in 1979, much new information came to light. The private papers of Anthony Eden, Harold Macmillan and Selwyn Lloyd were made available to their respective biographers, Robert Rhodes James, Alistair Horne and D.R. Thorpe; Philip Ziegler's *Mountbatten: The Official Biography* was published; among others who helped clear the air was Evelyn Shuckburgh in his *Descent to Suez: Diaries 1951–56*. Most important of all, the Public Record Office in 1987 opened the records of 1956 for scrutiny. Many hundred, if not thousand, files awaited inspection there; the volume of material released proved surprising, although much appeared to have been retained. Subsequently, Keith Kyle's exhaustive and near-definitive *Suez* was published in 1991, followed by various papers by Anthony Gorst and his collaborators, all these confirming our accounts of the doubt and turmoil at the heart of Government and within the senior military during the planning for and build-up to the operation.

Not only were all these sources denied to us, but many of the main participants were unwilling or reluctant to talk – understandably so. One of us, dining alongside Field Marshal Sir Gerald Templer, for whom he had worked in 1956, when the discussion turned to Suez was told in the officer's famously inimitable way that a full account was locked in the Chief of the

General Staff's safe at the Ministry of Defence and there it would "bloody well remain". Nevertheless, with one or two exceptions, we do feel that we managed to get the main thrust of the story right.

What now seems to be clearer is that the switch in early September from *Musketeer* to *Musketeer Revise* – the landing at Port Said rather than at Alexandria – was the consequence of military rather than political considerations. Statements by Stockwell and Beaufre were our authority for attributing this change solely to the politicians, but Rhodes James has shown that this was not so. Kyle has made clear that fear of heavy civilian casualties in an assault on Alexandria was a cause of deep concern to politicians and military alike. Also Macmillan's papers have revealed that, at the initial meeting of the Egypt Committee (otherwise described as the Inner Cabinet), the Chiefs of Staff were informed that the main objective of destroying Nasser was embodied in the *Musketeer* plans presented to the Egypt Committee on 10 August which involved a march on Cairo after Alexandria had been captured. The change in the proposed theatre of war from the heart of Egypt (the Cairo–Alexandria area) to Port Said and the Canal Zone appears to have obscured the original political aim of overthrowing Nasser; we were emphatic in our criticism of the lack of any political aim or objective in the *Revise* plans, and our views have been reinforced by all we have subsequently read. There seems to have been little or no clear thinking about how Egypt was to be governed, once it had been conquered, a belief supported by the rudimentary nature of the Military Government element in the invasion force. It is interesting that as late as 25 October the Chiefs of Staff were warning the politicians of their worries at having to occupy Cairo, and possibly Alexandria as well, a task they estimated as needing three or four full divisions and involving the withdrawal of a division from Germany and the prolonged retention of some of the reservists with the colours.

We emphasised also the consequences of Stockwell's ignorance of the Israeli involvement, an accusation that was made by Stockwell himself and implicitly echoed by Beaufre although how the French officer could have been unaware of what was going on

is difficult to imagine. This, like the volte-face of the Chiefs of
Staff, is another grey area, the full facts of which are unlikely ever
to be fully unravelled.

The charges we laid at the door of Anthony Eden and the
Government that he led were the absence of a clear and
achievable political aim; the deliberate deception of Parliament,
the public and our American ally by the concealment of its
intentions and misrepresentation of the motives for its actions;
the flouting of the will and resolutions of the UN; the lack of
military preparedness for the operation it contemplated; and the
failure to prepare adequately for the task of governing the
occupied country. To these Kyle adds another: that Ministers
during the Suez crisis ignored and by-passed the Civil Service
and largely ran the machine by themselves. Among the consequences were a mistrust of Government actions by the senior
military figures responsible for carrying them out, a disconcerted
Civil Service and a deeply divided public. Nutting's view was that
Eden divided the country, as it had never been since the Boer
War.

However great a shock Suez may have been at the time,
however much pre-conceptions of national power and influence
may have been upset, and however much the Government's
handling of events may have disturbed conceptions of national
moral standards, in retrospect the entire affair was, perhaps, in
global terms on too small a scale and of too little importance to
have become that act of national catharsis needed for a
fundamental change of direction. France, our partners in the
Suez adventure, recovered more quickly and within two years
had, in de Gaulle, restored to power a strong leader who was to
raise the standing of the country to new post-war levels of
strength and influence.

Our influence in the world deteriorated during the 1960s and
1970s to such an extent that, when we wrote the book in 1979, we
said that it had become fashionable to equate Britain with
Portugal or Greece. However, as a result of the actions of the
governments led by Margaret Thatcher in the 1980s and Tony
Blair from the mid-1990s, that is no longer thinkable in terms of
influence or power. In addition, the economic strength of the
nation and the material well-being of our people has vastly

increased and adjustment to the realities of the twenty-first
century seems to have been accomplished in a sound fashion, if
not always to universal approval.

Almost fifty years later, the parallels of Suez with the Iraqi war
of 2003 are striking. Although the United Kingdom was acting
not in opposition to the wishes of the United States but as its
junior partner and may have pressed the lessons of Suez upon
the US President, the later enterprise seems to have managed to
make many of the mistakes of its predecessor. When early in 2003
the indications of US intentions in Iraq became clear, one of us
began a lively correspondence with his then Labour MP, who was
to lose her seat to an anti-war Liberal Democrat in the elections
of 2005. He pointed out the possibilities of many of the Suez
errors being repeated were the Iraqi war to take place.

As in 1956, an aggressive war was mounted by the Allies
against the clearly expressed will of the UN. While the charge of
military unpreparedness in terms of the state of the Armed
Forces could not be said to be the case in 2003, the equally serious
one can be made of concealing the military intention from its
commanders until very late in the day and thus hampering full
and proper preparation in training and equipment for the
fighting war. The considerable variations in the reasons given
both before and since the event on both sides of the Atlantic to
justify pre-emptive war against Saddam Hussein have tended to
keep concealed what the true political aim might have been but
it is widely believed to be connected with control of a
considerable amount of the world's oil reserves, the
establishment of strong US military bases in the Middle East (but
away from the politically sensitive Saudi Arabia) and the
improved security of the state of Israel. The failure adequately to
understand the intensely tribal nature of the Iraqi nation and to
make effective preparation for its government after the easy part
– the defeat of its armed forces – had been accomplished, has
been made plain by daily events in that unhappy country.

The evidence that this country was split over the justification
for a war was provided by the great demonstration in London in
March 2003, apparently the largest public political protest ever to
take place in this country and the passions that drove it continue
to animate our society. And what goes on concerning many

people are that the shadows cast by the second Iraqi war remain to obscure the future of relationships between the Western nations and the Muslim world.

Suez was an act of supreme political folly on the part of the Government of the day. Views remain widely divided on whether Iraq should be similarly considered but, in the continuing and bloody aftermath of that war, the distant echoes of 1956 go on being heard.

As my good friend and co-author Geoffrey Powell sadly died before this revised Afterword was written, any new material is my work. I believe that, as throughout our collaboration, we would both have been in harmony about these later observations.

Roy Fullick
January 2006

NOTES

Chapter 1: NATIONALISATION

1. Neither President Nasser nor President Sadat had themselves any illusions on this subject. Nasser, Premier Gamal Abdul, *Egypt's Liberation: The Philosophy of the Revolution* (Washington, 1955), pp. 33–8, is illuminating. In Sadat, Colonel Anwar el, *Revolt on the Nile* (London, 1957), p. 68: "The moral weaknesses of irresolution, resignation, hypocrisy and fear" which had been "drilled into them by a long history of suffering and humiliation" is mentioned.
2. Introduction by Field-Marshal Hull in Kipping, Sir Norman, *The Suez Contractors* (London, 1969), p. 8.
3. Dayan, Moshe, *Story of My Life* (London, 1976), p. 146.
4. Literally "self-sacrifice".
5. Nutting, Anthony, *No End of a Lesson* (London, 1967), p. 25.
6. In Selwyn Lloyd, *Suez 1956* (London, 1978), p. 27, the writer states that a British official who was present at the meeting denied that Eden behaved in an "intolerable fashion" and adds that it would be very unlike Eden to be rude to a foreigner. For all that, Nasser clearly felt that Eden had slighted him.
7. Nutting, pp. 21–2.
8. Ibid, p. 29.
9. Ibid, pp. 34–5.
10. Nasser included among his many complaints the indignity which Egyptians had suffered by being kept waiting in the ante-rooms of the High Commission and the British Ambassador.

Chapter 2: THE IMPERIAL VISION

1. Nutting, pp. 47–8.
2. Love, Kenneth, *Suez: The Twice-Fought War: A History* (London, 1970), pp. 355–6, quoting Foster's cable in President Eisenhower's papers at Gettysburg. Selwyn Lloyd makes no reference to the incident.
3. *Hansard*, Commons, Vol. 557, Col. 1777, 27 July 1956.
4. Ibid, Col. 1613, 2 August 1956.
5. Ibid, Col. 1660, 2 August 1956.
6. *Daily Telegraph*, 28 July 1956.
7. *Punch*, 1 August 1956.
8. Ibid, 15 August 1956.
9. Shinwell, Emanuel, *I've Lived Through it All* (London, 1973).
10. Eden, Sir Anthony, *Full Circle* (London, 1960), p. 435.

11. Murphy, Robert, *Diplomat among Warriors* (London, 1964), pp. 462–3.
12. Macmillan, Harold, *Riding the Storm, 1956–1958* (London, 1971), p. 105.
13. Eisenhower, Dwight D., *The White House Years*, Vol. 2, *Waging Peace, 1956–61* (London, 1966), pp. 43–4.

Chapter 3: EARLY PLANS

1. Beaufre, Le Général André, *The Suez Expedition, 1956* (London, 1967), p. 26.
2. Ibid, p. 27.
3. Stockwell, General Sir Hugh, "Suez from the Inside", *Sunday Telegraph*, 30 October 1966.
4. Thomas, Hugh, *The Suez Affair* (London, 1966–7), p. 42.
5. *Hansard*, Commons, Vol. 597, Col. 1071, 16 December 1958.
6. Stockwell, *Sunday Telegraph*, 30 October 1966.
7. Ibid.
8. Beaufre, p. 28.
9. Interview.
10. Beaufre, p. 31.
11. Thomas, p. 68.
12. Beaufre, p. 28.
13. Butler, Lord, *The Art of the Possible* (London, 1971), p. 190.
14. Eisenhower, p. 40.
15. Eden, p. 437.
16. Murphy, p. 470.
17. Eisenhower, p. 45.
18. Thomas, p. 72.
19. Beaufre, p. 34.
20. Stockwell, *Sunday Telegraph*, 30 October 1966.
21. *The Times*, 15 May 1967.
22. Stockwell, 30 October 1966.
23. Ibid.
24. Beaufre, pp. 41–2.
25. Ibid, p. 26.
26. Ibid, p. 44.

Chapter 4: THE CONDITION OF THE WEAPON

1. *Statement on Defence, 1956*, Comnd 9691, H.M.S.O., February 1956.
2. Ibid.
3. *Hansard*, Commons, Vol. 512, Col. 845, 9 March 1953.
4. *Report on the Advisory Committee on Recruiting*, Cmnd. 545, para. 60, H.M.S.O., October 1958.
5. *Tonight*, B.B.C. 1, 10 November 1976.
6. Selwyn Lloyd, p. 109.
7. No other country finds it necessary to maintain such an establishment as The Royal Military College of Science at Shrivenham which carries out scientific and mathematical research and teaching in a military setting, and introduces the non-technical officer to matters technological in an attempt to remedy the shortcomings of his secondary education.

8. One of the authors admits with some reluctance, to having helped to write the scenario for this exercise.

9. The officer candidate school had, in fact, moved to Coëtquidan, but it was still known colloquially as St. Cyr.

Chapter 5: THE COLOSSUS MOVES

1. Cavenagh, Sandy, *Airborne to Suez* (London, 1965), p. 22.
2. Young, B. A., "Troops-Deck Ballad", *Punch*, 15 August 1956, p. 172.
3. This is very much a simplification of the complicated organisation of the British Army Reserve in 1956.
4. Thomas, p. 48.
5. Beaufre, pp. 40–1.
6. Selwyn Lloyd, p. 85, mentions the threat of the mounting of the military operation reinforcing political pressure.
7. Thomas, p. 63.
8. Eisenhower, pp. 39–40.
9. Kipping, p. 39ff.

Chapter 6: FRESH PLANS

1. Eden, p. 458.
2. Ibid, pp. 463–4.
3. Ibid, p. 467.
4. Ibid, p. 467.
5. Murphy, p. 470.
6. Robertson, Terence, *Crisis: The Inside Story of the Suez Conspiracy* (London, 1965), p. 111.
7. The description of the military planning of Suez is based primarily upon Stockwell and Beaufre, supplemented by personal discussion with officers who took part in it.
8. Beaufre, p. 47.
9. Ibid, p. 54.
10. Stockwell, *Sunday Telegraph*, 30 October 1966.
11. Beaufre, p. 55.
12. Fergusson, Bernard, *The Trumpet in the Hall* (London, 1970), p. 261.
13. Kelley, George Armstrong, *Lost Soldiers: The French Army and Empire in Crisis: 1947–62* (Cambridge, Mass., 1965), pp. 184–8.
14. Beaufre, p. 51.
15. *Punch*, 17 October 1956.
16. Eden, p. 483.
17. *The Times*, 10 October 1956.
18. Ibid, 23 November 1956.

Chapter 7: COLLUSION

1. Bar-Zohar, Michael, *The Armed Prophet: A Biography of Ben-Gurion* (London, 1967), p. 219.

2. Calvocoressi, P., *Suez—Ten Years After* (London, 1967), p. 67 quoting a statement by Ben-Gurion.
3. Eisenhower, p. 38.
4. Azeau, H., *Le Piège de Suez, 5 Novembre* (Paris, 1964), p. 124.
5. Dayan, Moshe, *Story of My Life* (London, 1976), p. 151.
6. Ibid, pp. 152–4.
7. Ibid, p. 141.
8. Pineau, Christian, *1956 Suez* (Paris, 1976), p. 128.
9. Except where otherwise stated, the account of the negotiations which follows is based primarily on the accounts of the four participants— Selwyn Lloyd, Nutting, Pineau and Dayan.
10. Robertson, p. 125, quoting Pineau, who himself does not mention the meeting.
11. Henriques, Colonel Robert, "The Ultimatum: A Dissenting View", *Spectator*, 6 November 1959, p. 525.
12. Bar-Zohar, p. 222.
13. Dayan, Moshe, *Diary of the Sinai Campaign* (London, 1966), p. 31.
14. Interview.
15. Dayan, *Story of My Life*, p. 163.
16. Ibid, p. 167.
17. Love, p. 458, also quotes a letter from Pineau which confirms that the occupation was "in the military plan" and "at the political level we all knew of it".
18. Beaufre, pp. 70–1.
19. Ibid.
20. Pineau, p. 135.
21. Eden, p. 512.
22. Nutting, p. 89.
23. Dayan, *Diary*, p. 59.
24. Thomas, pp. 96–7, quoting a senior Cabinet Minister.
25. "Suez: success or disaster", *Listener*, 4 November 1976, p. 563. Interview of General Sir Hugh Stockwell by Frank Gillard.
26. Nutting, p. 67.
27. Ibid, pp. 77–8, and Selwyn Lloyd, pp. 169–70, 179.
28. Pineau, p. 119.
29. Ibid, p. 115.
30. Nutting, p. 76.
31. Dayan, *Story of My Life*, p. 175.
32. Ibid, p. 180.
33. Selwyn Lloyd, p. 182.
34. Ibid, pp. 183–4.
35. There is some confusion about the date of this visit. Pineau had it take place on 22 October, but his memory seems frequently at fault. Selwyn Lloyd denies that it occurred.
36. Dayan, *Story of My Life*, p. 187. In his *Diary* he connects this incident to an earlier visit to Paris, but in this book he makes no mention of having been in France at the time of the Sèvres meeting.
37. Ibid, pp. 192–3 and Pineau, p. 149ff.

38. Pineau, p. 151.

39. Nutting, p. 102.

40. *Hansard*, Commons, Vol. 562, Col. 1491–4 and 1518, 20 December 1956.

41. Ibid, Vol. 507, Col. 1068, 18 December 1958.

Chapter 8: ULTIMATUM

1. In describing *Kadesh* we have relied primarily upon Dayan's two books, on Henriques, Robert, *One Hundred Hours to Suez* (London, 1957), and upon Luttwak, Edward and Horowitz, Dan, *The Israeli Army* (London, 1975).

2. Dayan, *Diary*, p. 210.

3. Flintham, V., "Suez 1956: A Lesson in Air Power", *Air Pictorial*, August 1966, p. 269.

4. Thomas, p. 123.

5. Henriques, p. 189.

6. Dayan, *Diary*, p. 218.

7. Keightley, General Sir Charles, "Operations in Egypt—November to December, 1956". Supplement to the *London Gazette*, 10 September 1957, p. 5329.

8. Nutting, pp. 111–12.

9. Eisenhower, p. 56.

10. Ibid.

11. Bar-Zohar, p. 234, and Robertson, p. 149.

12. Love, p. 511.

13. Bond, Brian, "Liddell Hart's Influence on Israeli Military Practice", *R.U.S.I. Journal*, Vol. 121, No. 2, June 1976, pp. 83–9.

14. Ibid, p. 89, n. 7. Sharon gave Ben-Gurion and not Dayan the credit for exonerating him. It was fortunate for Israel that the career of this brilliant officer, who was to prove such an outstanding general in the two subsequent wars, was not checked.

15. *Hansard*, Commons, Vol. 560, Col. 262, 31 October 1956.

16. Dayan, *Diary*, p. 115.

Chapter 9: AND MORE PLANS

1. Beaufre, pp. 54–5.

2. Massu, Jacques, *Verité sur Suez 1956* (Paris, 1978), p. 140.

3. Beaufre, p. 83.

4. Ibid, p. 81.

5. Ibid, p. 94.

6. Ibid, p. 93.

7. Massu, p. 146.

8. Beaufre, p. 88.

9. Stockwell, *Sunday Telegraph*, 13 November 1966.

10. Massu, p. 141.

11. Beaufre, p. 89.

12. Ibid.

13. Ibid, pp. 91, 97.

14. Dayan, *Diary*, pp. 160–1.
15. Eden, p. 540.
16. Beaufre, p. 97.

Chapter 10: THE AIR WAR

1. This chapter has primarily been compiled from secondary sources, details of which can be found in the bibliography, augmented by a number of interviews. So far as published material is concerned, the Royal Air Force is the silent service. Much more has been written about the Royal Navy's part in the campaign.
2. Liddell Hart, B. H., "Operation Musketeer", *Observer*, February 1957.
3. Keightley, p. 5330.
4. Kipping, p. 70.
5. Ibid, pp. 43–4.
6. Ibid, p. 62.
7. Keightley, p. 5331.
8. Fergusson, p. 262ff.
9. Ibid, p. 265.
10. Flintham, p. 271.
11. Thomas, pp. 110, 238.
12. Bromberger, Merry and Serge, *Secrets of Suez* (London, 1957), p. 104.
13. Interview.
14. Barker, A. J., *Suez: The Seven Days War* (London, 1967), p. 101.
15. Stockwell, *Sunday Telegraph*, 13 November 1966.

Chapter 11: THE AIRBORNE DROPS

1. Clark, D. M. J., *Suez Touchdown: A Soldier's Tale* (London, 1964), p. 37.
2. Ibid, pp. 37–8.
3. Beaufre, p. 81 and *Listener*, interview with Stockwell, p. 564.
4. See Chapter 16, p. 189.
5. Barker, p. 95.
6. Clark, p. 64.
7. *Hansard*, Commons, Vol. 560, Col. 247, 8 November 1956.
8. Clark, p. 61.
9. Barker, pp. 90–1.
10. The main sources for the accounts of the actions of 2 and 3 Para are officers who took part in the operations, including one of the authors.
11. Cavenagh, p. 106.
12. Leulliette, Pierre, *St. Michael and The Dragon* (London, 1964), p. 193. The account of the action by this *para* is vivid, but inaccurate in matters which he did not himself observe.
13. Massu, p. 159.
14. Cavenagh, p. 132.
15. Captain de Klee was in charge of this detachment. His account "A Jump with the French", *Household Brigade Magazine*, Spring 1957, complements that of Leulliette.

16. Leulliette, p. 203 and pp. 214–15.

17. Love, pp. 604–6, who interviewed both El Moguy and Butler, provides the most detailed account of these negotiations.

18. *Hansard*, Commons, Vol. 558, Col. 1965, 5 November 1956.

19. Eden, p. 553.

20. Keightley, pp. 5332–3.

21. Eden, p. 553.

22. Love, p. 605.

23. Ibid, pp. 608–9.

24. Eden, p. 554.

25. Love, pp. 609–10, 731.

26. Dayan, *Diary*, p. 184.

27. Beaufre, p. 104.

Chapter 12: THE ASSAULT FROM THE SEA

1. Clark, p. 69.

2. Stockwell, 6 November 1966.

3. Clark, pp. 79–80.

4. Cavenagh, pp. 168–9.

5. Ibid, p. 143.

6. Leulliette, p. 206.

7. The description of the trip ashore is based primarily upon Stockwell, Ibid, and Beaufre, pp. 109–15.

Chapter 13: EXPLOITATION

1. There was yet another lieutenant-general ashore. The Commandant-General of the Royal Marines had somehow hitched a lift into the battle. He had no business to be there at all.

2. Some accounts of the battle talk in G.M.T., others in local time, running two hours later. Some, including the Official Despatches appear to confuse the two. Unless otherwise stated, we have confined ourselves to local time, because G.M.T. is incongruous when related to dawn and dusk in Egypt in November.

3. Massu, p. 221.

4. Nutting, p. 137.

5. Murphy, p. 447.

6. Macmillan, p. 164.

7. Eden, p. 558.

8. Leulliette, p. 208.

9. Stockwell, 6 November 1966.

10. Beaufre, pp. 114–17.

11. Stockwell, ibid.

12. Churchill, Randolph S., *The Rise and Fall of Sir Anthony Eden* (London, 1959), p. 291.

13. Beaufre, p. 117.

Chapter 14: OCCUPATION

1. Burns, Lieutenant-General E. L. M., *Between Arab and Israeli* (London, 1962), p. 222.
2. Herbert, Sir Edwin, *Damage and Casualties in Port Said*, Cmnd. 47, H.M.S.O., December 1956, p. 26.
3. Fergusson, pp. 173–4.
4. Burns, p. 232.
5. Keightley, p. 5335.
6. Cavenagh, pp. 190–1.
7. Stockwell, 13 November 1966.
8. Interview.
9. Several versions of this incident have appeared. This, however, was related by the officer concerned.
10. Beaufre, p. 125. The author describes how the terms of the proclamation, which under the 1948 Geneva agreements should have been the legal basis for the occupation, had been under discussion between the allied commanders for months, how it was not ready when the landing took place and how the British Foreign Office decreed on 7 November that no proclamation should be made.

Chapter 15: WITHDRAWAL

1. Burns, pp. 197–201.
2. Ibid, p. 203.
3. Ibid, p. 212.
4. Ibid, p. 233.
5. Eden, pp. 565–6.
6. Butler, p. 195.
7. Beaufre, p. 125.
8. Leulliette, p. 214.
9. Beaufre, p. 125.
10. Burns, p. 228.

Chapter 16: HOW DID IT HAPPEN?

1. Terraine, John, *The Life and Times of Lord Mountbatten*, (London, 1968), p. 176.
2. Cavenagh, foreword.
3. *Hansard*, Lords, Vol. 238, Col. 1002–3, 16 March 1962.
4. Lewin, Ronald, *Slim: The Standard Bearer* (London, 1976), p. 304.
5. Baeyens, Jacques, *Un Coup d'Epée dans l'Eau du Canal* (Paris, 1976), p. 217.
6. Churchill, pp. 300–1.
7. Braddon, Russell, *Suez: Splitting of a Nation* (London, 1973), p. 139.
8. Ibid, p. 138.
9. Eden, p. 445.
10. Thomas, pp. 158, 243.
11. Selwyn Lloyd, p. 180.
12. Thomas, pp. 91–2.

13. Stockwell, 13 November 1966.
14. Ibid.
15. Ibid.
16. Fergusson, Bernard, *The Watery Maze* (London, 1961), p. 393.
17. Massu, p. 159.
18. Selwyn Lloyd, p. 121.
19. *Brassey's Annual* (London, 1957), ix.
20. Ibid.
21. Speech at the Mansion House, 10 November 1942.
22. Nasser, p. 109.
23. Ibid, pp. 107–9.

BIBLIOGRAPHY

Unpublished Sources

Manuscripts

Papers of Vice-Admiral Sir Maxwell Richmond, K.B.E., C.B., (The Imperial War Museum).

Manuscript by Reed, John, *History of the British Army in Egypt 1950–6* (Imperial War Museum).

Unpublished papers in possession of the Royal Armoured Corps Tank Museum.

Published Sources

Annual Register 1956.

Annual Statements on Defence, H.M.S.O.

Azeau, H., *Le Piège de Suez, 5 Novembre*. Robert Laffont, Paris, 1964.

Baeyens, Jacques, *Un Coup d'Epée dans l'Eau du Canal*, Fayard, Paris, 1976.

Barclay, Brigadier C. N., "Anglo-French Operations against Port Said", *The Army Quarterly*, April 1957.

Barker, A. J., *Suez: The Seven Days War*, Faber & Faber, 1967.

Barjot, L'Admiral P., "Refléxions sur les Operations de Suez 1956", *Revue de la Défense Nationale*, Paris, 1956.

Bar-Zohar, Michael, *The Armed Prophet: a Biography of Ben-Gurion*, trans. Len Ortzen, Arthur Barker, 1967.

Beaufre, Le Général André, *The Suez Expedition 1956*, trans. Richard Barry, Faber & Faber, 1967.

Berger, Morroe, *Military Elite and Social Change: Egypt since Napoleon*, Center for International Studies, Princeton University, 1960.

Berry, Captain P. S., "Suez Adventure", *Royal Armoured Corps Journal*, 1957.

Blaxland, Gregory, *Objective Egypt*, Frederick Muller, 1956.

Braddon, Russell, *Suez: Splitting of a Nation*, Collins, 1973.

Bromberger, Merry and Serge, *Secrets of Suez*, trans. James Cameron, Sidgwick & Jackson, 1957.

Buckley, Major W. K., "Operation Musketeer", *Household Brigade Magazine*, Spring 1957.

Burns, Lieutenant-General E. L. M., *Between Arab and Israeli*, George G. Harrap, 1962.

Butler, Lord, *The Art of the Possible*, Hamish Hamilton, 1971.

Calvocoressi, P., *Suez—Ten Years After*, ed. Antony Moncrieff, B.B.C., 1967.

Cavenagh, Sandy, *Airborne to Suez*, William Kimber, 1965.

"Chariot", "Musketeer", *The Naval Review*, April, 1957.

Childers, Erskine B., *The Road to Suez: A Study of Western Arab Relations*, Macgibbon & Kee, 1962.

Churchill, Randolph S., *The Rise and Fall of Sir Anthony Eden*, Macgibbon & Kee, 1959.

Clark, D. M. J., *Suez Touchdown: A Soldier's Tale*, Peter Davies, 1964.

Cromer, The Earl of, *Modern Egypt*, 2 vols, Macmillan, 1908.

Dayan, Moshe, *Diary of the Sinai Campaign*, Weidenfeld & Nicolson, 1966.

— *Story of My Life*, Weidenfeld & Nicolson, 1976.

De Fouquières, Colonel, "La Guerre des Six Jours", *Forces Aériennes Françaises*, Paris, May 1957.

De Klee, Captain M. P., "A Jump with the French", *Household Brigade Magazine*, Spring 1957.

De la Gorce, Paul-Marie, *The French Army: A Military-Political History*, trans. Kenneth Douglas, Weidenfeld & Nicolson, 1963.

Dodwell, Henry, *The Founder of Modern Egypt: A Study of Muhammed 'Ali*, Cambridge University Press, 1931.

Eden, Sir Anthony, *Full Circle*, Cassell, 1960.

Eisenhower, Dwight D., *The White House Years*, Vol. 2, *Waging Peace, 1956–61*, Heinemann, 1966.

Elgood, Lieutenant-Colonel P. G., *Egypt and the Army*, Oxford University Press, Humphrey Milford, 1962.

Ely, Général d'Armée Paul, *Mémoires: Suez . . . le 13 mai*, Plon, Paris, 1969.

Ernle-Erle-Drax, R. P., "Suez 1956: An Adventure in Grand Strategy", *The Naval Review*, April 1957.

Falls, Captain Cyril, "Operation Musketeer", *Brassey's Annual*, 1957.

Fergusson, Bernard, *The Watery Maze: The Story of Combined Operations*, Collins, 1961.

— *The Trumpet in the Hall*, Collins, 1970.

Finer, Herman, *Dulles over Suez: The Theory and Practice of his Diplomacy*, Heinemann, 1964.

Fleming, Captain J. B., "Port Said, 1956: Some Experiences of a Port Workshop, REME", *The Journal of the Royal Electrical and Mechanical Engineers*, 1958.

Flintham, V., "Suez 1956: A Lesson In Air Power", *Air Pictorial*, August and September, 1966.

Foot, M. R. D., *Men in Uniform: Military Manpower in Industrial Societies*, Weidenfeld and Nicolson for the Institute of Strategic Studies, 1961.

Fortescue, Hon. J. W., *A History of the British Army*, Vol. IV, Parts I and II, Macmillan, 1906.

Henriques, Robert, *One Hundred Hours to Suez: An Account of Israel's Campaign in the Sinai Peninsula*, Collins, 1957.

— "The Ultimatum: A Dissenting View", *Spectator*, 6 November, 1959.

Herbert, Sir Edwin, *Damage and Casualties in Port Said. Cmnd 47*, H.M.S.O., December 1956.

Hesseltine, W. B. and Wolf, H. C., *The Blue and Gray on the Nile*, The University of Chicago Press, 1961.

"J.S.", "The Aircraft Carrier Aspects of Suez", *The Naval Review*, April 1957.

Jackson, R., *The Israel Air Force Story*, Tom Stacey, 1970.

Johnson, Paul, *The Suez War*, Macgibbon & Kee, 1957.

Kyle, Keith, "Suez: What Really Happened", *The Listener*, 11 November 1976.

Keightley, General Sir Charles, "Operations in Egypt—November to December, 1956", Supplement to the *London Gazette*, Tuesday, 10 September 1957, H.M.S.O., 1957.

Kelly, George Armstrong, *Lost Soldiers: The French Army and Empire in Crisis: 1947–62*, MIT Press, Cambridge, Massachusetts, 1965.

Keesings Contemporary Archives.

Kipping, Sir Norman, *The Suez Contractors*, Kenneth Mason, 1969.

Leulliette, Pierre, *St. Michael and the Dragon: A Paratrooper in the Algerian War*, trans. Tony White, Heinemann, 1964.

Love, Kenneth, *Suez, The Twice-Fought War: A History*, Longman, 1970.

Luttwak, Edward and Horowitz, Dan, *The Israeli Army*, Allen Lane, 1975.

Macmillan, Harold, *Riding the Storm, 1956–1958*, Macmillan, 1971.

Mansfield, Peter, *The British in Egypt*, Weidenfeld & Nicolson, 1971.

Marlowe, John, *The Making of the Suez Canal*, Cresset Press, 1964.

Massu, Jacques (with Le Mire, Henri), *Verité sur Suez 1956*, Plon, Paris, 1978.

Menzies, Sir Robert, *Afternoon Light*, Cassell, 1967.

Munson, K., "Suez, 1956", *Aircraft Illustrated Extra*, November 1969.

Murphy, Robert, *Diplomat among Warriors*, Collins, 1964.

Nasser, Premier Gamal Abdul, *Egypt's Liberation: The Philosophy of the Revolution*, Public Affairs Press, Washington D.C., 1955.

Neguib, Mohammed, *Egypt's Destiny*, Victor Gollancz, 1955.

Nutting, Anthony, *No End of a Lesson: The Story of Suez*, Constable, 1967.

"Oscar", "The Seaborne Assault on Port Said", *The Naval Review*, January, 1957.

"Peregrine", "The Amphibious Assault on Port Said", *The Naval Review*, April, 1957.

Pineau, Christian, *1956 Suez*, Robert Lamont, Paris, 1976.

Polmar, Norman, *Aircraft Carriers: A Graphic History of Carrier Aviation and its Influence on World Events*, Doubleday, New York, 1969.

Richards, Lieutenant-Colonel L. F., "The Suez Emergency", *Royal Military Police Journal*, 1957.

Robertson, Terence, *Crisis: The Inside Story of the Suez Conspiracy*, Hutchinson, 1965.

Sadat, Colonel Anwar el, *Revolt on the Nile*, trans. Thomas Graham, Allen Wingate, 1957.

Schonfield, Hugh J., *The Suez Canal in Peace and War 1869–1969*, Valentine Mitchell, 1969.

Selwyn Lloyd, Lord, *Suez 1956: A Personal Account*, Jonathan Cape, 1978.

Shinwell, Emanuel, *I've Lived Through It All*, Victor Gollancz, 1973.

Stockwell, General Sir Hugh, "Suez from the Inside", *Sunday Telegraph*, 30 October, 6 and 13 November, 1966.

Terraine, John, *The Life and Times of Lord Mountbatten*, Hutchinson, 1968.

Thomas, Hugh, *The Suez Affair*, Weidenfeld and Nicolson, 1966–67.

Watt, D. C., *Documents on the Suez Crisis 26 July to 6 November 1956*, Royal Institute of International Affairs, 1957.

Williams, Philip, "The French Army", *Encounter*, December, 1961.

Wood, Sir Evelyn, "The Egyptian Army", *Encyclopedia Britannica*, Vol. IX, 1910.

MAPS

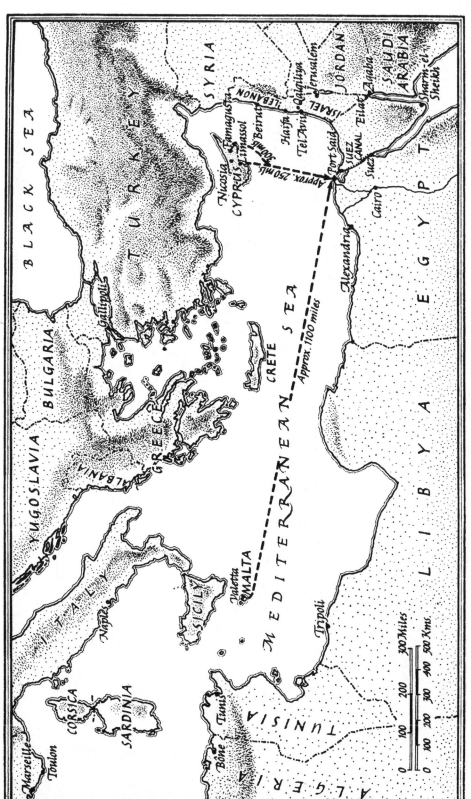

The Mediterranean

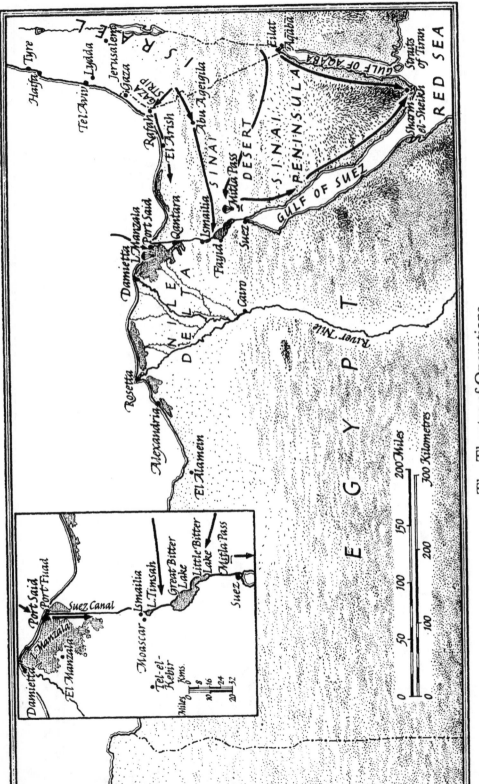

The Theatre of Operations

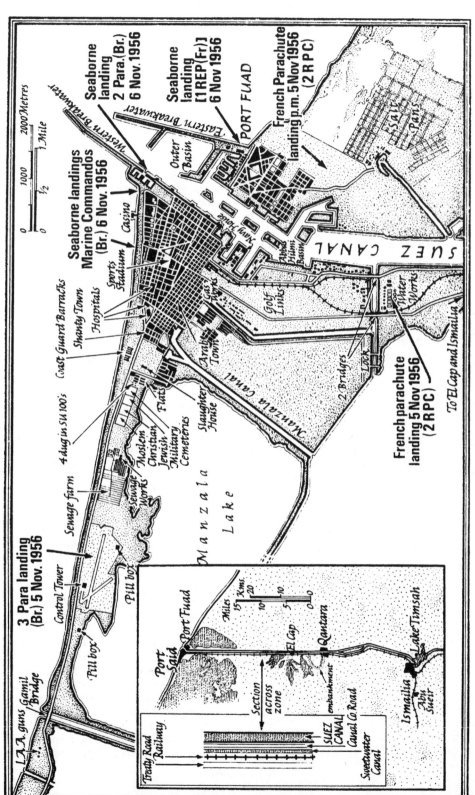

Port Said and Port Fuad

INDEX

United Nations Suez Clearance Organisation (UNSCO), 179
United Nations Truce Supervisory Organisation, 176
United States of America: withdraws support for Aswan High Dam project, 11; "special relationship" with Britain, 13, 36, 55; possible involvement in invasion of Egypt, 15; reasons for opposition to French and British plans for invasion, 23-4; excellence of military transport, 33; attitude to proposed Anglo-French invasion, 54-5, 140; opposition to British bombing of Egyptian air-

fields, 96; defines conditions of assistance to Britain, 160; benefitting from World War II, 196; attitude towards independence movements, 196

Verdict, Operation, 103
Villacoublay, 79, 80, 124

War of Independence, 68, 70
Wheeler, General, 179
Wigg, Colonel, 87
Winter Plan, 65-6, 75, 100; difficulties of, 65-6
Woods, Peter, 133